The Boogey Book

The Boogey Book

Matthew Edward Petchinsky

The Boogey Book
By: Matthew Petchinsky

Disclaimer:

This book, titled *"The Boogey Book"*, is a fan-made creation that draws thematic inspiration from the 1999 Disney Channel Original Movie, *"Don't Look Under the Bed."* However, this work is not affiliated with or endorsed by Disney or any of its subsidiaries. It is important to note that this book does **not** include any copyrighted material, characters, or specific plot elements from *"Don't Look Under the Bed."*

All characters, creatures, settings, ideas, and concepts presented in *"The Boogey Book"* are completely original and unique, crafted specifically for this project. Any similarities between the content of this book and other works, whether created by Disney or other parties, are purely coincidental and unintentional.

The Boogeyman and related themes, while loosely inspired by folklore, are represented here in an entirely new light, with brand-new interpretations, concepts, and methods of interacting with and combating the Boogeyman. The author, Matthew Petchinsky, has taken care to ensure that this work stands on its own as a unique and creative project, without infringing on the intellectual property rights of any established franchises.

This book is meant to be an enjoyable and creative fan tribute to the genre of childhood imagination and spooky fantasy, offering original insights and storytelling. All materials within this book are created solely for entertainment purposes, and no profit or claim to official material is being made in relation to Disney's work.

Thank you for supporting fan creations and original storytelling!

Introduction:
The Boogeyman Myth: A Global Legend

For centuries, tales of the Boogeyman have haunted the dreams of children worldwide. Known by different names across various cultures, the Boogeyman embodies the fear of the unknown and often represents the creeping anxiety of growing up. In most interpretations, this figure lurks in the shadows, hiding in closets, under beds, or behind doors, waiting for the moment when a child is alone, vulnerable, and gripped by fear. What makes the Boogeyman so terrifying is not just his presence but the unpredictability of his form. He is the shapeshifter of nightmares, taking on different appearances, feeding on fear, and thriving in the dark recesses of a child's mind.

From the "Bogeyman" of the United Kingdom to "El Coco" in Spain and Latin America, the Boogeyman has always played a role in controlling behavior, scaring children into obedience, or serving as a warning to avoid wandering into dark, forbidden places. But beyond his role in folklore, the Boogeyman touches on a deeper psychological fear: abandonment and loneliness. He is a symbol of what happens when we lose control of our imaginations and let fear take over, corrupting our dreams and our sense of security.

In *"The Boogey Book,"* we dive into this rich tapestry of the Boogeyman myth and unravel a new interpretation: the Boogeyman as the dark side of forgotten imaginary friends. While most stories present the Boogeyman as a simple monster under the bed, this book takes a different approach, exploring how our own imaginations, once left behind, can twist and transform into something far more sinister.

Imaginary Friends: Guardians of Childhood

As children, our imaginations are boundless. We create worlds, heroes, and companions that comfort us, entertain us, and sometimes even protect us. Imaginary friends are often seen as figments of a child's mind, but in many ways, they serve a greater purpose. These invisible companions represent creativity, innocence, and the freedom to explore emotions and situations without fear of judgment. They teach us how to cope with loneliness, frustration, and the many challenges of growing up.

But what happens when children abandon these companions? When the pressures of growing up, societal expectations, or the distractions of technology pull children away from the world of imagination, these once comforting friends can be left behind, forgotten. In *"The Boogey Book,"* we explore the concept that imaginary friends, when neglected or discarded, undergo a transformation. The vibrant, playful beings that once existed in harmony with a child's imagination can twist into something darker: a Boogeyman.

This transformation happens because, at its core, the Boogeyman is a reflection of loss and fear. The once-protective imaginary friend feels abandoned, rejected, and ultimately morphs into a creature driven by the need to regain attention—any attention, even if it's fueled by fear. This is why, in our version of the myth, the Boogeyman thrives on fear and negative emotions. The longer an imaginary friend is left forgotten, the stronger and more monstrous the Boogeyman becomes, feeding off the shadows and anxieties that grow in a child's mind.

This book isn't just about fighting monsters; it's about understanding the power of imagination and the importance of nurturing it. When children stop believing in their imaginary friends, they risk allowing those friends to become their darkest fears. By addressing the Boogeyman in this way, we hope to convey a deeper message: imagination is not something that should be abandoned—it's something that should be protected and cherished, no matter how old we become.

Restoring Balance: Why We Must Fight Back

The Boogeyman, in this interpretation, represents more than just a monster to be feared; he symbolizes the imbalance that occurs when imagination is suppressed, and fear is allowed to take root. The world of childhood is a delicate balance between light and dark, between fantasy and reality. When a child stops believing in the power of their imagination, darkness has the potential to creep in, and the Boogeyman seizes this opportunity to thrive.

It is vital to fight back against the Boogeyman, not only to defeat him but to restore the harmony that imagination brings to a child's life. The Boogeyman grows stronger as the world becomes darker, as fear overtakes creativity. This fight is not just about banishing the monster under the bed, but about reigniting the spark of creativity and reminding children—and even adults—that the imagination is a powerful tool for growth, healing, and understanding.

When we fight the Boogeyman, we fight for the restoration of wonder and the belief that our imaginations are still capable of creating beauty, hope, and joy. Without this fight, we risk losing more than just our imaginary friends—we risk losing the very essence of what makes childhood magical. The Boogeyman, in this sense, is not just a villain but a symbol of what happens when we let go of the imagination that once brought us comfort and joy.

The Power of Imagination and Facing Fear

In the chapters that follow, *"The Boogey Book"* will provide practical strategies, psychological tactics, and even magical rituals to help children—and the child in all of us—fight back against the Boogeyman. These methods are designed to not only defeat the Boogeyman but also to reawaken the imagination and restore the balance between light and dark.

By teaching children how to confront and overcome their fears, this book aims to empower readers to reclaim the power of their imagination. The Boogeyman is not unbeatable, but the key to victory lies in remembering that fear is a choice, and imagination is the antidote. Through visualization, creativity, and courage, the Boogeyman can be driven back to the shadows where he belongs, and imaginary friends, once lost, can be restored to their rightful place in the heart of a child's dreams.

So, as we embark on this journey through the pages of *"The Boogey Book,"* remember that the fight against the Boogeyman is more than just a battle against fear—it's a fight to preserve the magic of imagination. Let the light of creativity shine, and the shadows of the Boogeyman will fade.

Part 1: The Origins of Boogeymen

Chapter 1: The Birth of a Boogeyman

Imaginary friends are more than just the whimsical creations of a child's mind. They are companions in the world of make-believe, representing the boundless creativity, curiosity, and innocence that define childhood. For many children, imaginary friends serve as confidants, playmates, and protectors. These companions help children navigate the complexities of growing up by offering an outlet for emotions, fears, and frustrations. However, when these imaginary friends are forgotten or abandoned, they can take on a much darker form. This is the moment when an imaginary friend, neglected and cast aside, begins the transformation into a Boogeyman.

The Role of Imaginary Friends: Guardians of Creativity and Emotion

Imaginary friends serve a variety of crucial functions during a child's development. They are often created during early childhood when a child's mind is still forming its understanding of the world. These friends can take on any shape, personality, or form—sometimes mimicking real-life people or animals, and other times embodying fantastical creatures, superheroes, or beings that defy logic. They exist as extensions of a child's emotional and psychological state, often reflecting a child's needs, desires, and experiences.

1. **Companions in Solitude:** Many children invent imaginary friends during periods of isolation or loneliness. These friends become reliable companions, offering comfort and companionship when real-life friends or family members are unavailable. An imaginary friend can keep a child company in times of solitude, transforming moments of loneliness into adventures filled with joy, excitement, and play.

2. **Emotional Processing:** Imaginary friends act as mirrors to a child's inner world. They help children work through emotions like anger, sadness, fear, or confusion by offering a safe outlet for expressing these feelings. When a child feels frustrated or scared, they may turn to their imaginary friend for guidance or reassurance. In this way, these companions allow children to externalize their inner struggles and make sense of complex emotions.

3. **Exploring Boundaries:** Through their interactions with imaginary friends, children often explore the boundaries of their reality and imagination. They test limits, create rules, and break them within the safety of their make-believe world. Imaginary friends allow children to experience scenarios that they cannot control in the real world—like bravery in the face of danger or mastering a new skill—in a space where they are fully in control.

4. **Building Social Skills:** Interactions with imaginary friends help children develop important social and communication skills. By engaging in conversations, role-playing, and problem-solving with their imaginary companions, children learn how to navigate relationships and express themselves more clearly. These interactions often reflect real-world dynamics, giving children the opportunity to practice empathy, negotiation, and conflict resolution in a safe and controlled environment.

Imaginary friends, in essence, act as a bridge between the real world and a child's inner landscape. They are the embodiment of a child's creativity and emotional processing, helping them build resilience and imagination. But what happens when this connection to imagination is severed? What happens when a child grows older, moves on, or becomes distracted by the pressures and demands of reality? This is where the story takes a darker turn—this is the birth of the Boogeyman.

What Happens When a Child Stops Believing: The Transformation

As children grow older, their need for imaginary friends often diminishes. The transition from childhood to adolescence is marked by a shift toward reality, logic, and structure. The demands of school, social dynamics, and the expectations of adulthood can pull a child away from the imaginative world they once inhabited so freely. While this is a natural part of development, it leaves behind a profound sense of loss for the imaginary friend.

1. **The Feeling of Abandonment:** In this narrative, the imaginary friend experiences abandonment when the child stops believing in them. While an imaginary friend is a creation of the child's mind, they are not just a one-way construct; they are also deeply tied to the emotional energy of the child. When a child no longer interacts with or believes in their imaginary friend, the companion is left stranded in a state of limbo, disconnected from the child's creative energy.

The imaginary friend, once the source of joy and companionship, now feels abandoned, much like a child who has been left alone. This sense of rejection festers, and the positive energy that once fueled the imaginary friend begins to turn sour. The transition from light to dark, from playful to menacing, begins.

1. **The Darkness Creeps In:** As the imaginary friend is forgotten, they begin to change. The warmth and vibrancy that once defined their existence give way to coldness and shadows. The imaginary friend becomes a twisted version of their former self, feeding off the child's fears and insecurities. In the child's subconscious mind, this transformation manifests as the Boogeyman—the embodiment of all that is feared and unknown.

The Boogeyman thrives in darkness, not just the literal darkness of nighttime, but the metaphorical darkness of neglect and fear. As the imaginary friend fades from the child's memory, the Boogeyman grows in power, using fear as a fuel to sustain itself. The Boogeyman's form is mutable and ever-changing, a reflection of the forgotten imaginary friend's anguish. No longer bound by the rules of a child's imagination, the Boogeyman is free to roam the darker corners of the child's mind, seeking ways to instill fear and regain attention.

1. **The Desire for Attention:** One of the key motivations for the Boogeyman is to reclaim the child's attention—any attention, even if it's rooted in fear. While the imaginary friend was once content to engage with the child in joyful play, the Boogeyman craves recognition, even if it comes in the form of terror. The more the child fears the Boogeyman, the stronger the Boogeyman becomes.

The Boogeyman's ultimate goal is to be remembered, to be acknowledged once again by the child who has forgotten them. However, the only way they know how to achieve this is by instilling fear. Every creak in the closet, every shadow under the bed, every whisper in the dark is the Boogeyman's attempt to draw the child's attention back to them. It is a tragic reversal of the once-loving relationship between child and imaginary friend—where once there was love and laughter, now there is only fear and dread.

1. **The Transformation Complete:** Over time, the Boogeyman's form solidifies. No longer a mere shadow of the imaginary friend, the Boogeyman becomes a fully independent entity, driven by fear and sustained by darkness. Their presence is a reminder of what happens when imagination is cast aside—when creativity is replaced by conformity and fear is allowed to take root. The child, now too afraid to confront their forgotten friend, becomes trapped in a cycle of fear, unable to reclaim the imaginative power that once brought them joy.

The Boogeyman thrives in this environment, growing stronger as the child's imagination fades into the background. The relationship between the child and the Boogeyman becomes one of mutual destruction—the more the child fears, the more powerful the Boogeyman becomes, and the harder it is for the child to return to a place of imagination and wonder.

Reversing the Transformation: Reclaiming Imagination

The transformation from imaginary friend to Boogeyman is not inevitable, nor is it irreversible. The Boogeyman exists as a manifestation of the child's abandonment of imagination, but imagination itself is a powerful force. The key to defeating the Boogeyman lies in the child's ability to reclaim their imagination, to reawaken the creative energy that once fueled their connection to the imaginary world.

1. **Facing Fear with Imagination:** To reverse the transformation, the child must confront their fear and remember the power of imagination. The Boogeyman can only thrive in the absence of creativity and belief, but when the child rekindles their imaginative spirit, the Boogeyman begins to lose their power. The child can turn the Boogeyman back into an imaginary friend by remembering the joy and comfort they once found in their creative companion.
2. **Restoring Balance:** When the child restores their connection to imagination, they restore balance to their inner world. The Boogeyman, once a terrifying force of fear, can be transformed back into a playful, protective presence. This transformation not only banishes the darkness but also reintroduces creativity, joy, and resilience into the child's life.
3. **A Cautionary Tale:** The birth of the Boogeyman serves as a cautionary tale about the dangers of forgetting imagination. While growing up is a natural part of life, it's important to remember that imagination and creativity are vital components of who we are. When we abandon these parts of ourselves, we risk allowing fear to take over. The Boogeyman is a reminder of what can happen when we let go of the magic that makes childhood so special.

Conclusion

The birth of a Boogeyman is a process fueled by fear, neglect, and abandonment. It begins with the forgotten imaginary friend, who, in their loneliness and rejection, transforms into a creature of darkness. The Boogeyman thrives on fear, but their origins lie in the child's own imagination. The key to defeating the Boogeyman is to reclaim that imagination, to face fear head-on, and to remember the power that creativity holds. In doing so, the child can not only banish the Boogeyman but restore balance to their world, bringing light back into the darkness.

Chapter 2: The Transformation Process

The transformation of an imaginary friend into a Boogeyman is a gradual, multi-faceted process that is both psychological and, in our fictional context, tinged with a touch of magic. It is the product of emotional abandonment, fear, and the growing distance between a child and their once-beloved companion. When a child outgrows their imaginary friend, or neglects them due to the pressures of growing up, this once-loving and protective figure begins to morph into something darker and more menacing: the Boogeyman.

From Companion to Creature: How an Imaginary Friend Morphs into a Boogeyman

Imaginary friends are born from the vibrant, unbound creativity of children. They embody hope, playfulness, and emotional support. But when this bond is broken—whether through the natural progression of childhood, external pressures, or the child's growing preference for the real world—the imaginary friend is left in an emotional and creative void. Here's how that journey unfolds:

1. **The First Signs of Neglect:** At first, the imaginary friend notices subtle changes. The child may engage with them less frequently, preferring to spend time with real-world friends, toys, or electronic devices. As the child grows older, school and social pressures begin to take precedence. The imaginary friend, once a constant presence, becomes less relevant. During this phase, the imaginary friend still exists, but their presence in the child's world begins to fade.

Emotionally, the imaginary friend feels confused. They still exist within the child's mind, but they're no longer part of the child's everyday life. The imaginative energy that once sustained them is now diverted elsewhere, leaving them disconnected. This is the initial seed of transformation: a sense of abandonment.

1. **The Void of Abandonment:** As the child grows more distant, the imaginary friend becomes trapped in a state of limbo. No longer actively participating in the child's world, they are left to exist on the fringes of the child's imagination. This is a crucial stage in the transformation process, as the imaginary friend is left without purpose or interaction.

The once joyful presence of the imaginary friend begins to decay. They experience an overwhelming sense of loneliness, a loss of identity, and a growing frustration. This void in the imaginary friend's existence becomes fertile ground for darker emotions to take root. The longer they remain forgotten, the more these negative feelings intensify, leading to the next phase of transformation: resentment.

1. **The Rise of Resentment:** Resentment is a powerful catalyst in the transformation of the imaginary friend into a Boogeyman. As the child's attention drifts further away, the imaginary friend feels an increasing sense of betrayal. They were once a source of comfort and joy,

but now they are cast aside, forgotten, and ignored. In their growing loneliness, they begin to question their existence: *Why did the child abandon me? Why am I no longer important?*

This stage is marked by an emotional shift within the imaginary friend. The positive energy that once defined their relationship with the child—love, joy, playfulness—begins to sour. Resentment festers and morphs into anger and bitterness. The imaginary friend still craves the child's attention, but now that desire is tinged with darker intentions. Instead of wanting to play, they want to be noticed again, even if that attention comes through fear.

The friend's form begins to change as well, shifting from a benign, friendly figure into something darker, more distorted. Their physical appearance, once tied to the child's creative vision, becomes influenced by the darker emotions within them. Features that were once soft and comforting become sharp, eerie, and unsettling.

1. **Manifesting Fear:** As resentment turns into frustration, the imaginary friend's energy becomes intertwined with the child's growing fears. The Boogeyman, at this stage, emerges not just from loneliness, but from the fears that naturally arise as the child matures. Whether those fears are of the dark, of being alone, or of something unknown lurking in the shadows, the imaginary friend begins to embody them.

This fear acts as a bridge between the child and the now-twisting imaginary friend. The friend, desperate for attention, begins to manipulate these fears, manifesting in ways that frighten the child. They might create sounds in the closet, shadows under the bed, or a sense of unease in the dark. The once-playful friend has now become a creature of fear—shifting into the Boogeyman.

The Boogeyman doesn't merely want to terrify the child; they want the child to remember them, to notice them again. Even if that attention comes through screams or sleepless nights, the Boogeyman feeds on the energy of fear, drawing power from the child's terror. The imaginary friend has completed its metamorphosis into the Boogeyman: a being of darkness and fear, born from abandonment and fueled by the child's own anxieties.

Psychological Elements: The Emotional and Mental Shift

The transformation from imaginary friend to Boogeyman is deeply rooted in psychological processes. For children, imaginary friends represent a sense of control and comfort in a world where they are often powerless. When a child stops believing in this friend, they abandon a part of their emotional coping mechanisms, leaving behind unresolved feelings of fear, loneliness, and insecurity.

1. **Attachment and Loss:** Children form strong emotional attachments to their imaginary friends. When these friends are suddenly neglected or forgotten, it mirrors the real-world experience of loss or rejection. The imaginary friend, though a creation of the child's mind, represents a part of the child's emotional support system. The loss of this connection leads to feelings of abandonment, which manifest as the Boogeyman.

2. **Fear as a Projection of Internal Conflict:** The Boogeyman represents the externalization of a child's internal fears and conflicts. As the child grows older, they encounter new sources

of anxiety—whether it's fear of the dark, fear of growing up, or fear of loneliness. These fears, which may be too overwhelming for the child to process directly, are projected onto the Boogeyman.

In many ways, the Boogeyman serves as a psychological coping mechanism for these fears. By giving form to the child's anxieties, the Boogeyman allows the child to confront them in a tangible way, even if that confrontation is terrifying. The Boogeyman is a product of the child's subconscious mind, a figure that embodies all the fears the child has yet to process or understand.

1. **The Need for Recognition:** Psychologically, the Boogeyman's desire for attention reflects the child's own need for validation and emotional recognition. When the imaginary friend is forgotten, the Boogeyman emerges as a way for the child to confront the unresolved emotions surrounding that abandonment. Even though the child may no longer consciously think about their imaginary friend, the emotional impact of losing that connection remains.

The Boogeyman, as a projection of the child's subconscious, craves recognition because the child, on some level, still craves emotional resolution. The child must learn to face their fears and address the underlying emotions that gave rise to the Boogeyman in order to overcome it.

Magical Elements: The Enchantment of Imagination

While the psychological aspects of the transformation are grounded in the child's emotional state, the magical elements of this process draw from the creative and mystical aspects of imagination. In the context of *"The Boogey Book,"* the transformation from imaginary friend to Boogeyman is not only a psychological journey but also one that taps into the magic of belief and creativity.

1. **The Power of Belief:** Imagination is a form of magic in itself. Children's minds are capable of creating entire worlds and beings out of thin air, and imaginary friends are the most tangible form of this creative magic. When a child stops believing in their imaginary friend, it's as if the magical energy that once sustained them is cut off. This loss of belief is not just an emotional blow to the imaginary friend—it's a literal severing of the magical energy that kept them alive.

Without belief, the imaginary friend begins to decay. Their form becomes warped, and the light of creativity dims, allowing darker forces to take hold. This is where the transformation into the Boogeyman begins to take on a magical dimension. The Boogeyman is not just a manifestation of psychological fears but also a magical creature born from the decay of lost imagination.

1. **The Influence of Fear:** Fear, in the world of *"The Boogey Book,"* is a form of dark magic. Just as belief in the imaginary friend once empowered them, fear now fuels the Boogeyman's transformation. Fear has the power to warp reality, turning innocent shadows into menacing figures and ordinary sounds into terrifying noises. The Boogeyman harnesses this magical energy, using it to grow stronger and more real in the child's mind.

This is why the Boogeyman becomes most powerful at night, when fear is at its peak and the child's imagination runs wild. In the dark, the Boogeyman's form solidifies, and their ability to manipulate the environment around them—creaking floors, flickering lights, shifting shadows—grows stronger. The more the child fears them, the more powerful the Boogeyman becomes.

1. **The Boogey Dimension:** As the imaginary friend transforms into the Boogeyman, they gain access to a magical realm known as the **Boogey Dimension**. This is a shadowy, distorted mirror of the child's world, where the rules of reality are warped by fear and imagination. The Boogey Dimension is where the Boogeyman retreats when they are not actively haunting the child, and it is where they gather strength and power.

The Boogey Dimension is an ever-expanding realm, growing in size and complexity the longer the Boogeyman remains connected to the child's fears. It is filled with the remnants of forgotten imaginary friends, twisted and corrupted by their descent into darkness. The Boogeyman can manipulate this dimension, using it as a hiding place, a prison, or even a battleground in their encounters with the child.

The Final Transformation: From Friend to Foe

The transformation from imaginary friend to Boogeyman is a tragic and inevitable consequence of neglect and fear. Once a beacon of joy and comfort, the imaginary friend becomes a creature of darkness, driven by the desire to reclaim the child's attention—no matter the cost. This transformation is fueled by both psychological and magical forces, intertwining the child's emotional abandonment with the power of imagination and fear.

The Boogeyman, once fully formed, is no longer a friend but a formidable enemy. They are the embodiment of fear and loss, and they will not stop until the child confronts their fears and reclaims the imagination that once fueled their friendship.

The next step in the child's journey is learning how to fight back—how to face the Boogeyman, overcome fear, and restore the balance between light and dark. Only by understanding the transformation process can the child hope to defeat the Boogeyman and return their world to a place of safety, creativity, and wonder.

Chapter 3: Famous Boogeymen in History

The concept of the Boogeyman is one of the oldest and most persistent across cultures, appearing in various forms throughout the ages. Although the appearance and characteristics of the Boogeyman differ from one culture to another, the underlying theme remains consistent: a figure born from fear, often used to keep children obedient, and lurking in the dark places where the imagination wanders. While the Boogeyman is typically associated with childhood fears, many of these legendary figures have deep ties to the idea of abandoned or forgotten imaginary companions. As we explore famous Boogeymen throughout history, it becomes clear how these creatures tie into the collective myth of neglected imagination.

1. El Coco (Spain and Latin America)

Perhaps one of the most well-known Boogeymen figures, *El Coco* (or *El Cucuy* in Mexico) is a terrifying creature often invoked by parents to scare children into good behavior. Described as a dark, shapeless figure or an old man with a sack, El Coco is said to snatch children who misbehave or refuse to go to sleep. His legend is so ingrained in Spanish and Latin American cultures that the phrase, *"Duérmete niño, que viene el Coco,"* or "Go to sleep, child, or the Coco will come," is commonly used as a warning.

Connection to Forgotten Imaginary Friends:

In some interpretations of the El Coco myth, the creature is thought to be a shadowy reflection of a child's deepest fears—fear of the dark, fear of being alone, or fear of being forgotten. El Coco's ability to take children away if they misbehave reflects the emotional abandonment felt by a neglected imaginary friend. Once a protector and companion, the imaginary friend may evolve into El Coco if the child dismisses them, transforming into a lurking presence that feeds on fear. El Coco represents the darker side of imagination when it is left untended.

2. **The Boggart (England)**

In English folklore, *Boggarts* are mischievous or malevolent creatures that inhabit dark places such as under beds, inside cupboards, or in forests. They are known to cause household chaos—moving furniture, breaking dishes, and sometimes pulling blankets off sleeping children. In some stories, Boggarts can be invisible, making it difficult to track or expel them. Unlike some Boogeymen, Boggarts can attach themselves to specific families, following them wherever they move, which makes them nearly impossible to escape.

Connection to Forgotten Imaginary Friends:

The Boggart can be seen as a manifestation of an imaginary friend who has been completely forgotten, leaving the child's world but staying tied to the family home. The invisible, trickster nature of the Boggart suggests a being who was once playful and engaging but now feels resentment and seeks to cause mischief in retaliation for being abandoned. The Boggart's tendency to disrupt the comfort and safety of the home mirrors how a neglected imaginary friend might turn from a source of comfort into a source of disruption in a child's emotional life.

3.Baba Yaga (Slavic Folklore)

Baba Yaga is a powerful and terrifying figure in Slavic folklore, often depicted as a witch who lives in a hut that stands on chicken legs, deep within the forest. She is a complex figure—sometimes a helpful guide, other times a dangerous, child-eating monster. Baba Yaga represents both the nurturing and the destructive aspects of the mother figure. She tests those who seek her help, and while she may provide guidance or a solution, her demands are often frightening and challenging.

Connection to Forgotten Imaginary Friends:

Baba Yaga's dual nature—both a source of wisdom and a figure of fear—mirrors the relationship between a child and their imaginary friend. An imaginary friend, when nurtured, can be a source of guidance, creativity, and emotional support. However, when abandoned or feared, that same imaginary friend can become something far darker, much like Baba Yaga's fearsome nature. As a figure who tests the courage of those who seek her, Baba Yaga represents the emotional journey of confronting the fear of loss—whether it be the loss of innocence, imagination, or companionship.

4. The Namahage (Japan)

Namahage are demon-like figures from Japanese folklore, particularly in the Akita region. Traditionally, men dress as Namahage during New Year's celebrations, wearing fearsome masks and wielding knives while going door to door, asking if any lazy children or misbehaving people live in the house. Namahage act as a warning for children to behave properly, and their visits are said to ward off misfortune for the coming year. Though frightening in appearance, the Namahage are ultimately protectors of the home and family.

Connection to Forgotten Imaginary Friends:

The Namahage serve as a physical embodiment of the fears that a child might experience when they neglect their imaginary friend. Their dual role as both terrifying and protective figures reflects the complex emotional role that imaginary friends play. When an imaginary friend is neglected, they may take on a darker, more frightening aspect, but like the Namahage, their purpose is not purely malevolent. Instead, they serve to remind the child of important lessons—such as discipline, respect, and responsibility—mirroring the lessons that an imaginary friend might teach when engaged in play. The Namahage can be seen as a reflection of the imaginary friend's shift from playful companion to enforcer of boundaries, especially when neglected.

5. The Black Annis (England)

Black Annis is a horrifying hag from English folklore, said to live in a cave in the Dane Hills of Leicestershire. She is depicted as a blue-skinned woman with iron claws, known for her tendency to snatch children who stray too far from home or misbehave. Black Annis hides in the shadows, waiting for an opportunity to capture her victims and is said to use their skins to make clothing for herself.

Connection to Forgotten Imaginary Friends:

Black Annis represents the ultimate fear of abandonment and the destructive potential of neglected imagination. Her role as a predatory figure, lurking in the shadows and stealing children, parallels how a forgotten imaginary friend, once a protector, might transform into something dangerous and uncontrollable. Black Annis's craving for children's skins can be interpreted symbolically as a reflection of the imaginary friend's desire to reclaim the emotional connection with the child. Once the child outgrows their imaginary friend, the friend may become a figure like Black Annis, who waits in the dark, ready to consume the child's remaining sense of wonder and innocence

6. **The Wendigo (Algonquian Native American Mythology)**

In the mythology of the Algonquian-speaking peoples, the *Wendigo* is a malevolent, cannibalistic spirit that can possess humans and cause them to commit acts of extreme violence, especially cannibalism. The Wendigo is associated with winter, starvation, and the dangers of isolation. It is said to grow stronger as it consumes more, becoming an insatiable monster that is never satisfied. The Wendigo is not only a literal danger but also a metaphor for the destructive power of unchecked greed and isolation.

Connection to Forgotten Imaginary Friends:

The Wendigo's hunger and insatiability can be compared to the way an abandoned imaginary friend transforms into a Boogeyman. The longer the imaginary friend is neglected, the more their emotional hunger grows, and the more they crave attention—whether positive or negative. This endless desire for recognition mirrors the Wendigo's never-ending appetite. Additionally, the Wendigo's association with isolation ties into the theme of an imaginary friend who is left alone for too long, gradually becoming a fearsome and monstrous figure as a result of emotional starvation.

7.The Krampus (Central European Folklore)

Krampus is a horned, demonic figure from Central European folklore who punishes children who have been naughty during the Christmas season. The counterpart to Saint Nicholas, Krampus is known for terrifying children into good behavior, often depicted as a hairy, devilish figure with chains and bells, wielding a bundle of birch sticks to swat misbehaving children. In some legends, Krampus is said to carry a sack or basket in which he hauls away particularly bad children, either to his lair or to drown, eat, or otherwise punish them.

Connection to Forgotten Imaginary Friends:

Krampus's role as the punisher of bad behavior ties into the emotional response of a forgotten imaginary friend. While an imaginary friend might start off as a supportive, playful companion, they may eventually become a force of punishment and fear if abandoned. Much like Krampus's transformation from folklore figure to Christmas demon, the imaginary friend's shift into a Boogeyman can be seen as a consequence of emotional neglect. The child's refusal to engage with their imaginary friend transforms that friend into a punishing figure—one who haunts the child and demands recognition through fear, just as Krampus does during the Christmas season.

8. The Jumbie (Caribbean Folklore)

In Caribbean folklore, *Jumbies* are malevolent spirits that come out at night to cause harm or mischief. They are often associated with dark places, particularly forests, graveyards, or abandoned homes. Jumbies are known to prey on children who wander away from their homes or misbehave, and their appearance is usually accompanied by a chilling sense of dread or unease. They are often depicted as shape-shifters, capable of taking on different forms to deceive and frighten their victims.

Connection to Forgotten Imaginary Friends:

Jumbies, with their association with dark and abandoned places, can be seen as a reflection of the emotional state of a forgotten imaginary friend. Left alone and untended, the imaginary friend retreats into the dark corners of the child's mind, where they eventually transform into something more sinister. The Jumbie's ability to shape-shift mirrors the Boogeyman's mutable form, which changes according to the child's fears. The emotional abandonment of the imaginary friend leaves them vulnerable to becoming a Jumbie-like figure, one who lingers in the shadows and strikes fear into the child's heart.

Conclusion: Boogeymen as Universal Figures of Fear

Across cultures, the Boogeyman appears in many forms—some frightening, some tragic, and some cautionary. These figures all reflect a deep-seated fear of abandonment, punishment, and the unknown, which is often tied to childhood. But when we look deeper, many of these legendary Boogeymen also reveal the consequences of neglecting the imagination and the emotional connections we forge in our early years.

Whether through the shadowy Boggart, the punishing Krampus, or the monstrous Wendigo, the Boogeyman's transformation from an abandoned imaginary friend into a fearsome creature teaches us that the imagination must be nurtured and tended. Left unchecked, the imaginative energies that once brought comfort can become the very things that haunt us, lurking in the dark corners of our minds and feeding on our deepest fears.

The Boogeyman is not just a figure of punishment or fear but a symbol of the delicate balance between creativity and neglect, between light and darkness. To fight the Boogeyman is to reclaim control over our fears and, ultimately, to restore the power of imagination.

Here are some more examples, about 135 more examples of Boogiemen:

1. **The Bicho Papão (Portugal/Brazil)**

A traditional Portuguese and Brazilian Boogeyman figure, *Bicho Papão* is a monster that parents use to scare their children into obedience. The phrase "O Bicho Papão vai te pegar!" is often used to warn children to behave or sleep.

2. **The Sack Man (Spain/Portugal)**

The *Sack Man* is a Boogeyman-like figure who kidnaps naughty children by putting them into a sack. This figure is often used as a cautionary tale to ensure children obey their parents.

3. **Baba Roga (Slavic Folklore)**

In Slavic cultures, *Baba Roga* is similar to Baba Yaga, but with more of a focus on terrifying children. She's depicted as a scary old woman who comes to take away misbehaving kids.

4. **The Karakoncolos (Turkey)**

A winter-time figure, the *Karakoncolos* is a hairy, goblin-like creature that lures children out into the cold and causes mischief during long winter nights.

5. Struwwelpeter (Germany)

Struwwelpeter is a character in German folklore and literature who frightens children who don't care for their appearance. He's often depicted with long, unruly hair and nails, symbolizing neglect.

6. The Pooka (Celtic Mythology)

The *Pooka* is a shape-shifting creature from Irish folklore, often appearing as a black horse or goat. It is known for causing chaos and frightening children who wander too far from home.

7. The Erlking (Germany)

The *Erlking* is a supernatural creature that appears in the form of an old man who lures children to their deaths. His appearance is often associated with mist and darkness.

8. The Nain Rouge (France)

In French folklore, the *Nain Rouge* is a small, red dwarf who causes chaos and brings misfortune to those who see him. He is considered a harbinger of doom and bad luck.

9. The Nukekubi (Japan)

A *Nukekubi* is a being whose head detaches from its body at night to fly around and terrorize people, especially children. It's said to bite and harass its victims before returning to its body by dawn.

10. The Gashadokuro (Japan)

The *Gashadokuro* is a giant skeleton that roams the countryside, especially at night. It is the ghost of those who died from starvation, and it sneaks up on its victims to crush them.

11. The Bugbear (England)

A creature similar to the Boogeyman, the *Bugbear* is often depicted as a bear-like monster that terrorizes children. The term "bugbear" is now used to describe an irrational fear.

12. The Jinn (Middle Eastern Folklore)

In Islamic and Middle Eastern folklore, *Jinn* are supernatural beings made from smokeless fire. Some Jinn can be malevolent, haunting or possessing people, and terrifying children.

13. The Banshee (Irish Folklore)

The *Banshee* is a female spirit whose wail is said to signal death. Though not directly a Boogeyman, her terrifying appearance and association with death make her a fearsome figure in Irish mythology.

14. The Slender Man (Modern Urban Legend)

A modern addition to the pantheon of Boogeyman-like figures, *Slender Man* is a tall, faceless figure who abducts and terrorizes children, primarily existing in the digital folklore of the internet age.

15. The Leshy (Russian Folklore)

The *Leshy* is a forest spirit in Russian folklore who can take the form of a giant or shrink to the size of a blade of grass. He is known for kidnapping children and leading them deep into the forest.

16. The Kallikantzaros (Greece)

The *Kallikantzaros* are mischievous goblins that come to the surface during the twelve days of Christmas to create chaos, destroy things, and frighten children.

17. The Cuca (Brazilian Folklore)

The *Cuca* is a witch-like figure in Brazilian folklore who kidnaps children who don't go to bed. She is often depicted as an old hag or alligator-woman.

18. The Alp (Germany)

The *Alp* is a malevolent spirit or demon in German folklore that sits on the chest of sleeping individuals, causing nightmares. The Alp preys on fear, similar to the Boogeyman.

19. The Chaneques (Mexico)

Chaneques are small, mischievous creatures from Mexican folklore. They are known to protect the forests but will abduct children who wander too far from home.

20. The Ijiraq (Inuit Mythology)

An *Ijiraq* is a shapeshifter from Inuit mythology who kidnaps children and hides them away from their families. It is often associated with getting lost in the wilderness.

21. The Tokoloshe (Southern African Folklore)

The *Tokoloshe* is a small, malevolent creature in Southern African folklore, often invoked to frighten children or adults. It can make itself invisible and attack at night, typically targeting the weak or unsuspecting.

22. The Wendigo (Algonquian Native American Mythology)

The *Wendigo* is a terrifying spirit of cannibalism and starvation in Algonquian folklore. It embodies greed and excess, often preying on children or adults who have lost their moral compass.

23. The Yule Cat (Iceland)

The *Yule Cat* is a monstrous feline from Icelandic folklore that prowls during Christmas time, devouring anyone who hasn't received new clothes for the holiday season. It's meant to scare children into good behavior.

24. The Groac'h (Breton Folklore)

The *Groac'h* is a malevolent water spirit in Breton folklore. She lures children and adults to her underwater lair, where she drowns them or turns them into fish.

25. The Dzoavits (Shoshone Mythology)

A malevolent figure in Shoshone mythology, *Dzoavits* is known for kidnapping children and carrying them away to his cave, where they are never seen again.

26. The Jorōgumo (Japanese Mythology)

A *Jorōgumo* is a spider spirit that can transform into a beautiful woman. She lures young men into her web, trapping and consuming them, representing deceptive and predatory behavior.

27. The Nachzehrer (Germany)

A *Nachzehrer* is a type of vampire in German folklore. Unlike traditional vampires, it feeds on the life force of others, particularly children, by consuming corpses or draining energy from the living.

28. The Kappa (Japan)

Kappa are water spirits in Japanese mythology, known to drag children into rivers and lakes to drown them. They are both feared and revered, as they are capable of both helping and harming.

29. The Striga (Albania)

The *Striga* is a vampiric witch in Albanian folklore that preys on children, particularly at night, by draining their life force. They are considered a malevolent force of the supernatural.

30. The Encantado (Brazilian Folklore)

Encantados are shape-shifting dolphin spirits from the Amazon River. Though typically benevolent, they have been known to lure children away from their families with magical music and take them to an underwater world.

31. The Nokken (Scandinavian Folklore)

The *Nokken* is a water spirit in Scandinavian folklore that plays enchanting music to lure people, especially children, into rivers or lakes where they drown.

32. The Djieien (Iroquois Mythology)

A giant spider in Iroquois mythology, *Djieien* spins webs to trap its victims, particularly children who wander too far into the forest. It represents entrapment and isolation.

33. The Patasola (Colombian Folklore)

The *Patasola* is a vampire-like creature in Colombian folklore, appearing as a beautiful woman to lure men and children into the jungle, where she reveals her true, hideous form and attacks them.

34. The Lamia (Greek Mythology)

The *Lamia* was once a beautiful queen who turned into a child-eating monster after losing her own children. She hunts down and devours the children of others, embodying maternal grief turned into destructive rage.

35. The Aswang (Philippine Folklore)

The *Aswang* is a shape-shifting, vampiric creature in Filipino mythology that preys on children, especially pregnant women and newborns, by consuming their flesh or blood.

36. Pontianak (Malaysia)

Description: The *Pontianak* is a vengeful female spirit that often appears as a beautiful woman, luring men before transforming into a monster that attacks and kills them. **Link to Imaginary Friend:** The *Pontianak* could represent an imaginary friend who feels abandoned, particularly after a traumatic experience such as betrayal. In her transformation from nurturing to vengeful, she mirrors the emotional shift from an imaginary friend who was once comforting to a creature of resentment, seeking revenge on those who forgot her.

37. La Llorona (Mexico)

Description: *La Llorona* is the ghost of a woman who drowned her children and now wanders the earth in eternal grief, weeping and searching for them. **Link to Imaginary Friend:** *La Llorona* is driven by the unbearable pain of loss, similar to an imaginary friend who feels deeply betrayed or abandoned by the child who created her. This deep emotional pain transforms her into a ghostly, terrifying figure, much like how a forgotten imaginary friend may become a Boogeyman to gain attention through fear.

38. Strigoi (Romania)

Description: The *Strigoi* are undead, vampiric creatures who return from the grave to haunt and feed on the living. **Link to Imaginary Friend:** The *Strigoi* can be seen as an imaginary friend who, after being left behind, returns to "haunt" the child, seeking attention through negative means. Their vampiric nature—draining life force—parallels how an imaginary friend might drain emotional energy from the child through fear and nightmares.

39. Gualichu (Mapuche Mythology)

Description: *Gualichu* is an evil spirit in Mapuche mythology that causes misfortune and illness. **Link to Imaginary Friend:** *Gualichu* represents an imaginary friend who has become malevolent, perhaps after being forgotten or cast aside. Its influence over a person's wellbeing mirrors how an abandoned imaginary friend might morph into a source of fear, causing emotional or psychological harm as a way to demand recognition.

40. Hodag (North American Folklore)

Description: The *Hodag* is a mythical creature said to inhabit the forests of Wisconsin, often described as fearsome and grotesque. **Link to Imaginary Friend:** The *Hodag* could represent an imaginary friend who, once playful and adventurous, has become a wild, uncontrollable force due to being abandoned. Its monstrous appearance may be a reflection of how the imaginary friend's personality and form have become distorted through neglect.

41.The Dullahan (Ireland)

Description: The *Dullahan* is a headless horseman who rides through the night, often seen as a harbinger of death. **Link to Imaginary Friend:** The *Dullahan* could symbolize an imaginary friend whose identity and purpose have been "severed" by the child's lack of belief. This disconnection mirrors the physical headlessness of the *Dullahan*, and the transformation into a harbinger of death represents the imaginary friend's shift from protector to a figure of fear.

42. Adze (Ewe Mythology, Ghana)

Description: The *Adze* is a vampiric being that can take the form of a firefly and possess humans, feeding on their blood. **Link to Imaginary Friend:** The *Adze*'s transformation from a harmless insect into a malevolent spirit mirrors the shift of an imaginary friend from a source of light (firefly) to a dark, vampiric creature. The possession aspect can represent how an imaginary friend, once abandoned, invades the child's mind, becoming a tormenting presence.

43. Penanggalan (Malaysia)

Description: A *Penanggalan* is a type of vampiric spirit whose head and organs detach from its body to fly around at night, seeking blood. **Link to Imaginary Friend:** The horrific transformation of the *Penanggalan*—from human to flying monster—parallels how an imaginary friend, once a loving companion, can become a disembodied terror seeking to regain control over the child's imagination through fear.

44. The Azeman (Suriname)

Description: The *Azeman* is a vampire-like figure from Surinamese folklore that transforms into an animal at night and preys on humans. **Link to Imaginary Friend:** The *Azeman* can represent an imaginary friend who has morphed into something primal and predatory after being abandoned. The shape-shifting quality symbolizes how the imaginary friend's role and form have changed, becoming a predator rather than a protector.

45. Gorgon (Greek Mythology)

Description: The *Gorgons*, including Medusa, are monstrous women with snakes for hair, whose gaze can turn people to stone. **Link to Imaginary Friend:** The *Gorgon* can represent an imaginary friend who has been rejected due to fear or misunderstanding. The transformation into a monster with the power to petrify others reflects the emotional freezing or "petrification" of a once-loving relationship, with the imaginary friend turning dangerous after abandonment.

46. La Diablesse (Caribbean Folklore)

Description: *La Diablesse* is a seductive, deceptive woman who lures men into danger. She is often associated with betrayal and manipulation. **Link to Imaginary Friend:** *La Diablesse* can represent an imaginary friend who feels betrayed and thus becomes a manipulative, dangerous figure. Once abandoned, this friend might resort to trickery or deception, symbolized by *La Diablesse*, to draw attention back to themselves through fear or seduction.

47. Tikbalang (Philippine Mythology)

Description: The *Tikbalang* is a humanoid creature with the head of a horse that causes travelers to become lost in the woods. **Link to Imaginary Friend:** The *Tikbalang* represents an imaginary friend who, once neglected, leads the child astray emotionally. Rather than providing guidance and comfort, the friend now creates confusion and disorientation, much like the *Tikbalang* who misleads travelers.

48. The Gritty (American Urban Legend)

Description: *The Gritty* is a modern urban legend originating from sports culture, often depicted as a large, monstrous figure with an unsettling presence. **Link to Imaginary Friend:** *The Gritty* can symbolize an imaginary friend who, after abandonment, has grown into something unsettling and bizarre. Its playful yet grotesque form mirrors how an imaginary friend can become distorted over time, blending elements of fun with fear.

49. El Sombrerón (Guatemala)

Description: *El Sombrerón* is a short man with a large hat who enchants young women, tying up their hair and casting spells to prevent them from sleeping. **Link to Imaginary Friend:** *El Sombrerón*'s enchanting and controlling nature mirrors how an imaginary friend might become possessive after abandonment. Rather than bringing joy and comfort, the friend now disrupts sleep and peace, using enchantments as a way to regain influence over the child.

50. The Nilbog (Modern Fantasy)

Description: *Nilbog* is a creature from modern fantasy lore that has the ability to reverse the effects of healing, feeding on positive energy to grow stronger. **Link to Imaginary Friend:** The *Nilbog* represents an imaginary friend who, rather than healing or comforting the child, has become a reverse force—feeding on positivity and turning it into fear. This inversion of purpose mirrors the emotional reversal an imaginary friend experiences when neglected.

51. Nure-onna (Japan)

Description: The *Nure-onna* is a serpent-woman who lures people to rivers with her childlike cries, only to drag them into the water and drown them. **Link to Imaginary Friend:** The *Nure-onna* represents an imaginary friend who manipulates a child's emotions to regain attention. Her childlike cries reflect the friend's desire to return to their former relationship, but her deadly nature shows how far the friend has transformed, now using fear and manipulation.

52. Cipactli (Aztec Mythology)

Description: *Cipactli* is a primordial sea monster in Aztec mythology, often depicted as a crocodile or fish-like creature. **Link to Imaginary Friend:** *Cipactli* represents an imaginary friend who has become a primal, uncontrollable force after abandonment. Their shift into a monstrous sea creature symbolizes how deeply buried emotions—once imaginative—can transform into dangerous entities lurking in the subconscious.

53. Oni (Japan)

Description: *Oni* are large, demon-like creatures known for their strength and ferocity. They are often used to frighten people, particularly children. **Link to Imaginary Friend:** The *Oni*'s transformation from protector to aggressor mirrors the path of an imaginary friend turned Boogeyman. Once a source of strength and companionship, the friend now uses their power to instill fear and dominate the child's imagination.

54. Golem (Jewish Folklore)

Description: The *Golem* is a creature made of clay or earth, brought to life by magic to serve and protect, but sometimes becomes uncontrollable. **Link to Imaginary Friend:** The *Golem* represents an imaginary friend who was once created to serve a protective role but, after being abandoned, has grown uncontrollable. Its raw, elemental nature reflects how the friend has become something too powerful and independent, now acting as a Boogeyman.

55. Baba Yaga (Slavic Folklore)

Description: *Baba Yaga* is a witch who lives in a hut on chicken legs and has both nurturing and malevolent qualities. She tests those who seek her help. **Link to Imaginary Friend:** *Baba Yaga*'s dual nature mirrors the transformation of an imaginary friend from benevolent to malevolent. The imaginary friend's original nurturing role turns into a test of courage, with the friend becoming more menacing to demand the child's attention.

56. The Hecatoncheires (Greek Mythology)

Description: The *Hecatoncheires* are giant creatures with a hundred hands and fifty heads, representing chaos and overwhelming force. **Link to Imaginary Friend:** The overwhelming form of the *Hecatoncheires* can represent the chaotic emotions of an abandoned imaginary friend. Their many hands and heads reflect the myriad ways the friend tries to regain attention, becoming an unstoppable force of fear rather than comfort.

57. Impundulu (Southern Africa)

Description: The *Impundulu* is a lightning bird that can take human form and serve witches. It feeds on blood and is often used to frighten children. **Link to Imaginary Friend:** The *Impundulu* represents an imaginary friend who has aligned with darker forces after being abandoned, using its once-helpful abilities for harm. The lightning imagery reflects how quickly and dramatically an imaginary friend can transform into a terrifying figure.

58. Huggin' Molly (American Folklore)

Description: *Huggin' Molly* is a ghostly figure who hugs people tightly, almost to the point of suffocation, before disappearing. **Link to Imaginary Friend:** *Huggin' Molly* represents an imaginary friend who, after abandonment, becomes possessive and overbearing. The suffocating hugs symbolize the friend's desperate attempt to cling to the child, even if it causes discomfort or fear.

59. Cucafera (Catalonian Folklore)

Description: *Cucafera* is a dragon-like creature that kidnaps children and carries them away to her lair. **Link to Imaginary Friend:** The *Cucafera* represents an imaginary friend who has become possessive and controlling after being forgotten. Instead of providing comfort, the friend now traps the child in a world of fear, much like the dragon who carries children away.

60. Ogopogo (Canada)

Description: *Ogopogo* is a lake monster said to live in Okanagan Lake in British Columbia. It is both feared and revered. **Link to Imaginary Friend:** The *Ogopogo*'s mysterious and elusive nature reflects how an imaginary friend can fade into the subconscious after being forgotten, only to resurface as a fearsome presence, lurking beneath the surface of the child's mind.

61. Hákarl (Iceland)

Description: *Hákarl* is a shark that has been fermented and is associated with Icelandic tradition, but its fearsome reputation in myth links it to danger. **Link to Imaginary Friend:** The *Hákarl* can represent an imaginary friend who has been "preserved" in the child's mind, becoming toxic and fearsome after being forgotten. Its association with danger mirrors how the friend's memory becomes a source of fear rather than comfort.

62. Vetala (Hindu Mythology)

Description: The *Vetala* is a spirit that haunts cemeteries and can possess corpses, using them to frighten and terrorize the living. **Link to Imaginary Friend:** The *Vetala* represents an imaginary friend who has taken over darker elements of the child's psyche, haunting them from the shadows and using fear as a way to maintain control, much like the possession of a corpse.

63. Akabeko (Japanese Folklore)

Description: The *Akabeko* is a red cow believed to protect against illness, especially smallpox. Though benevolent, its strong association with disease makes it a powerful figure in folklore. **Link to Imaginary Friend:** The *Akabeko* represents an imaginary friend who, after being abandoned, takes on protective but fearsome qualities. While still caring for the child, the friend's new form is intimidating and frightening, creating a sense of unease in the child.

64. Chullachaqui (Peruvian Amazon)

Description: The *Chullachaqui* is a forest spirit that lures people away with the appearance of someone they know before trapping them in the jungle. **Link to Imaginary Friend:** The *Chullachaqui* represents an imaginary friend who uses deception to regain attention. By taking on a familiar form, the friend leads the child deeper into emotional isolation, much like the spirit leading people into the jungle.

65. Baba Harbhajan (Indian Folklore)

Description: *Baba Harbhajan* is a military ghost said to protect soldiers along the Indian-Chinese border. Though benevolent, his spirit is seen as both protective and somewhat unsettling. **Link to Imaginary Friend:** *Baba Harbhajan* represents an imaginary friend who continues to "protect" the child even after being forgotten. However, this protection now comes in a ghostly, unsettling form, blurring the lines between comfort and fear.

66. Churels (Indian Mythology)

Description: *Churels* are the spirits of women who died violently or during childbirth and return as vengeful ghosts, often targeting men. **Link to Imaginary Friend:** The *Churels* represent an imaginary friend who, after being abandoned in a moment of emotional trauma, returns as a vengeful force. Their need for revenge mirrors the emotional hurt caused by abandonment, transforming love into fear.

67. El Pombero (Argentina)

Description: *El Pombero* is a small, mischievous creature known for causing mischief in rural areas, sometimes kidnapping or harassing people. **Link to Imaginary Friend:** *El Pombero* represents an imaginary friend who has become mischievous and uncontrollable after being forgotten. What was once playful has turned destructive, with the friend using mischief as a way to gain the child's attention.

68. Nzambi (Congo)

Description: *Nzambi* is a powerful spirit associated with death and the underworld in Congolese folklore. **Link to Imaginary Friend:** *Nzambi* represents an imaginary friend who has transitioned into a figure associated with death and endings. After being forgotten, the friend adopts a role of finality and fear, reminding the child of the emotional consequences of abandonment.

69. Yowie (Australia)

Description: The *Yowie* is a large, ape-like creature said to inhabit the wilderness of Australia, often considered a dangerous and elusive being. **Link to Imaginary Friend:** The *Yowie* represents an imaginary friend who has become distant and feral after abandonment. No longer connected to the child's playful world, the friend now exists as a wild, fearsome figure lurking on the fringes of the child's imagination.

70. The Golem (Eastern Europe)

Description: The *Golem* is a creature made of clay, brought to life to serve but often becomes uncontrollable. **Link to Imaginary Friend:** The *Golem*'s transformation from a servant to an uncontrollable being mirrors the journey of an imaginary friend who was once protective but becomes a force of fear after being neglected.

71. The Tiyanak (Philippines)

Description: The *Tiyanak* is a vampiric creature that takes the form of a baby to lure people in before attacking them. **Link to Imaginary Friend:** The *Tiyanak* represents an imaginary friend who uses their once-innocent form to manipulate the child into re-engaging, only to reveal their darker, more dangerous nature as a Boogeyman.

72. The White Lady (Global Folklore)

Description: The *White Lady* is a ghostly figure often associated with tragedy, grief, and vengeance. **Link to Imaginary Friend:** The *White Lady* represents an imaginary friend who, after being abandoned, has transformed into a ghostly, tragic figure seeking acknowledgment through fear. Her connection to grief mirrors the emotional pain of abandonment.

73. Asema (Suriname)

Description: The *Asema* is a vampiric witch in Surinamese folklore, capable of shape-shifting and preying on victims at night. **Link to Imaginary Friend:** The *Asema* represents an imaginary friend who has become predatory after abandonment, using shape-shifting and fear to manipulate the child into paying attention.

74. The Anaye (Navajo Mythology)

Description: The *Anaye* are monstrous beings in Navajo mythology, often considered enemies of humanity. **Link to Imaginary Friend:** The *Anaye* represent an imaginary friend who has transformed into a monstrous figure, turning against the child and embodying all the fears and anxieties that arise from emotional neglect.

75. The Pishacha (Indian Mythology)

Description: The *Pishacha* are demonic spirits that haunt graveyards and feed on human energy. **Link to Imaginary Friend:** The *Pishacha* represent an imaginary friend who, after abandonment, becomes a parasitic force in the child's mind. No longer a source of creativity, the friend now drains the child's emotional energy through fear and nightmares.

76. The Wendish Werewolf (Germany)

Description: The *Wendish Werewolf* is a shapeshifter that takes the form of a wolf to terrorize villages and forests. **Link to Imaginary Friend:** The *Wendish Werewolf* symbolizes an imaginary friend who has taken on a predatory, wild form after abandonment. Their once-friendly shape has become dangerous, hunting the child's peace of mind.

77. The Tenome (Japan)

Description: The *Tenome* is a ghostly figure with eyes on its hands, known for chasing and devouring its victims. **Link to Imaginary Friend:** The *Tenome* represents an imaginary friend who has become grotesque and dangerous, symbolizing how distorted and frightening a once-comforting figure can become when forgotten. The eyes on its hands reflect the friend's desperate search for recognition and attention.

78. Nain Rouge (Detroit Folklore)

Description: The *Nain Rouge* is a red dwarf that brings misfortune and disaster to those who encounter him. **Link to Imaginary Friend:** The *Nain Rouge* represents an imaginary friend who has become a harbinger of bad luck after being forgotten. No longer a source of joy, the friend now appears in times of fear and anxiety, feeding off the child's negative emotions.

79. The Wraith (Global Mythology)

Description: A *Wraith* is a ghostly figure that represents death or doom, often seen before a person's demise. **Link to Imaginary Friend:** The *Wraith* represents an imaginary friend who has taken on a haunting, ghostly form after abandonment, symbolizing the emotional death of the once-loving relationship and the fear that follows.

80. The Grim Reaper (Western Culture)

Description: The *Grim Reaper* is the personification of death, often depicted as a cloaked figure wielding a scythe. **Link to Imaginary Friend:** The *Grim Reaper* represents the final stage of an imaginary friend's transformation, where they become a figure of death or finality. The once-joyful relationship is now severed completely, with the friend serving as a reminder of the emotional consequences of neglect.

81. Morgens (Welsh Folklore)

Description: The *Morgens* are water spirits who drown people, particularly children, who venture too close to the water. **Link to Imaginary Friend:** The *Morgens* represent an imaginary friend who lures the child into danger, using once-playful methods to regain attention, now twisted into malevolent manipulation.

82. The Skinwalker (Navajo)

Description: A *Skinwalker* is a malevolent witch who can transform into an animal, often associated with dark magic and danger. **Link to Imaginary Friend:** The *Skinwalker* represents an imaginary friend who has embraced dark, predatory instincts after abandonment. No longer serving the child's imagination, the friend now uses fear and shape-shifting to regain attention in a destructive manner.

83. Goblins (Global)

Description: *Goblins* are mischievous and often malevolent creatures that cause trouble, steal, and disrupt households. **Link to Imaginary Friend:** Goblins represent an imaginary friend who has turned into a mischievous and chaotic force after abandonment. No longer a benign presence, the friend now uses disruption and trickery to remind the child of their existence.

84. Shades (Greek Mythology)

Description: *Shades* are the spirits of the dead, often depicted as ghostly, shadow-like figures who wander the underworld. **Link to Imaginary Friend:** *Shades* represent an imaginary friend who has become a ghost of their former self, haunting the child from the recesses of their mind. Their presence serves as a reminder of what once was, but now lingers as a source of fear.

85. The Myling (Scandinavian Mythology)

Description: The *Myling* is the spirit of an unbaptized child that haunts the living, often seeking vengeance for their abandonment. **Link to Imaginary Friend:** The *Myling* represents an imaginary friend who feels abandoned and now haunts the child as a form of vengeance. The emotional neglect is symbolized by the ghostly, tragic figure who seeks to regain attention through fear.

86. Werehyenas (African Folklore)

Description: *Werehyenas* are shape-shifting humans who take the form of hyenas, often feared for their predatory nature. **Link to Imaginary Friend:** *Werehyenas* symbolize an imaginary friend who has embraced a predatory, animalistic form after abandonment. No longer a source of playful companionship, the friend now uses fear and predation to dominate the child's thoughts.

87. The Gray Man (American Folklore)

Description: The *Gray Man* is a ghostly figure that appears before hurricanes, warning people of impending danger. **Link to Imaginary Friend:** The *Gray Man* represents an imaginary friend who now serves as a harbinger of fear, warning the child of emotional turmoil. Though not directly harmful, their presence is unsettling, reflecting the friend's shift from protector to a source of anxiety.

88. The Tizheruk (Inuit Mythology)

Description: The *Tizheruk* is a giant sea serpent that lurks in the waters near Alaska, dragging people and animals into the depths. **Link to Imaginary Friend:** The *Tizheruk* represents an imaginary friend who has become a lurking, dangerous presence in the child's subconscious. Once a playful creation, the friend now drags the child into emotional depths, symbolizing the overwhelming fear of abandonment.

89. The Spring-Heeled Jack (England)

Description: *Spring-Heeled Jack* is a Victorian-era figure who terrorized people by leaping great distances and breathing fire, known for his unsettling appearance. **Link to Imaginary Friend:** *Spring-Heeled Jack* represents an imaginary friend who has become unpredictable and frightening after abandonment. The friend now jumps into the child's life in unexpected and terrifying ways, seeking attention through shock and fear.

90. Chaneques (Mexican Folklore)

Description: *Chaneques* are small forest spirits known for causing mischief and leading people astray, particularly children. **Link to Imaginary Friend:** The *Chaneques* represent an imaginary friend who has become mischievous and manipulative after being forgotten. Rather than bringing joy, the friend now leads the child into confusion and fear.

91. Pelesit (Malaysia)

Description: The *Pelesit* is a spirit that possesses people, causing them to act against their will. **Link to Imaginary Friend:** The *Pelesit* represents an imaginary friend who has taken control of the child's mind after abandonment. Rather than serving the child's imagination, the friend now manipulates their thoughts and actions, becoming a dark, controlling presence.

92. Trolls (Norwegian Folklore)

Description: *Trolls* are large, monstrous beings that live in caves or forests, often depicted as hostile or mischievous toward humans. **Link to Imaginary Friend:** The *Trolls* represent an imaginary friend who has become monstrous after abandonment, hiding in the dark corners of the child's mind. Once playful, the friend now embodies the child's fear of isolation and loneliness.

93. The Rougarou (Louisiana)

Description: The *Rougarou* is a werewolf-like creature from Louisiana folklore, said to stalk people who break Lent or behave badly. **Link to Imaginary Friend:** The *Rougarou* represents an imaginary friend who has taken on a fearsome, predatory form after abandonment. No longer guiding the child toward fun or creativity, the friend now stalks them with the intention of enforcing rules through fear.

94. Kornbock (Germany)

Description: The *Kornbock* is a creature associated with the harvest, often seen as a punishment for those who neglect their duties. **Link to Imaginary Friend:** The *Kornbock* represents an imaginary friend who punishes the child for forgetting them. Their once-playful demeanor has turned into a reminder of the consequences of neglect, now enforcing their presence through fear of punishment.

95. Domovoi (Slavic Mythology)

Description: The *Domovoi* is a household spirit that protects the home but can become mischievous if neglected or disrespected. **Link to Imaginary Friend:** The *Domovoi* represents an imaginary friend who, after abandonment, shifts from a protective force to a mischievous or frightening presence. The friend's need for recognition leads them to cause disruption and fear in the household.

96. Rusalka (Russian Mythology)

Description: *Rusalka* are water nymphs that lure people, especially men, into rivers or lakes, where they drown them. **Link to Imaginary Friend:** The *Rusalka* represents an imaginary friend who has become seductive and dangerous after abandonment. Once playful and innocent, the friend now lures the child into emotional danger, seeking attention through manipulation.

97. Tiyanak (Filipino Mythology)

Description: The *Tiyanak* is a vampiric creature that takes the form of a baby to lure people in before attacking them. **Link to Imaginary Friend:** The *Tiyanak* represents an imaginary friend who uses their once-innocent form to manipulate the child into re-engaging, only to reveal their darker, more dangerous nature as a Boogeyman.

98. Cadejo (Central American Folklore)

Description: The *Cadejo* is a supernatural dog that can be either good or evil, protecting or attacking travelers. **Link to Imaginary Friend:** The *Cadejo*'s dual nature reflects how an imaginary friend can transform from a protector into a fearsome adversary after abandonment. The once-loyal companion now haunts the child, deciding whether to offer protection or terror.

99. Nightmare (Germanic Folklore)

Description: *Nightmares* are creatures that sit on the chest of sleeping people, causing terrifying dreams. **Link to Imaginary Friend:** The *Nightmare* represents an imaginary friend who has become a literal source of fear in the child's dreams. No longer a comforting presence, the friend now haunts the child's sleep, turning their imagination against them.

100. Black Shuck (British Folklore)

Description: *Black Shuck* is a ghostly black dog said to appear as an omen of death or misfortune. **Link to Imaginary Friend:** *Black Shuck* represents an imaginary friend who has transformed into a dark, looming presence after abandonment. Once playful, the friend now brings fear and anxiety into the child's life, serving as a harbinger of emotional turmoil.

101. Wepwawet (Egyptian Mythology)

Description: *Wepwawet* is a god associated with war and death, often depicted as a wolf or jackal. **Link to Imaginary Friend:** *Wepwawet* represents an imaginary friend who has adopted a more aggressive, warlike demeanor after abandonment. The friend's transformation into a figure associated with death mirrors the emotional severing between them and the child.

102. Tarasque (French Folklore)

Description: The *Tarasque* is a dragon-like creature that terrorizes villages in French folklore, eventually tamed by a saint. **Link to Imaginary Friend:** The *Tarasque* represents an imaginary friend who has become wild and uncontrollable after being forgotten. The friend's transformation into a dangerous creature reflects the emotional turmoil caused by abandonment.

103. Qalupalik (Inuit Mythology)

Description: The *Qalupalik* is a sea monster that lures children to the water's edge and drags them into the depths. **Link to Imaginary Friend:** The *Qalupalik* represents an imaginary friend who uses emotional manipulation to lure the child back into their world. Once a playful companion, the friend now drags the child into a dark, fearsome place, symbolizing the danger of neglect.

104. Manananggal (Philippine Folklore)

Description: The *Manananggal* is a vampiric creature that detaches its upper body to fly around and prey on pregnant women. **Link to Imaginary Friend:** The *Manananggal* represents an imaginary friend who has become a predatory, parasitic force after abandonment. Their once-whole form has become divided, symbolizing the emotional fragmentation caused by the child's neglect.

105. The Headless Mule (Brazilian Folklore)

Description: The *Headless Mule* is a cursed woman who transforms into a headless creature, galloping through the night and causing destruction. **Link to Imaginary Friend:** The *Headless Mule* represents an imaginary friend who has been cursed by abandonment, losing their identity and becoming a destructive force in the child's life.

106. The Bogey (Old English Folklore)

Description: *The Bogey* is a traditional Boogeyman figure who hides in closets or under beds, waiting to scare children. **Link to Imaginary Friend:** *The Bogey* represents the quintessential imaginary friend turned Boogeyman. Once a comforting figure, the friend now lurks in the child's subconscious, using fear to regain attention.

107. The Cuca (Brazilian Folklore)

Description: The *Cuca* is a witch-like figure who kidnaps children who don't go to bed. **Link to Imaginary Friend:** The *Cuca* represents an imaginary friend who has become controlling and punishing after being forgotten. The friend now enforces rules through fear, using their once-nurturing role as a way to instill terror.

108. Momo (Modern Urban Legend)

Description: *Momo* is a modern internet urban legend, depicted as a grotesque figure who communicates with people through social media, causing fear and panic. **Link to Imaginary Friend:** *Momo* represents an imaginary friend who has adapted to modern technology to haunt the child. Their distorted, grotesque form reflects how an abandoned friend can evolve into a fearsome presence in the digital age.

109. The Domovoi (Slavic Mythology)

Description: The *Domovoi* is a household spirit that protects the home but can become mischievous if neglected. **Link to Imaginary Friend:** The *Domovoi* represents an imaginary friend who, after abandonment, turns to mischief and fear as a way to regain the child's attention. No longer a comforting protector, the friend now causes chaos in the household.

110. The Ebu Gogo (Indonesian Folklore)

Description: *Ebu Gogo* are small, humanoid creatures known for stealing food and children in Indonesian folklore. **Link to Imaginary Friend:** The *Ebu Gogo* represent an imaginary friend who has become greedy and manipulative after abandonment. Rather than offering companionship, the friend now takes from the child, using fear and theft to assert their presence.

111. Adaro (Solomon Islands)

Description: The *Adaro* are malevolent sea spirits that bring harm to those who encounter them. **Link to Imaginary Friend:** The *Adaro* represent an imaginary friend who, after abandonment, becomes a malevolent force associated with danger. The friend's transformation into a sea spirit reflects the emotional depths and turmoil caused by neglect.

112. Nukekubi (Japan)

Description: The *Nukekubi* is a being whose head detaches from its body at night to fly around and terrorize people. **Link to Imaginary Friend:** The *Nukekubi* represents an imaginary friend whose identity has become fragmented after abandonment. Once whole, the friend now uses their disembodied form to haunt the child, seeking attention through fear.

113. Kelpie (Scotland)

Description: The *Kelpie* is a shape-shifting water spirit that lures people to their deaths by drowning. **Link to Imaginary Friend:** The *Kelpie* represents an imaginary friend who uses manipulation and emotional allure to regain the child's attention. Once playful, the friend now lures the child into dangerous emotional territory, symbolizing the fear of abandonment.

114. Haltija (Finland)

Description: *Haltija* are guardian spirits that protect the natural world, but can become dangerous if angered. **Link to Imaginary Friend:** The *Haltija* represent an imaginary friend who has become vengeful after being forgotten. Once a guardian, the friend now punishes the child through fear and manipulation, using their former protective role as leverage.

115. El Cadejo (Guatemala)

Description: *El Cadejo* is a supernatural dog that can be either good or evil, protecting or attacking travelers. **Link to Imaginary Friend:** The *Cadejo* represents an imaginary friend who has become a dual-natured figure after abandonment. The friend's shift from protector to predator mirrors the emotional tension between loyalty and fear.

116. The Drude (Germany)

Description: The *Drude* is a witch-like figure that causes nightmares by sitting on the chest of sleeping people. **Link to Imaginary Friend:** The *Drude* represents an imaginary friend who, after abandonment, becomes a literal source of nightmares. Rather than comforting the child, the friend now haunts their sleep, turning their dreams into a source of fear.

117. Zashiki-warashi (Japan)

Description: The *Zashiki-warashi* are childlike spirits that bring good fortune to households, but can become mischievous if disrespected. **Link to Imaginary Friend:** The *Zashiki-warashi* represent an imaginary friend who, after being forgotten, turns to mischief and disruption. Once a source of joy and good fortune, the friend now causes confusion and fear to regain attention.

118. The Skadegamutc (Mi'kmaq Mythology)

Description: The *Skadegamutc* are undead witches who prey on the living, often appearing at night to attack and feed on their victims. **Link to Imaginary Friend:** The *Skadegamutc* represent an imaginary friend who has taken on a vampiric, predatory form after abandonment. Their transformation into an undead figure reflects the emotional death of the friendship and the friend's new role as a Boogeyman.

119. The Gwyllgi (Welsh Mythology)

Description: The *Gwyllgi* is a spectral black dog that haunts roads and crossroads, often seen as an omen of death or danger. **Link to Imaginary Friend:** The *Gwyllgi* represents an imaginary friend who, after abandonment, has become a haunting, fearsome presence. Once playful, the friend now looms over the child's thoughts, serving as a reminder of the emotional toll of neglect.

120. Abaasy (Yakut Mythology)

Description: The *Abaasy* are evil spirits that live underground and are associated with death and destruction. **Link to Imaginary Friend:** The *Abaasy* represent an imaginary friend who has descended into darkness after abandonment. Once a source of joy, the friend now resides in the child's subconscious, using fear and destruction to gain attention.

121. The Korrigan (Breton Mythology)

Description: *Korrigans* are small, mischievous creatures known for their beauty and treachery, often luring people to their doom. **Link to Imaginary Friend:** The *Korrigan* represents an imaginary friend who, after abandonment, uses their once-playful nature to deceive and frighten the child. Their beauty masks a darker intent, symbolizing the emotional danger of neglect.

122. The Night Hag (Scandinavian Folklore)

Description: The *Night Hag* is a spirit that sits on the chest of sleeping people, causing nightmares and paralysis. **Link to Imaginary Friend:** The *Night Hag* represents an imaginary friend who has transformed into a literal source of fear in the child's sleep. Once a comforting presence, the friend now uses their influence over the child's imagination to create nightmares.

123. Mare (Germanic Folklore)

Description: The *Mare* is a spirit that causes nightmares by sitting on the chest of sleepers, similar to the *Night Hag*. **Link to Imaginary Friend:** The *Mare* represents an imaginary friend who has become a source of psychological torment after abandonment. The friend's once-positive influence over the child's dreams has now turned into a fearsome presence, haunting the child at night.

124. The Ojáncanu (Spanish Folklore)

Description: The *Ojáncanu* is a giant, monstrous being that terrorizes villages, often kidnapping and devouring children. **Link to Imaginary Friend:** The *Ojáncanu* represents an imaginary friend who has grown into a monstrous figure after abandonment. Once playful and caring, the friend now uses fear and physical presence to dominate the child's imagination.

125. Aziza (West African Folklore)

Description: The *Aziza* are small, fairy-like creatures that live in forests and grant magical knowledge, but can also be mischievous. **Link to Imaginary Friend:** The *Aziza* represent an imaginary friend who, after abandonment, turns to mischief and manipulation to regain attention. Their once-helpful nature has now become a source of confusion and fear for the child.

126. Berbalang (Philippine Folklore)

Description: The *Berbalang* are vampiric creatures that feast on human flesh, particularly that of the dead. **Link to Imaginary Friend:** The *Berbalang* represent an imaginary friend who has become predatory and parasitic after abandonment. No longer a playful presence, the friend now seeks to feed off the child's fears and anxieties, becoming a Boogeyman in the process.

127. The Pishacha (India)

Description: The *Pishacha* are demonic spirits that haunt graveyards and feed on human energy. **Link to Imaginary Friend:** The *Pishacha* represent an imaginary friend who, after abandonment, becomes a parasitic force in the child's mind. No longer a source of creativity, the friend now drains the child's emotional energy through fear and nightmares.

128. The Yuki-onna (Japan)

Description: The *Yuki-onna* is a beautiful but deadly spirit associated with snowstorms, luring people to their deaths in the cold. **Link to Imaginary Friend:** The *Yuki-onna* represents an imaginary friend who uses their beauty and allure to manipulate the child into emotional danger. Once a source of warmth and companionship, the friend now leads the child into isolation and fear.

129. Baba Dochia (Romanian Folklore)

Description: *Baba Dochia* is a figure associated with the end of winter and the coming of spring, often depicted as a witch-like character. **Link to Imaginary Friend:** *Baba Dochia* represents an imaginary friend who, after abandonment, has become a controlling, witch-like figure. The friend's shift from nurturing to punishing mirrors the emotional change that comes with neglect.

130. Strix (Roman Folklore)

Description: The *Strix* is a vampiric bird that preys on children, often associated with night and death. **Link to Imaginary Friend:** The *Strix* represents an imaginary friend who has transformed into a predatory, vampiric figure after abandonment. Once a playful presence, the friend now haunts the child's nights, preying on their emotional fears.

131. The Vodyanoy (Slavic Folklore)

Description: The *Vodyanoy* is a water spirit that drowns people, especially those who disrespect the water. **Link to Imaginary Friend:** The *Vodyanoy* represents an imaginary friend who, after abandonment, has become a dangerous force lurking in the child's subconscious. No longer a protector, the friend now seeks to drag the child into emotional depths, using fear as leverage.

132. The Aatxe (Basque Mythology)

Description: The *Aatxe* is a red bull that appears during storms, often as a protector of the innocent but a punisher of the guilty. **Link to Imaginary Friend:** The *Aatxe* represents an imaginary friend who has become a dual-natured figure after abandonment. While still protective, the friend now uses their power to punish the child, reflecting the emotional tension between care and fear.

133. The Bannik (Russia)

Description: The *Bannik* is a spirit that lives in bathhouses, protecting them but also punishing those who disrespect the space. **Link to Imaginary Friend:** The *Bannik* represents an imaginary friend who, after abandonment, becomes vengeful and punishing. Once a source of comfort, the friend now enforces rules through fear, reminding the child of the consequences of neglect.

134. The Gulon (Scandinavian Mythology)

Description: The *Gulon* is a creature that devours its prey, often depicted as a large, ferocious beast. **Link to Imaginary Friend:** The *Gulon* represents an imaginary friend who has become predatory and uncontrollable after abandonment. No longer a playful companion, the friend now devours the child's sense of security, using fear as their primary tool.

135. El Tunchi (Peruvian Amazon)

Description: *El Tunchi* is a spirit that lives in the jungle, often appearing as a whistle in the wind, luring people to their doom. **Link to Imaginary Friend:** *El Tunchi* represents an imaginary friend who has become a distant, haunting presence after abandonment. No longer playful, the friend now uses subtle means to lure the child into fear and confusion, symbolizing the emotional toll of neglect.

These mythical creatures provide a fascinating lens through which to explore the transformation of imaginary friends into Boogeymen. Each figure reflects different aspects of abandonment, fear, and the complex emotional journey that both children and their creations experience when left behind. Through this exploration, we gain insight into the deeper psychological and cultural roots of the Boogeyman myth.

Chapter 4: The Psychology of Fear

Fear is a powerful emotion, especially in childhood, when the world is full of unknowns and the boundary between imagination and reality is often blurred. For children, the Boogeyman represents the embodiment of that fear, lurking in shadows, under the bed, or in closets, waiting to strike at their most vulnerable moments. The Boogeyman feeds off this fear, growing stronger with every nightmare, sleepless night, and anxious glance over the shoulder. But why do children fear the Boogeyman so intensely, and how does that fear become the source of the Boogeyman's strength?

This chapter delves into the psychological mechanisms behind childhood fear, the development of the Boogeyman myth, and how fear itself can turn an abandoned imaginary friend into a malevolent force.

Why Children Fear the Boogeyman

1. Developmental Psychology: The Unknown and Unseen

Children are naturally predisposed to fear the unknown. In the early years of life, their cognitive abilities are still developing, and their understanding of the world is limited. They have not yet learned to distinguish between what is real and what is imaginary. This is why imaginary friends play such a large role in their emotional and social development—they help children process emotions and situations that are still beyond their grasp.

But when imagination takes a dark turn, so too does the child's perception of reality. As children grow, they become aware of their vulnerabilities—of the fact that there are things they cannot control, things they do not understand, and things that could harm them. The Boogeyman becomes the personification of these fears. It is the unknown threat hiding just out of sight, a representation of the dangers they can't fully comprehend but sense on a primal level.

Psychologically, this fear is fueled by:

- **Lack of Control:** Children are often in situations where they feel powerless—whether it's over their routines, environment, or emotions. The Boogeyman embodies this lack of control, as he is an omnipresent figure who can strike at any time without warning.
- **Vivid Imaginations:** Children have wild imaginations, which allows them to create elaborate scenarios of danger. A small noise at night can spark an entire narrative where the Boogeyman is creeping toward their bed.
- **Separation Anxiety:** Many children experience fear of separation from their parents or caregivers, especially at night. The dark and isolation make children feel vulnerable, and the Boogeyman becomes a stand-in for the fears associated with being alone and unprotected.

2. The Dark as a Metaphor for the Unknown

For many children, fear of the dark is one of their earliest and most persistent fears. The absence of light represents the absence of certainty. In the dark, shadows play tricks on the mind, and the lack of visual clarity makes it easy for the imagination to run wild. Without visual input to anchor their sense of reality, children are more prone to imagining that something dangerous is lurking just out of sight.

The Boogeyman, as a figure who resides in the dark, thrives in this uncertainty. His existence is tied to the shadows, to the corners of the room that remain hidden once the lights go out. This is why the Boogeyman so often "lives" under the bed or in the closet—places that are always shrouded in darkness, where it is easy for children to project their fears.

3. Fear of Abandonment and Emotional Isolation

Fear of abandonment is another deep-seated fear that children may experience, and this can tie directly into the transformation of an imaginary friend into a Boogeyman. When children first create imaginary friends, these companions serve as a source of comfort, joy, and emotional support. But as they grow older, they may begin to lose interest in these imaginary figures, abandoning them in favor of real-world interactions or more "grown-up" activities.

In psychological terms, this abandonment creates a sense of emotional isolation for the imaginary friend, which mirrors the child's own fears of being left alone. The Boogeyman, in this case, is a reflection of the child's unresolved emotions about abandonment. The child may subconsciously project their own fear of being forgotten or abandoned onto the Boogeyman, making him a figure who is not only frightening but also emotionally tied to their own feelings of loneliness and neglect.

How Fear Fuels the Boogeyman's Strength

Fear is not just an emotion; it is a primal response that engages both the mind and body. The physiological effects of fear, such as increased heart rate, heightened senses, and adrenaline rushes, create a state of hyper-awareness. In the context of the Boogeyman myth, this heightened state of fear serves as fuel for the Boogeyman, allowing him to grow stronger and more present in the child's mind.

1. The Boogeyman as a Psychological Projection

The Boogeyman is often a projection of the child's internal fears and anxieties. In this sense, the more a child fears the Boogeyman, the more real he becomes. The Boogeyman does not exist in a physical form, but rather as a manifestation of the child's psychological state. As the child's fear grows, so too does the Boogeyman's presence in their mind.

Psychologically, this process can be explained through **cognitive-behavioral theory**:

- **Fear as a Feedback Loop:** When a child fears the Boogeyman, they may experience physiological symptoms such as sweating, trembling, or an increased heart rate. These symptoms, in turn, reinforce the fear, making the Boogeyman seem even more real. The child's mind creates a feedback loop where fear leads to physical symptoms, which then increase the child's belief that the Boogeyman is present, thereby amplifying the fear.

- **Self-Fulfilling Prophecy:** As the child's fear grows, they may begin to interpret any small sound or shadow as confirmation that the Boogeyman is real. This leads to a self-fulfilling prophecy, where the child's fear actively contributes to the creation and strength of the Boogeyman in their imagination.

2. Fear as Energy: The Boogeyman Feeds on Fear

In many myths and stories, the Boogeyman is said to feed on the fear of children, growing stronger with every frightened thought. This concept has deep psychological roots, as fear itself can be an incredibly consuming emotion. Fear monopolizes a child's attention, often pushing aside rational thought and other emotions, creating an environment where the Boogeyman thrives.

In the context of an imaginary friend who has been abandoned, fear becomes a way for the Boogeyman to reestablish a connection with the child. When the child stops believing in their imaginary friend, the friend may feel cast aside and forgotten. But fear can force the child to pay attention once again. The Boogeyman, now transformed from a forgotten friend into a creature of terror, uses fear to gain back the emotional energy that was once freely given through love, play, and companionship.

3. The Boogeyman as a Symbol of Unresolved Fear

The Boogeyman's power comes from more than just surface-level fear of the dark or the unknown; he also represents the child's deeper, unresolved fears. These could include:

- **Fear of growing up and losing innocence.**
- **Fear of failure or disappointing parents.**
- **Fear of being unloved or unwanted.**

The Boogeyman thrives on these unresolved fears because they provide a constant source of emotional energy. As long as the child has unresolved anxieties, the Boogeyman has something to feed on. This is why, in many cases, confronting and addressing these underlying fears is the key to defeating the Boogeyman.

4. Fear of the Boogeyman as a Coping Mechanism

Interestingly, fearing the Boogeyman can also serve as a coping mechanism for children. In a world that often feels chaotic and out of control, the Boogeyman provides a tangible, albeit terrifying, outlet for children to channel their fears. Rather than facing abstract concepts like death, loneliness, or failure, the Boogeyman allows children to externalize these fears into something concrete—something they can imagine, fight, or escape from.

In this way, the Boogeyman can paradoxically serve as a way for children to gain some sense of control over their emotions. By creating a figure that embodies their fears, they can begin to understand and confront those fears in a more manageable way.

5. How Fear Sustains the Boogeyman's Existence

The longer a child fears the Boogeyman, the more real he becomes. This is not just true in a psychological sense but also in the context of the Boogeyman's mythos. The Boogeyman is often portrayed as a creature who cannot exist without fear. He is not a physical being but rather an entity born from and sustained by the fear of the children who believe in him.

In some stories, the Boogeyman can only harm children who are afraid of him. This creates a symbiotic relationship between the Boogeyman and the child's fear. As the child's fear grows, so does the Boogeyman's power. Conversely, if the child can overcome their fear, the Boogeyman loses his strength and eventually fades away. This idea reinforces the notion that fear is not just an emotion but a form of energy that the Boogeyman needs to survive.

Breaking the Cycle of Fear: Confronting the Boogeyman

Understanding the psychology of fear is the first step in breaking the cycle of fear that fuels the Boogeyman's power. Children can take control of their fear by recognizing that the Boogeyman is a manifestation of their own imagination. By addressing the underlying anxieties that give rise to the Boogeyman—whether it's fear of abandonment, fear of the dark, or fear of growing up—children can strip the Boogeyman of his strength.

Many strategies can help children confront their fear of the Boogeyman:

- **Rationalization:** Helping children understand that the Boogeyman is not real and cannot harm them.
- **Imagination as a Tool:** Encouraging children to use their imagination to reimagine the Boogeyman as something less frightening or even friendly.
- **Empowerment:** Teaching children coping mechanisms, such as visualization or breathing exercises, to control their fear.
- **Parental Support:** Providing reassurance and comfort so that the child feels safe and secure.

The Boogeyman may seem invincible at the height of a child's fear, but understanding the psychology behind that fear reveals that the Boogeyman's strength is dependent entirely on the child's emotional state. By addressing the root causes of fear, the Boogeyman can be weakened and ultimately defeated, restoring the balance of imagination and allowing the child to feel empowered rather than terrorized.

In the next chapter, we will explore the origins of the Boogeyman myth in various cultures and how these cultural interpretations reflect deeper societal fears. By understanding the historical context of the Boogeyman, we can further uncover how this figure has evolved to represent different aspects of human fear and imagination across time.

Part 2: Identifying a Boogeyman

Chapter 5: Signs of a Boogeyman Infestation

When a Boogeyman begins to manifest in a child's life, the signs can be subtle at first but become increasingly difficult to ignore as fear grows. As with any supernatural presence, there are key indicators of an infestation—an invasion of fear that seeps into the child's mind, home, and daily life. Recognizing these signs early is crucial in stopping the Boogeyman from gaining full control over the child's imagination and emotions. In this chapter, we'll explore the various manifestations of a Boogeyman infestation, from eerie shadows to strange noises and unusual behavior in both the child and their environment.

1. Changes in Shadows: The Boogeyman's Presence in the Dark

One of the most common and telling signs of a Boogeyman infestation is the appearance of unnatural shadows in the child's room or surrounding areas. These shadows may start out small and harmless, but as the Boogeyman feeds on the child's fear, they grow darker, more distorted, and more ominous.

Signs to Watch For:

- **Shadows that Don't Match Their Source:** One of the earliest signs of a Boogeyman infestation is the appearance of shadows that don't seem to correlate with any object or light source in the room. These shadows may move in unnatural ways, slinking across the walls or floor when nothing else is moving.
- **Shadows That Appear to Watch:** Children often describe feeling as though the shadows in their room are "watching" them. These shadows may take on vaguely humanoid shapes or resemble creatures lurking in the corners. They tend to appear in places associated with the Boogeyman, such as under the bed, in closets, or behind doors.
- **Shadows That Follow the Child:** In more advanced stages of infestation, children may report seeing their own shadow behave differently, such as lingering longer than normal or moving out of sync with their body. They might also notice shadows trailing them in the house, appearing in places where there should be no shadows at all.

Psychological Impact:

These shadowy figures prey on the child's fear of the dark, amplifying their anxiety. The child may feel watched or stalked, leading to sleepless nights and increasing dread, which only strengthens the Boogeyman's presence.

2. Strange Noises: The Boogeyman's Auditory Tactics

The Boogeyman often announces his presence through eerie sounds and noises that defy explanation. These sounds can range from soft, unsettling whispers to loud thumps or creaks that seem to come from nowhere.

Common Sounds Associated with the Boogeyman:

- **Scratching or Tapping:** One of the first signs of a Boogeyman infestation is the sound of scratching or tapping, often coming from within walls, under the bed, or inside the closet. These sounds may start off faint and intermittent but grow louder and more persistent as the infestation progresses.
- **Whispers and Breathing:** Some children report hearing whispers or the sound of breathing, especially when they are alone or lying in bed at night. These noises are often faint, making the child doubt whether they are real or imagined. The whispers may seem to come from dark corners of the room, drawing the child's attention and fear.
- **Footsteps or Creaking Floors:** In more advanced cases, children may hear the sound of footsteps approaching their room, often accompanied by the creaking of floorboards or the soft thud of footsteps. These sounds stop abruptly when an adult enters the room, increasing the child's sense of isolation and helplessness.

Psychological Impact:

The auditory signs of the Boogeyman are particularly effective at fostering a sense of dread because they often occur when the child is alone, heightening their vulnerability. These sounds are designed to make the child feel watched, followed, and unsafe even in their own bed, a place that should be a sanctuary.

3. Unusual Behavior in Children: The Boogeyman's Psychological Hold

One of the clearest signs that the Boogeyman has taken hold is the child's sudden and unexplained change in behavior. As fear grows, the child's reactions to their environment and interactions with others begin to shift, often in alarming ways. These behavioral changes reflect the Boogeyman's growing influence over their mind and emotions.

Common Behavioral Changes:

- **Reluctance or Refusal to Sleep:** A child experiencing a Boogeyman infestation may develop a strong reluctance to go to bed or enter their bedroom, fearing that the Boogeyman is waiting for them in the dark. They may ask for the lights to stay on, refuse to sleep alone, or become increasingly anxious as bedtime approaches.
- **Nightmares and Night Terrors:** The Boogeyman feeds off fear during sleep, often manifesting in the child's dreams. Frequent nightmares or night terrors, in which the child wakes up screaming or in a panic, are key indicators of the Boogeyman's influence. These nightmares often feature recurring themes of being chased, trapped, or watched by shadowy figures.
- **Increased Anxiety and Clinginess:** Children who are aware of the Boogeyman's presence often exhibit heightened anxiety during the day as well, not just at night. They may become clingy, unwilling to be left alone even for short periods, or develop a sudden fear of going into certain rooms or areas of the house, particularly closets or under the bed.
- **Disruptions in Daily Routines:** Children affected by the Boogeyman may experience a range of disruptions in their daily lives, such as difficulty concentrating at school, loss of appetite, or irritability. These disruptions are the result of the growing fear and lack of sleep caused by the Boogeyman's presence.

Psychological Impact:

The Boogeyman uses these behavioral changes to isolate the child, making them feel alone in their fear. The child's increasing anxiety may be dismissed by adults as irrational, which only intensifies their feelings of helplessness. This emotional vulnerability gives the Boogeyman more power to manipulate and control the child's mind.

4. Physical Manifestations: The Boogeyman's Grip on Reality

As a Boogeyman infestation deepens, his influence may extend beyond the child's psychological state, resulting in physical manifestations that affect the environment around them. These manifestations serve as proof that the Boogeyman is not just a figment of the child's imagination, but a tangible force feeding off their fear.

Common Physical Manifestations:

- **Objects Moving or Being Displaced:** Children may notice that their belongings—especially toys or items in the closet—are moved or disturbed when no one else is around. These disturbances may start off subtle, like a door being left ajar or a toy being out of place, but can escalate to furniture being moved or items going missing.
- **Temperature Drops:** One of the classic signs of supernatural presence is an unexplained drop in temperature. A child's room may suddenly feel colder than the rest of the house, particularly in the areas where the Boogeyman is most active, such as near the bed or in the closet.
- **Doors Opening or Closing on Their Own:** In more severe cases of infestation, children may witness doors or closet doors opening or closing by themselves. These moments are often accompanied by a growing sense of dread, as though the Boogeyman is signaling his presence.

Psychological Impact:

These physical manifestations serve to further convince the child that the Boogeyman is real, deepening their fear and anxiety. As objects move or doors open on their own, the line between reality and imagination blurs, making it harder for the child to rationalize their fear or seek comfort. The environment itself becomes a battleground, with the Boogeyman gaining more control over the physical space.

5. Signs in the Child's Artwork or Writing: The Boogeyman in the Subconscious

Children often express their deepest fears and emotions through creative outlets, such as drawing, writing, or imaginative play. When a Boogeyman infestation begins to take hold, these fears can start to show up in the child's artwork or stories, even if they haven't explicitly talked about the Boogeyman.

Common Signs in Artwork and Writing:

- **Dark and Disturbing Imagery:** If the child's drawings suddenly take on a darker tone, featuring shadowy figures, monsters, or scenes of danger, it may be a sign that the Boogeyman is present in their subconscious. These images may show the child being watched, trapped, or chased by a figure resembling the Boogeyman.
- **Recurring Themes of Fear or Isolation:** Children affected by the Boogeyman may create stories or scenarios in which characters are alone, afraid, or unable to escape from danger. These stories often mirror the child's own fears of being trapped in a situation where they are vulnerable to the Boogeyman's influence.
- **Secret or Hidden Drawings:** In some cases, children may hide their more disturbing artwork, drawing the Boogeyman or other frightening imagery in places they think adults won't find. This can be a sign that the child feels unable to talk about their fear and is using art as an outlet for their emotions.

Psychological Impact:

Artwork and writing can be a window into the child's subconscious, revealing the depth of their fear and how the Boogeyman is influencing their thoughts. These creative expressions provide insight into the child's internal struggle, offering clues about how the Boogeyman is manifesting in their imagination and daily life.

6. The Emotional Aura of the Room: The Boogeyman's Domain

Finally, a more subtle but telling sign of a Boogeyman infestation is the emotional aura that seems to settle over the child's room or home. This aura is not necessarily something that can be measured or seen, but it is felt—by the child and sometimes even by others who enter the space.

Signs of a Negative Emotional Aura:

- **A Sense of Dread:** Children often report feeling a sense of dread or unease when entering certain rooms, especially their bedroom or closet. This feeling may be difficult to describe but is unmistakable—a gut reaction that something is wrong or dangerous.
- **Sudden Emotional Swings:** Children affected by the Boogeyman may experience sudden mood swings, especially when they enter spaces where the Boogeyman's presence is strongest. They may go from calm to anxious or happy to fearful without any clear cause.
- **Pets Reacting to the Environment:** Sometimes, animals in the household—especially cats or dogs—will react to the Boogeyman's presence. They may refuse to enter certain rooms, growling or hissing at seemingly empty spaces. Pets' heightened senses often pick up on the negative energy created by the Boogeyman's growing power.

Psychological Impact:

The emotional aura of a Boogeyman-infested space can deepen the child's feelings of isolation and fear. Even when no visible signs are present, the pervasive sense of dread can make the child feel as though they are constantly in danger, further weakening their emotional defenses and allowing the Boogeyman to tighten his grip.

Conclusion: Recognizing the Signs and Taking Action

Recognizing the signs of a Boogeyman infestation is the first step in fighting back. By paying attention to changes in shadows, noises, behavior, and environment, parents and guardians can intervene before the Boogeyman gains too much power. While these signs may seem subtle at first, they are indicators that fear is taking root, giving the Boogeyman the strength he needs to thrive.

The next chapter will explore various tactics and strategies for confronting and weakening the Boogeyman, including psychological methods, magical defenses, and practical tips for helping children reclaim their imagination and sense of safety. Understanding the signs is key to mounting a defense and restoring balance in the child's world.

Chapter 6: Differences Between Imaginary Friends and Boogeymen

Imaginary friends play a crucial role in childhood development, often providing companionship, comfort, and an outlet for creativity. However, under certain circumstances—particularly when a child outgrows or neglects their imaginary friend—these once-benign entities can undergo a dark transformation, becoming a source of fear rather than joy. This chapter explores the key differences between imaginary friends and Boogeymen, focusing on the traits that define each, and the subtle changes that occur as an imaginary friend begins to turn into a Boogeyman.

The Role of Imaginary Friends: Companions and Protectors

Imaginary friends are an important part of childhood, offering emotional support, companionship, and a safe outlet for expressing thoughts and emotions that may be difficult for a child to share with others. They are often created during periods of change or uncertainty, such as starting school, moving to a new place, or facing social challenges. Imaginary friends are uniquely positioned to fill emotional gaps, helping children feel understood, supported, and in control of their imaginative world.

Key Traits of Imaginary Friends:

1. **Companionship:** Imaginary friends are created by children to provide a sense of friendship and comfort, particularly during times when real-life friends may not be available. They often play games, go on adventures, and engage in comforting activities.
2. **Empowerment:** Imaginary friends frequently serve as figures of empowerment for children. They allow the child to take on a leadership role, providing a sense of control over their imaginative world. This helps children build confidence and resilience in their day-to-day lives.
3. **Emotional Support:** When children face anxiety or fear, their imaginary friends often act as protectors, offering words of encouragement and helping to soothe their worries. This makes the imaginary friend a positive force in the child's emotional development.
4. **Creativity and Play:** Imaginary friends often emerge in a child's imaginative play. They encourage storytelling, creative thinking, and problem-solving, allowing the child to explore different scenarios and roles in a safe, controlled environment.

In short, imaginary friends serve as companions who foster emotional growth and creativity. They are an extension of the child's imagination, born from a desire for connection and emotional support.

The Role of Boogeymen: Manifestations of Fear

Boogeymen, on the other hand, are creatures of fear and terror. Unlike imaginary friends, whose role is to provide comfort and companionship, Boogeymen exist to frighten and control. They often feed on a child's fears and anxieties, using those emotions to grow stronger and more malevolent. While an imaginary friend is created out of love and joy, a Boogeyman thrives in an atmosphere of fear, isolation, and emotional distress.

Key Traits of Boogeymen:

1. **Isolation and Fear:** Boogeymen prey on a child's sense of loneliness and vulnerability. They isolate the child emotionally, using fear to keep the child from seeking comfort or protection from others. This fear often leads to feelings of helplessness and despair.

2. **Manipulation:** Unlike imaginary friends, who empower children, Boogeymen use manipulation to control and dominate. They play on the child's fears and insecurities, making the child feel powerless. The Boogeyman's influence can cause the child to question their sense of reality, feeding the cycle of fear.

3. **Nightmares and Dread:** Boogeymen manifest in the dark corners of a child's mind, often appearing in nightmares and disturbing thoughts. They may take on many forms, but their primary goal is to create a constant state of anxiety, making the child feel unsafe even in familiar spaces.

4. **Longevity:** While imaginary friends often fade as children grow older, Boogeymen tend to linger. They remain in the background, waiting for moments of vulnerability to reemerge. Boogeymen are persistent, clinging to the child's subconscious, and they often grow stronger with time if left unchecked.

In essence, Boogeymen are the opposite of imaginary friends. Where imaginary friends bring joy and security, Boogeymen bring fear and despair. They thrive on the emotional turmoil that often arises when a child feels abandoned, forgotten, or afraid.

Subtle Changes: The Shift from Imaginary Friend to Boogeyman

The transformation from an imaginary friend to a Boogeyman is rarely sudden. Instead, it occurs gradually, as the child's relationship with their imaginary friend changes or deteriorates. Understanding these subtle changes is crucial for recognizing when an imaginary friend is beginning to turn dark.

1. Emotional Distance: The Beginning of Neglect

The first sign of an imaginary friend's transformation is often emotional distance. When children begin to outgrow their imaginary friends, they may spend less time interacting with them, either because they are developing real-world friendships or because their interests are shifting toward more mature activities.

During this period, the imaginary friend may feel abandoned or neglected. While the child may not be aware of this change, the imaginary friend begins to experience a sense of loss. At first, this may manifest as a subtle shift in the tone of interactions. The imaginary friend, once playful and joyful, may become quieter, more reserved, or even melancholic.

Example: A child's imaginary friend, who used to suggest exciting games and adventures, might begin to withdraw, offering fewer ideas and becoming more passive. The friend may seem less eager to engage, mirroring the child's decreasing interest.

2. Shifts in Behavior: From Playful to Possessive

As the emotional distance between the child and their imaginary friend grows, the friend may become possessive or demanding, seeking to regain the child's attention. The once-lighthearted interactions may take on a more intense, even desperate tone. The imaginary friend may start to monopolize the child's time, discouraging them from interacting with real friends or participating in other activities.

Example: The imaginary friend might insist on playing the same games repeatedly, refusing to let the child engage in other activities. The friend may begin to criticize or sabotage the child's real-world friendships, causing the child to feel conflicted or anxious.

This shift in behavior marks the early stages of the imaginary friend's transformation into a Boogeyman. The friend's desperation for attention turns into possessiveness, and their positive influence begins to fade.

3. Fear and Control: The Friend Becomes the Enemy

The most significant change occurs when the imaginary friend begins to use fear as a means of maintaining control. At this point, the friend has crossed the threshold from companion to Boogeyman. Fear replaces joy as the primary motivator for interaction. The imaginary friend, once a source of comfort, now instills dread in the child.

Example: The child may start to feel uneasy around their imaginary friend, sensing a darker presence in their games or stories. The friend might suggest frightening scenarios or challenge the child in unsettling ways. What was once a game of adventure now becomes a test of endurance, with the friend introducing elements of fear and danger.

This is where the Boogeyman's power begins to take hold. The child may feel trapped, unable to escape the relationship with their once-beloved friend. The friend's ability to evoke fear allows them to maintain a presence in the child's life, even as the child tries to distance themselves emotionally.

4. Physical Manifestations: From Play to Nightmares

As the transformation progresses, the imaginary friend may begin to manifest in darker, more physical ways. This often includes the appearance of shadows, strange noises, or unsettling dreams. These manifestations are the Boogeyman's way of asserting dominance over the child's imagination and emotions.

Example: The child may start to experience nightmares in which their imaginary friend appears as a frightening or distorted figure. They may hear the friend's voice whispering at night or see their shadow moving in places where it shouldn't be. These physical manifestations reinforce the child's growing fear, making it harder for them to dismiss the friend as mere imagination.

At this stage, the Boogeyman has fully emerged. The imaginary friend is no longer a source of comfort but a figure of terror, using fear to maintain control and stay connected to the child's emotional world.

Distinguishing Traits: Imaginary Friend vs. Boogeyman

As the transformation from imaginary friend to Boogeyman progresses, it is important to distinguish the traits that define each. Below is a comparison of the key characteristics of imaginary friends and Boogeymen:

Trait	Imaginary Friend	Boogeyman
Role	Companion, protector, and emotional support	Creature of fear, isolation, and manipulation
Emotional Impact	Comfort, joy, and empowerment	Fear, anxiety, and helplessness
Behavior	Playful, creative, and imaginative	Possessive, manipulative, and controlling
Interactions	Positive, encouraging, and fun	Threatening, fear-inducing, and unsettling
Manifestations	Engages in imaginative play	Appears in nightmares, shadows, and noises
Source of Power	Draws strength from love and imagination	Feeds on fear and anxiety

Recognizing the Shift: How to Intervene

Recognizing the subtle changes in an imaginary friend's behavior is key to preventing their full transformation into a Boogeyman. When a child begins to feel uneasy or afraid of their imaginary friend, it's important for parents or guardians to step in and help the child navigate these emotions. Encouraging open communication, providing reassurance, and addressing the child's fears are essential steps in preventing the imaginary friend from turning into a Boogeyman. Here's how to recognize and address the shift before it escalates:

5. Open Communication: Encouraging the Child to Share Their Fears

When a child starts to experience fear or discomfort related to their imaginary friend, it's important to create an environment where they feel safe discussing their feelings. Sometimes children may be reluctant to talk about their fears because they think adults won't understand or take them seriously. However, acknowledging their fear can be the first step in dismantling the Boogeyman's power.

Steps to Foster Communication:

- **Create a Safe Space:** Let the child know it's okay to talk about their fears without judgment. Ask them open-ended questions about their imaginary friend and how they feel during their interactions.
- **Validate Their Emotions:** Even if the fear seems irrational, it's important to validate the child's emotions. Fear is a powerful motivator, and by validating their feelings, you show them that their concerns are taken seriously.
- **Provide Reassurance:** Reassure the child that they are safe and that imaginary friends, like all things in their imagination, can be controlled by them. Reinforce the idea that they have power over their own thoughts and fears.

By encouraging open communication, parents and guardians can help the child process their fears and provide them with the tools to address those fears before they become overwhelming.

6. Reclaiming Control: Empowering the Child

One of the key differences between imaginary friends and Boogeymen is the role of control. Imaginary friends encourage children to feel empowered, while Boogeymen thrive on making them feel helpless. To prevent the shift from imaginary friend to Boogeyman, it's essential to help the child reclaim control over their imaginative world.

Ways to Empower the Child:

- **Encourage Imaginative Solutions:** Have the child imagine ways to "disarm" their imaginary friend if they start to feel afraid. They could create magical objects or scenarios where they gain control, such as imagining a superhero version of themselves who defeats the Boogeyman.
- **Introduce Positive Reinforcement:** Teach the child positive visualization techniques, where they can transform their fear into something friendly. For example, if they're afraid of shadows in their room, encourage them to imagine the shadows are playful animals or friendly figures.
- **Creative Expression:** Allow the child to express their fears through art, storytelling, or role-playing games. By creating stories where they overcome their fears or make friends with the Boogeyman, they can take ownership of their emotions and feel less vulnerable.

By giving the child tools to manage their imagination and fears, you help them understand that they are in control of the narrative, preventing the imaginary friend from turning into something darker.

7. Addressing Nightmares and Sleep Issues

Nightmares and trouble sleeping are common signs that an imaginary friend may be morphing into a Boogeyman. These fears often manifest at night when children are alone with their thoughts. Addressing sleep-related anxiety early on can help prevent the Boogeyman from gaining too much influence over the child's subconscious mind.

Steps to Address Nightmares:

- **Nighttime Routine:** Establish a comforting bedtime routine that helps the child feel safe and secure. This can include reading a comforting story, using a nightlight, or practicing calming breathing exercises before bed.
- **Dream Catchers or Protective Objects:** Some children find comfort in having a symbolic object that "protects" them from nightmares, such as a dream catcher or a special stuffed animal that keeps the Boogeyman away.
- **Guided Visualizations:** Teach the child to use guided visualizations before bed, where they imagine a safe, happy place where nothing can harm them. This helps shift their focus from fear to comfort as they fall asleep.

By addressing sleep issues head-on, you prevent the Boogeyman from using the child's most vulnerable moments—nighttime—to exert influence over them.

8. Balancing Reality and Imagination

While imaginary friends are valuable for a child's emotional and creative development, it's also important to help them distinguish between imagination and reality, especially when their fears start to blur those lines. Teaching the child how to balance these two worlds can prevent an imaginary friend from turning into a Boogeyman.

Techniques to Help the Child Balance Imagination and Reality:

- **Teach Boundaries Between Fantasy and Reality:** Help the child understand that their imagination is powerful, but it exists in a different space than reality. Encourage them to talk about their imaginary friend in a way that keeps them grounded in reality, such as recognizing that the friend is part of their creative world but doesn't have control over their real life.
- **Set Limits for Imaginative Play:** If the child's imaginary friend begins to take up too much of their time or affect their ability to interact with others, setting boundaries can help. Limit the time they spend with their imaginary friend and encourage more social interaction with peers or family members.
- **Use Reality Testing:** When the child expresses fear of their imaginary friend or the Boogeyman, guide them through reality testing. This involves helping them examine the situation logically—such as checking for real sources of the shadows or noises they're afraid of—to ground them in the real world.

By balancing imagination with reality, you help the child keep their imaginary world as a positive outlet for creativity rather than allowing it to become a source of fear.

Conclusion: Understanding the Transformation

Imaginary friends and Boogeymen exist on opposite ends of the emotional spectrum, but the line between them can blur when fear takes hold. Understanding the differences between these two entities and recognizing the subtle changes that occur as an imaginary friend turns into a Boogeyman is crucial for intervening before fear takes control.

By fostering open communication, empowering the child, addressing sleep issues, and balancing reality with imagination, parents and guardians can help children navigate the emotional complexities of their imaginative world. In doing so, they can prevent the Boogeyman from gaining a foothold and ensure that imaginary friends remain a source of comfort and joy rather than fear and dread.

In the next chapter, we will explore practical strategies and defenses for combating the Boogeyman, from psychological tactics to magical rituals, giving children the tools they need to reclaim their imagination and banish the Boogeyman for good.

Chapter 7: The First Encounter

Most children have their first encounter with the Boogeyman during a seemingly ordinary night. It's a moment shrouded in mystery, fear, and uncertainty. It begins when the shadows in the room seem to stretch a little further than usual, the familiar shapes of toys and furniture distort into something unfamiliar, and a faint sense of being watched creeps over the child. This is how the Boogeyman enters their world—not with a bang, but with a quiet, unsettling shift in the air.

How Most Children Encounter Their First Boogeyman

The first encounter often happens between the ages of four and six, when a child's imagination is vivid but their understanding of the world is still developing. It usually occurs in the safety of their own bedroom, a place that, until now, has been filled with comforting bedtime stories and soft, warm blankets. But this night is different. The child may hear a strange noise, see a flicker of movement in the corner of their eye, or simply sense a presence that doesn't belong.

For some, the encounter begins with the creak of the closet door, or a rustle beneath the bed. Others might see a shadow stretch unnaturally across the wall or feel an eerie, unexplainable chill in the room. These subtle cues are how the Boogeyman makes his presence known. He doesn't burst into the room or appear with a dramatic flair. Instead, he thrives on subtlety, using the child's own fear and imagination to fuel his power.

At this stage, the Boogeyman remains a shadowy figure, lurking in the periphery of the child's vision. He often appears as a vague, shifting shape, sometimes resembling a familiar form—like a tall, cloaked figure or a grotesque distortion of a favorite toy. The Boogeyman's form is fluid, constantly changing to reflect the child's deepest fears. No two encounters are ever quite the same, as the Boogeyman adapts to each child's unique imagination and vulnerabilities.

Reactions: The Child's Fear and Instincts

The child's initial reaction to the Boogeyman is almost always fear—intense, primal, and overwhelming. Their heart races, their body freezes, and the room, once familiar, becomes an alien landscape. For a few moments, they may be paralyzed, unable to scream, call for help, or even move. This is the Boogeyman's power—he feeds off the fear, growing stronger the more terrified the child becomes.

In the moments following the first encounter, children may react in one of three ways:

1. **Flight**: Many children instinctively run, throwing off their blankets and racing to their parents' room or another safe space. Their hearts pound, and they may not even look back, convinced that something is chasing them. In some cases, children may try to hide under their covers or curl into a tight ball, believing the darkness of their blanket will protect them from the lurking figure.

2. **Freeze**: Others freeze in place, their eyes wide and their bodies stiff with terror. They may remain completely still, hoping that if they don't move, the Boogeyman won't notice them. This is the most dangerous reaction, as the Boogeyman thrives in the stillness, using the child's fear to grow closer and more tangible.

3. **Fight**: A rare few might attempt to "fight" the fear, using stuffed animals, pillows, or even their own small voices to shout at the Boogeyman. These children often have a strong sense of self-confidence or protection from a loved one's words, but while they are brave, their efforts are usually met with little success. The Boogeyman is not a foe that can be vanquished by ordinary means.

What to Do Immediately

Parents and guardians play a crucial role in helping a child navigate their first encounter with the Boogeyman. Here are some steps that should be taken immediately to help the child feel safe and diminish the Boogeyman's power:

1. **Stay Calm**: The first step is for parents to remain calm, even if their child's fear is intense. A calm, reassuring presence immediately weakens the Boogeyman's hold, as he relies on the atmosphere of fear. Speak in soothing tones and avoid dismissing the child's fears as "just a nightmare" or "their imagination." The child needs to feel heard and validated.

2. **Turn on the Lights**: The Boogeyman thrives in darkness, where shadows can play tricks on the mind. Turning on the lights immediately diminishes his power, transforming him from a lurking menace into a mere shadow, barely visible in the brightness. Let the child see that the light exposes the truth—that there is nothing tangible to fear.

3. **Explore the Room Together**: Gently explore the room with your child. Look under the bed, open the closet door, and show them that these spaces are safe. Encourage the child to do this with you, so they can see for themselves that the Boogeyman has no physical form. By engaging with their environment, the child can begin to regain control of the space.

4. **Empower the Child**: Offer the child a "tool" to ward off the Boogeyman. This could be a stuffed animal that acts as a guardian, a special flashlight, or even a "protective" blanket. These symbols of safety give the child a sense of power and control, which the Boogeyman cannot easily overcome.

5. **Create a Nighttime Ritual**: To prevent future encounters, establish a calming bedtime routine. Reading a favorite book, listening to soothing music, or using a nightlight can help set a peaceful atmosphere that the Boogeyman will find difficult to penetrate. The more secure and confident the child feels in their room, the weaker the Boogeyman becomes.

6. **Teach the Power of Belief**: Remind the child that the Boogeyman only has as much power as they allow. He is a creature of fear and imagination, and while he may seem frightening, the child's belief in their own strength and safety is stronger. Empower the child by helping them understand that their bravery and confidence are the key to keeping the Boogeyman at bay.

Conclusion

The first encounter with the Boogeyman can be a terrifying experience, but it is also a moment where a child learns resilience and the power of their imagination. With the right support, guidance, and coping strategies, a child can overcome this fear and take back control of their nighttime world. The Boogeyman may lurk in the shadows, but he is no match for a child armed with confidence, comfort, and the love of those who protect them.

Part 3: Tools and Weapons to Fight Boogeymen

Chapter 8: DIY Boogeyman Busters

When the Boogeyman strikes, fear can paralyze even the bravest of children. But what many don't realize is that the household is filled with powerful items that can serve as makeshift weapons against the Boogeyman. In this chapter, we explore simple yet effective tools that any child (or even adults) can use to protect themselves, turning ordinary objects into "Boogeyman Busters." These items might not physically harm the Boogeyman—who exists in the shadowy spaces between fear and imagination—but they can weaken his power and give the child the courage to stand strong.

The Power of Belief: Why DIY Boogeyman Busters Work

The Boogeyman is a creature that feeds on fear, thriving in the dark and in moments of uncertainty. While he cannot be physically harmed in the traditional sense, his power can be diminished by a child's belief in their ability to defend themselves. A Boogeyman Buster works not because of its physical properties, but because it instills confidence in the user, helping them fight back against fear and reclaim their space.

Household Items as Makeshift Weapons

1. **The Flashlight of Justice**

   Boogeymen love the dark, and nothing banishes the darkness faster than a flashlight. The bright beam of a flashlight can be aimed into corners, under beds, or into closets where the Boogeyman is lurking. It serves as a "weapon" that dispels shadows and weakens the Boogeyman's hold on the room. For added effect, children can name their flashlight something powerful like "The Flashlight of Justice" or "The Light of Valor," making it feel like a magical tool that repels fear.

   - **How to Use**: Keep the flashlight close to the bed. If the child feels scared or senses the Boogeyman, they should immediately grab the flashlight and shine it in the direction of their fear. They can say something brave, like "I see you, and you're not welcome here!" to strengthen the effect.

2. **Stuffed Animal Guardians**

A favorite stuffed animal can transform into a fierce protector in the face of the Boogeyman. Children already form deep bonds with their plush friends, and these items can become symbols of safety. In the battle against the Boogeyman, a stuffed animal is not just a toy—it's a guardian that watches over the child while they sleep.

- **How to Use**: Give the stuffed animal a special name and purpose. It could be "Brave Bear" or "Lionheart," a fierce creature that stands between the child and the Boogeyman. The child can place the stuffed animal on guard near the bed or hold it tight if they sense danger. Involving the child in "training" their stuffed animal to protect them enhances their sense of safety.

3. **The Blanket of Invincibility**

The blanket has long been a classic defense against monsters and boogeymen. Draped over the child, it acts as a shield, making them invisible to the Boogeyman. With the right amount of imagination, any blanket can be imbued with protective magic.

- **How to Use**: Before bed, the child can drape the blanket over themselves and imagine it glowing with protective light. They can even perform a little ritual, like patting the edges of the blanket and saying, "This is my shield, no fear can pass, no Boogeyman can last." This creates a mental boundary that the Boogeyman cannot penetrate.

4. **The Spray of Courage**

A simple spray bottle filled with water can become a potent tool in the fight against the Boogeyman. Children can label it as "Boogeyman Repellent" and believe that a spritz of this magical liquid will drive away fear and keep the creature at bay. To enhance the effect, parents can add a drop of lavender oil or other soothing scents, turning the spray into both a calming and empowering tool.

- **How to Use**: If the child feels uneasy, they can grab the spray and give a few firm spritzes into the air, focusing on dark corners or spaces where the Boogeyman might be hiding. As they spray, they should say something like, "Be gone, Boogeyman! You're not welcome here!" The scent, combined with the child's belief, drives away fear.

5. **The Shield of Shadows**

A large pillow can serve as a makeshift shield, helping children feel protected as they face the Boogeyman. This shield doesn't just block the Boogeyman—it absorbs his power, rendering him weak and ineffective. Children can imagine that their pillow glows with a protective aura when held up as a barrier between them and the Boogeyman.

- **How to Use**: If the child feels afraid, they can grab the pillow, hold it in front of them, and imagine it glowing with light. As they do, they should say something powerful like, "This shield blocks all darkness!" They can use the pillow to "push" the Boogeyman back, reclaiming control over their space.

6. **The Mirror of Truth**

A small hand mirror can be used to reflect the Boogeyman's true form. Since he thrives in fear and uncertainty, catching him in a mirror shows him for what he really is—a shadowy figment of the imagination. Children can use a mirror to "trap" the Boogeyman and reflect his image back at him, diminishing his power.

- **How to Use**: The child can keep a small hand mirror nearby. When they sense the Boogeyman, they hold up the mirror and say, "Show yourself, Boogeyman! You can't hide!" By looking into the mirror, they imagine the Boogeyman's fear bouncing back at him, weakening his presence in the room.

7. **The Music Box of Peace**

Music has a calming effect on the mind and spirit. A simple music box or even a playlist of soothing songs can act as a powerful Boogeyman Buster by creating an atmosphere of peace and serenity. Boogeymen despise calm because it makes it harder for them to thrive on fear.

- **How to Use**: Before bed, the child can play the music box or listen to calming music. They should imagine the notes wrapping around them like a protective cocoon, keeping them safe from the Boogeyman. If fear creeps in during the night, turning on the music again will disrupt the Boogeyman's grip.

8. **The Nightlight of Protection**

A nightlight serves as a powerful deterrent against the Boogeyman, who prefers the dark and shadowy corners. The soft glow of the nightlight keeps fear at bay, creating a barrier the Boogeyman struggles to cross. While the Boogeyman may be able to lurk in total darkness, even the faintest light weakens him.

- **How to Use**: Keep a nightlight on in the child's room to maintain a comforting glow. Explain to the child that this light is their "guardian" that watches over them all night, keeping the Boogeyman far away. Some children may prefer a nightlight with special colors or shapes that make them feel even more protected.

Preparing for Battle: The Mental Fortitude of a Boogeyman Buster

While the items listed above can provide comfort and security, the true strength of a Boogeyman Buster lies in the mind. Children should be encouraged to embrace their inner courage and feel empowered by their tools. Role-playing scenarios during the day can help prepare the child for the night, allowing them to practice using their Boogeyman Busters with confidence.

Parents can help their child create a "Boogeyman Buster Kit," collecting their chosen tools into a special box or bag that they can keep near their bed. The child should feel involved in the creation of their kit, choosing items that resonate with them and assigning each one a special role. The more ownership they feel over their defense, the more effective these items will be in building their sense of security.

Conclusion

The Boogeyman may thrive in the shadows, but with a little imagination and some well-chosen household items, every child can become a Boogeyman Buster. These makeshift weapons, infused with belief and courage, are more than enough to turn the tide in the battle against fear. After all, the most powerful tool of all is the child's own bravery. By giving them these everyday objects and teaching them how to use them, we empower children to face the Boogeyman head-on and reclaim the night as their own.

Chapter 9: Boogey Light: The Power of Light

The Boogeyman, like many creatures that thrive on fear, exists in the shadows. Darkness is his domain, where he manipulates the unknown and preys upon the imaginations of children. However, light—whether it's from the sun, a lamp, or even the flicker of a candle—has the unique ability to strip away the shadows and reveal the Boogeyman's true nature. This chapter delves into the power of light and how different types of light can weaken or even expose the Boogeyman, allowing children and their families to reclaim their nighttime peace.

The Boogeyman and His Relationship with Darkness

The Boogeyman's power is drawn from the darkness, both literal and figurative. In darkness, the mind can play tricks, and fear is amplified. The child's uncertainty and inability to see what lurks in the shadows give the Boogeyman strength. His form, ever-changing and elusive, thrives in low visibility. Darkness provides the Boogeyman with the perfect cover—he can move unseen, manipulating the child's fear of the unknown. This is why light is his greatest enemy.

Light, on the other hand, represents clarity, truth, and safety. It's a force that pushes back against the shadows and exposes what hides within. By introducing light into the space, the Boogeyman is weakened, his form becomes less menacing, and, in some cases, he may be completely revealed, showing him for what he truly is—a creature of fear and imagination.

Types of Light and Their Effectiveness

1. **Natural Sunlight: The Ultimate Boogeyman Buster**

   Sunlight is the most powerful and purifying light in existence. Its bright, warming rays are said to completely banish the Boogeyman. Since he thrives in the darkest corners of the night, the first rays of dawn strip away all his power. When sunlight enters a room, the Boogeyman has no choice but to retreat until night falls again.

○ **How to Use**: At sunrise, open the curtains or blinds and let the sunlight flood the room. If the child has experienced a frightening encounter with the Boogeyman during the night, standing in the sunlight can help them feel re-energized and safe. The Boogeyman cannot return while the sun is shining, and knowing this helps children feel secure during the day.

2. **Nightlights: A Constant Source of Protection**

Nightlights are one of the most popular tools used to keep the Boogeyman at bay. Their soft, consistent glow throughout the night creates a buffer of safety, filling the room with just enough light to diminish the shadows. Nightlights are particularly effective because they provide a constant source of light without being too bright, allowing the child to sleep comfortably while also feeling secure.

○ **How to Use**: Place the nightlight in a strategic location, such as near the child's bed or in a corner where shadows might gather. Explain to the child that the nightlight is their guardian, keeping watch over them while they sleep. Some nightlights even come with fun shapes or colors, like stars or animals, making them even more comforting for the child.

3. **Flashlights: The Weapon of Choice in a Boogeyman Emergency**

Flashlights are not only practical but also empowering for children during a Boogeyman encounter. The ability to control where the light goes allows the child to actively search for the Boogeyman and "banish" him from the dark corners of their room. Flashlights are especially useful when a child feels immediate fear or senses movement in the shadows.

○ **How to Use**: Keep a flashlight near the child's bed, either on their nightstand or under their pillow. Teach them to use it as their "weapon" against the Boogeyman. When they feel scared, they can grab the flashlight and shine it into dark areas like the closet, under the bed, or in the corners of the room. As they do this, encourage them to say something brave like, "I see you, Boogeyman! You can't hide from me!" This act of shining light empowers the child and weakens the Boogeyman's influence.

4. **Lamps and Overhead Lights: Brightening the Entire Room**

Lamps and overhead lights provide broad illumination, filling the entire room with brightness. The sudden switch from darkness to light can disorient the Boogeyman, forcing him to retreat. Turning on a lamp in the middle of the night can serve as an immediate way to weaken the Boogeyman and help the child feel more secure.

○ **How to Use**: Encourage the child to use a bedside lamp if they wake up feeling afraid. By simply turning on the light, they can chase away the shadows and reduce the Boogeyman's ability to hide. Some children may prefer to sleep with a lamp on if their fear of the dark is strong, but this is entirely up to their comfort level. Overhead lights can be used as a last resort if the fear becomes too overwhelming.

5. **Candles: A Flicker of Ancient Power**

Candles, with their warm, flickering glow, have long been associated with warding off evil spirits and keeping darkness at bay. While they aren't practical for children to use on their own, parents can use candles during a bedtime ritual to create a calming and protective atmosphere. The soft light of a candle can fill a room with a sense of peace, reminding the child that light always overcomes the dark.

- **How to Use**: Light a candle before bed and let its soft glow fill the room as you read a bedtime story or talk about the child's day. If the child expresses fear of the Boogeyman, explain that the candlelight is a symbol of protection, keeping the Boogeyman away. Once the child is ready to sleep, blow out the candle with a little ritual, such as saying, "With this light, I send away all fear."

6. **String Lights: Decorative Protection**

String lights, often used as room decor, can also serve as an effective Boogeyman deterrent. Their soft, twinkling glow can create a magical atmosphere that makes the child feel safe and secure. String lights are particularly useful because they can be left on all night without being too bright, and they cover a large area, filling the room with light.

- **How to Use**: Hang string lights along the walls, around the bed, or across the ceiling. The child can be involved in choosing the design, whether it's stars, moons, or fun shapes, turning the act of decorating into a ritual of protection. The twinkling lights create a barrier that the Boogeyman will find difficult to penetrate.

7. **Glow-in-the-Dark Objects: Ever-Present Light**

Glow-in-the-dark stickers, stars, or toys are another creative way to introduce light into a child's room. While they don't provide the same level of brightness as a nightlight or lamp, they offer a comforting glow that lingers even after the lights are turned off. Glow-in-the-dark objects serve as reminders that light is always present, even in the darkest hours of the night.

- **How to Use**: Place glow-in-the-dark stars on the ceiling or walls, or give the child a glow-in-the-dark toy to keep by their bedside. As they fall asleep, the soft glow will remind them that they are not alone in the dark and that the Boogeyman cannot thrive where light exists.

8. **Motion-Sensor Lights: Surprising the Boogeyman**

Motion-sensor lights are an advanced tool in the fight against the Boogeyman. These lights turn on when they detect movement, surprising the Boogeyman when he tries to sneak into the room. The sudden burst of light catches him off guard, forcing him to retreat before he can establish a foothold.

- **How to Use**: Install motion-sensor lights in key areas of the child's room, such as near the door, under the bed, or inside the closet. Explain to the child that these lights will "catch" the Boogeyman if he tries to sneak into their room, making it impossible for him to approach undetected. The surprise of light will make the child feel safer, knowing that the Boogeyman is no match for modern technology.

Rituals of Light: Empowering the Child

Introducing light into a child's room can be more than just flipping a switch—it can be turned into a ritual that empowers the child and banishes the Boogeyman. Here are a few light-based rituals that parents and children can perform together:

1. **The Light of Courage Ritual**: Before bed, the child can "activate" their nightlight, flashlight, or string lights by saying a short phrase like, "This light protects me from all fear." This ritual gives the child ownership of their safety and reinforces the idea that light is their ally.
2. **The Sunstone Charm**: A small, sun-shaped object, like a toy or charm, can be placed by the child's bed as a symbol of the sun's power. The child can hold it before going to sleep and imagine it filling the room with sunlight, even in the dark of night.
3. **The Circle of Light**: If the child has a fear of a particular spot in the room, like the closet or under the bed, use a flashlight to "draw" a circle of light around that area, saying, "This circle keeps the Boogeyman out." The child can then go to sleep knowing that their room is protected.

Conclusion: The Power of Light in the Battle Against the Boogeyman

Light is the most powerful weapon against the Boogeyman because it exposes him for what he truly is—a creature of shadow and fear. Whether it's the warm glow of a nightlight, the sudden flash of a motion-sensor light, or the protective rays of the sun, light banishes darkness and brings comfort and security to the child. By incorporating different types of light into the bedroom, parents can help their children feel safe, empowered, and ready to face whatever the night may bring.

The Boogeyman may rule the shadows, but where there is light, there is always hope. And with the right combination of belief, imagination, and illumination, every child can sleep peacefully, knowing that the Boogeyman has no place in their world.

Chapter 10: Creating Protective Circles

Boundaries are an essential part of both the physical and mental defense against the Boogeyman. By creating protective circles and safe zones in your home, you establish a sanctuary where fear cannot penetrate. These circles serve as a powerful mental and emotional shield, giving children a tangible way to assert control over their space and reduce the Boogeyman's power. In this chapter, we'll explore the importance of boundaries and guide you through the process of creating effective protective circles using various techniques that blend imagination, intention, and simple household items.

The Importance of Boundaries

Boundaries, both visible and invisible, play a crucial role in combating fear. For children, the Boogeyman represents an entity that has crossed the boundary between safety and danger, between the known and the unknown. The creation of protective circles gives children a way to visualize and enforce those boundaries, making it clear that there is a safe space where the Boogeyman cannot enter. These boundaries also empower children by giving them a sense of control over their environment, which directly weakens the Boogeyman's hold.

Boundaries work on multiple levels:

1. **Physical Boundaries**: These include the actual space within a room or home, such as the bed, a corner, or an area where the child plays. Creating a physical safe zone helps the child define where they feel most secure.
2. **Emotional Boundaries**: These are created by rituals, intentions, and beliefs. When a child establishes a protective circle, they're not just creating a physical barrier, but an emotional one, which strengthens their sense of security.
3. **Energetic Boundaries**: These boundaries exist in the realm of imagination and energy. The child believes that they are surrounded by a force field or protective barrier that prevents the Boogeyman from crossing. This belief alone can be incredibly powerful, as it transforms fear into confidence.

Step-by-Step Guide to Creating Protective Circles

There are many ways to create protective circles, depending on the materials at hand, the child's preferences, and the level of involvement the parent wishes to have. Below are several methods, each with its own unique approach.

Method 1: The Circle of Light

The Circle of Light is one of the simplest and most effective ways to create a protective boundary. It uses light as the primary element of protection, invoking the idea that light always drives away darkness and fear.

1. **Materials**: Flashlight, nightlight, or any light source.
2. **How to Create**:
   - Before bedtime, have the child hold the flashlight or nightlight. They should stand in the center of their room or near their bed.
   - Turn on the light and slowly walk in a circle around the room, shining the light along the walls, under the bed, and into dark corners.
   - As you walk, have the child say something like, "This light protects me, no darkness can enter." Encourage the child to repeat this or a similar phrase with confidence.
   - Once the circle is complete, place the light source in a prominent location, such as by the bed, as a symbol of ongoing protection.

This circle, once created, remains active throughout the night, as the power of the light continues to shield the room from the Boogeyman.

Method 2: The Chalk or Salt Circle

Chalk or salt has long been used in folklore and superstition as a means to create protective barriers. Both substances can be used to form a visible circle, giving the child a tangible reminder of their safe space.

1. **Materials**: Chalk or salt, small stones or crystals (optional).
2. **How to Create**:
   - Begin by explaining to the child that salt or chalk has special powers that can create an invisible wall around them.

- Choose an area where the child wants to create their safe zone, such as around their bed, play area, or a reading nook.
- With the child's help, slowly sprinkle salt or use chalk to draw a circle around the chosen space. As you do this, encourage the child to visualize the Boogeyman being unable to cross the boundary.
- If desired, add small stones or crystals at intervals around the circle to reinforce the barrier. You can explain that these stones act as "anchors" to keep the protective energy in place.
- Once the circle is complete, have the child step inside and say something like, "This is my safe space, no fear can enter here."

The circle of chalk or salt can be redrawn as needed and serves as a physical representation of the boundary the child has created.

Method 3: The Blanket of Protection Circle

The Blanket of Protection Circle uses a familiar and comforting object—a blanket—to create a portable and personal safe zone. This method works especially well for children who feel most secure with their favorite blanket or stuffed animal.

1. **Materials**: A blanket (preferably one the child already loves), and a pillow (optional).
2. **How to Create**:
   - Begin by having the child choose their favorite blanket. Explain to them that this blanket is special and can create a circle of safety wherever they go.
   - Spread the blanket on the floor and have the child sit or lie in the center of it.
   - As the child sits or lies on the blanket, tell them to imagine that the edges of the blanket are glowing with protective light.
   - Have the child say, "This is my circle of protection, no Boogeyman can cross it."
   - If the child has a favorite stuffed animal, they can place it at the edge of the blanket as a "guardian" to watch over the circle while they sleep or play.

This method works particularly well because it ties the idea of safety to an object the child is already attached to, making the protective circle feel even more personal and comforting.

Method 4: The Candlelight Circle

Candles provide a sense of peace and can be used as a focus point for creating an invisible circle of protection. This method is ideal for older children, as it involves the use of fire (under adult supervision).

1. **Materials**: A small candle (real or battery-operated), a lighter or matches.
2. **How to Create**:

- Place the candle in the center of the room or the space the child wishes to protect, such as near their bed or in the center of their play area.
- Light the candle (or turn on the battery-operated candle). As the flame flickers, explain to the child that the light from the candle will create a circle of warmth and safety that the Boogeyman cannot penetrate.
- Slowly walk around the candle, imagining the flame expanding outward until it forms a full circle of light around the room.
- Have the child stand or sit inside the circle and say, "This light keeps me safe, nothing can harm me here."
- Leave the candle burning for a short while, or if using a battery-operated candle, let it stay on throughout the night as a reminder of the protective circle.

Candles offer both a literal and symbolic form of light, reinforcing the idea that warmth and brightness protect against the dark forces of fear.

Method 5: The Sound Circle

Sometimes, sound can be just as powerful as light in creating boundaries. Soft music, chimes, or even spoken words can form a circle that soothes the mind and creates a space of peace and safety.

1. **Materials**: A small bell, wind chimes, or a soft music player.
2. **How to Create**:
    - Begin by choosing a sound that the child finds calming, whether it's the gentle ring of a bell, the tinkle of wind chimes, or the sound of soft music.
    - Start by playing or ringing the sound in the center of the room. Explain to the child that the sound will create a circle of peace and safety, driving away any fear or negative energy.
    - Slowly walk around the room, ringing the bell or allowing the music to fill the space. Imagine the sound forming an invisible wall that surrounds the entire area.
    - As you walk, encourage the child to repeat a phrase such as, "This sound keeps me safe and happy, no fear can enter my circle."
    - Once the circle is complete, leave the sound playing softly in the background or return to the center of the room to finish with a final ring of the bell.

Sound has a unique ability to create a calming atmosphere, and this method is particularly effective for children who respond to music or other auditory cues.

Conclusion: The Power of Protective Circles

Creating protective circles is a powerful way to empower children in their battle against the Boogeyman. By giving them tangible methods to create boundaries, children gain a sense of control over their environment, which directly reduces their fear and anxiety. These circles are more than just physical spaces—they are mental and emotional tools that allow children to feel safe, secure, and in charge.

Whether using light, sound, or simple objects like a blanket or chalk, the act of creating a protective circle teaches children that they have the power to defend themselves against fear. The Boogeyman may lurk in the shadows, but within the boundaries of their protective circle, children can rest easy knowing that they are safe from harm.

Chapter 11: The Power of Music

Music is a universal force that has long been used to calm, comfort, and heal. But music is not only a tool for relaxation—it can also serve as a powerful weapon against fear, particularly when it comes to repelling or weakening the Boogeyman. In this chapter, we explore how different types of tunes and sounds can be used to drive away the Boogeyman, creating a sonic shield that helps children feel safe and protected in their homes.

Why Music Works Against the Boogeyman

The Boogeyman thrives in an atmosphere of silence and fear. He lurks in the quiet corners of the night, creeping in when the house is still and the only sound is the faint rustling of the wind. In this silence, a child's imagination runs wild, and every creak or murmur becomes a potential threat. Music, however, disrupts this silence. It fills the space with rhythm, melody, and harmony, drowning out the whispers of fear. By introducing sound into the room, music creates a barrier that the Boogeyman cannot easily penetrate.

But beyond mere noise, music also has emotional and psychological effects. Certain tunes can evoke feelings of calm, safety, and joy—emotions that directly counteract the fear that the Boogeyman feeds on. As fear diminishes, so does the Boogeyman's power. Music, therefore, becomes a powerful tool for both defense and comfort.

Types of Tunes and Sounds That Repel the Boogeyman

Different types of music and sounds have varying effects on the Boogeyman. Some sounds create a protective shield, while others actively repel him, forcing him to retreat into the shadows. Here are some of the most effective types of music for driving away the Boogeyman.

1. Lullabies: Calming Protection

Lullabies are soft, soothing songs that have been used for centuries to lull children to sleep. Their gentle melodies create a calming atmosphere that immediately dispels fear and anxiety. When a child listens to a lullaby, they feel safe, loved, and protected. The Boogeyman, who feeds on fear and uncertainty, finds it difficult to enter a space where lullabies are playing.

- **How to Use**: Play a lullaby softly as the child is getting ready for bed. The melody can play in the background as part of the bedtime routine, creating a comforting environment. Some parents prefer to sing a lullaby themselves, as the sound of a parent's voice adds an extra layer of security. Whether sung or played from a device, lullabies help create a protective shield that weakens the Boogeyman's influence.
- **Recommended Lullabies**:
  - *Brahms' Lullaby*
  - *Twinkle, Twinkle, Little Star*
  - *Hush, Little Baby*

Each of these lullabies carries a gentle rhythm that reassures the child and pushes back against the darkness.

2. Classical Music: A Symphony of Defense

Classical music, with its intricate melodies and harmonies, has a powerful effect on both the mind and the environment. Compositions by great masters such as Mozart, Beethoven, and Debussy can fill a room with a sense of order and balance, creating a space that the Boogeyman finds difficult to enter. Classical music works particularly well because of its emotional range—it can be both soothing and uplifting, banishing fear while instilling a sense of peace and protection.

- **How to Use**: Select a classical music playlist or album to play during the evening or before bedtime. Choose pieces that are calm and melodic, avoiding anything too fast or intense, as this could disrupt the relaxing atmosphere. Play the music softly in the background as the child falls asleep, creating a constant flow of sound that protects the room from the Boogeyman's presence.
- **Recommended Classical Pieces**:
  - *Clair de Lune* by Claude Debussy
  - *Moonlight Sonata* by Ludwig van Beethoven
  - *Eine kleine Nachtmusik* by Wolfgang Amadeus Mozart

These pieces are gentle and melodic, creating a safe and harmonious environment where fear cannot take root.

3. White Noise: Filling the Silence

White noise is a steady, consistent sound that can mask other noises in the environment, such as creaking floors or distant wind, which might otherwise trigger a child's imagination and invite the Boogeyman. White noise machines, fans, or recordings of rain or ocean waves can help fill the silence in a child's room, creating a sonic barrier that the Boogeyman struggles to penetrate.

- **How to Use:** Place a white noise machine or fan in the child's room, or use a recording of soft environmental sounds like rain or waves. The key is to create a background of steady sound that masks the stillness of the night. This method works especially well for children who are sensitive to sudden noises, as the white noise provides a continuous blanket of sound that keeps them feeling safe.
- **Recommended White Noise Sounds:**
  - Gentle rain falling
  - Ocean waves lapping the shore
  - A steady fan or air purifier

White noise works by keeping the environment stable and predictable, making it harder for the Boogeyman to creep in unnoticed.

4. Chimes and Bells: Warding Off Shadows

The sound of bells and chimes has long been associated with warding off evil spirits and keeping dark forces at bay. The clear, bright tones of wind chimes or a small hand bell can disrupt the Boogeyman's energy and force him to retreat. Bells work because their sound is sharp and piercing, cutting through the silence and dispersing any negative energy lingering in the room.

- **How to Use:** Hang wind chimes near the child's window or place a small bell near their bed. Before going to sleep, the child can gently ring the bell or listen to the chimes, imagining the sound driving away the Boogeyman. Some families create a bedtime ritual where the bell is rung three times, with each ring symbolizing protection and safety.
- **Recommended Chimes:**
  - Small wind chimes with a soft, tinkling sound
  - A handheld bell or small set of jingle bells

Chimes and bells are particularly effective when used as part of a nightly ritual, reinforcing the idea that sound can protect against the Boogeyman.

5. Upbeat and Joyful Music: The Sound of Happiness

Music that is upbeat, joyful, and filled with energy can have a profound effect on dispelling fear. Songs that make children smile or want to dance lift their spirits and create an atmosphere where the Boogeyman has no power. When the room is filled with laughter and happiness, the Boogeyman becomes weak and eventually fades away.

- **How to Use**: In the morning or during playtime, play some of the child's favorite happy songs. Encourage them to dance, sing along, or clap their hands. By filling the space with joyful energy, the child creates an emotional barrier that keeps the Boogeyman from returning.
- **Recommended Upbeat Songs**:
    - *Here Comes the Sun* by The Beatles
    - *You've Got a Friend in Me* from *Toy Story*
    - *Happy* by Pharrell Williams

These songs not only create a positive atmosphere but also fill the room with sounds that banish fear and invite feelings of warmth and security.

6. Personalized Comfort Sounds: Songs from Family or Tradition

Sometimes the most powerful sounds are those tied to personal memories, family traditions, or cultural roots. Whether it's a song a parent used to sing or a melody passed down through generations, these sounds carry with them a deep sense of belonging and safety. The Boogeyman finds it especially difficult to invade a space where the child is surrounded by the sounds of love and protection.

- **How to Use**: Sing or play songs that are special to your family, especially those that have comforting or protective meanings. These could be lullabies, religious hymns, or folk songs from your family's culture. The sound of these familiar melodies will create an emotional connection to feelings of safety and love, strengthening the child's ability to repel the Boogeyman.
- **Recommended Personal Comfort Songs**:
    - A family lullaby or traditional song
    - A hymn or prayer melody
    - A favorite childhood song sung by a parent or grandparent

By connecting to family traditions, these personalized sounds carry extra emotional weight, making them particularly powerful in protecting against the Boogeyman.

Creating a Musical Ritual: Strengthening the Power of Sound

Music is most effective against the Boogeyman when it's used consistently as part of a bedtime or daily ritual. Establishing a regular routine that includes protective sounds will help the child associate music with safety, reinforcing the idea that sound keeps the Boogeyman away. Here's how to create a simple musical ritual:

1. **Choose the Right Music**: Select the type of music that resonates most with your child, whether it's a soothing lullaby, white noise, or a joyful song. Allow your child to have a say in the music choices, as this will make them feel more involved in the process.
2. **Play the Music at a Consistent Time**: Whether it's during the bedtime routine or right before the lights go out, play the music at the same time each night. This consistency will help the child feel secure and establish a routine that the Boogeyman can't disrupt.
3. **Pair the Music with a Positive Phrase**: As the music begins, encourage your child to say something empowering, such as, "This music keeps me safe. The Boogeyman can't stay here." By connecting the sound to a verbal affirmation, you reinforce the protective power of music.
4. **Keep the Music Playing**: If your child is comfortable, allow the music to play softly throughout the night. The continuous sound will serve as a protective barrier, making it harder for the Boogeyman to enter the room.

Conclusion: Harnessing the Power of Music

Music has an incredible ability to shape emotions, create atmosphere, and protect against fear. By choosing the right tunes and incorporating them into a daily or nightly routine, you can help your child feel safe, secure, and empowered in the battle against the Boogeyman. Whether it's a gentle lullaby, the sound of ocean waves, or the bright tones of wind chimes, music fills the room with an energy that repels darkness and invites peace.

The Boogeyman may thrive in silence, but in the presence of music, his power fades. With the right sounds on their side, every child can rest easy, knowing that they are safe from harm.

Part 4: Understanding Boogeyman Tactics

Chapter 12: How Boogeymen Lurk

Boogeymen are creatures of mystery and fear, often found hiding in the places where shadows linger and darkness thrives. To better understand how to protect yourself from them, it's important to explore where Boogeymen hide and why certain spaces seem to be their favorite lurking spots. This chapter delves deep into the psychology and habits of the Boogeyman, shedding light on the corners of your home where he might be hiding—and how to reclaim those spaces as safe, comforting zones.

The Nature of the Boogeyman: Why He Lurks in the Shadows

Before exploring the specific places where Boogeymen hide, it's essential to understand *why* they gravitate toward certain areas. The Boogeyman is a creature born from fear and thrives in places where darkness reigns and imagination runs wild. These are places that tend to be out of sight, creating an unknown, and for children, the unknown is a blank canvas for fear to manifest.

The Boogeyman is not merely attracted to physical darkness; he also finds strength in emotional darkness—the fears, uncertainties, and vulnerabilities that children experience when they are alone. For the Boogeyman, darkness offers a perfect hiding place, where he can move unnoticed and amplify the fears that children may already have.

Wherever there are shadows, uncertainty, or isolation, the Boogeyman can lurk. And for children, certain areas of their bedroom and home create the perfect environment for him to manifest.

Classic Hiding Spots of the Boogeyman

Though the Boogeyman can appear anywhere darkness and fear combine, there are a few places that are his most common haunts. These are the spots children often associate with the Boogeyman and where they are most likely to imagine his presence. Let's take a closer look at each one.

1. Under the Bed: The Most Famous Hideout

Perhaps the most infamous of the Boogeyman's hiding spots, *under the bed* has long been a place where children's imaginations run wild. The space beneath the bed is dark, often cluttered with forgotten toys, books, and objects that cast odd, unsettling shadows. Because it's out of sight, children can't see what's lurking down there once the lights go out—leaving it open to all sorts of fearful possibilities.

The Boogeyman is drawn to the space under the bed for a few reasons:

- **It's dark and hidden**: When a child is lying in bed, they cannot see what's beneath them. This lack of visibility creates the perfect environment for fear to grow.
- **It's physically close to the child**: Since the bed is where a child sleeps—and often feels most vulnerable—the Boogeyman likes to lurk nearby, feeding on the child's fear and imagination.
- **It plays into common fears**: Many children have an instinctual fear of things hiding beneath them. The idea of a creature lying in wait just out of sight is a powerful fear trigger.

How to Reclaim the Space Under the Bed

While the Boogeyman might love the darkness under the bed, there are several ways to make this space less inviting for him:

- **Use a nightlight or under-bed light**: Installing a small light that illuminates the area under the bed can drive away the Boogeyman's shadows. Even a string of fairy lights can work wonders by ensuring that nothing remains hidden in the darkness.
- **Keep the space clean and clutter-free**: Boogeymen are drawn to clutter because it creates confusing shapes and shadows. By keeping the area under the bed clear of unnecessary objects, you remove the visual distortions that can trigger fear.
- **Create a protective barrier**: Encourage your child to imagine a force field or barrier around the bed that the Boogeyman cannot cross. This invisible shield can provide comfort and keep the space beneath the bed free of fear.

2. In the Closet: A Doorway to the Unknown

The closet is another prime hiding spot for the Boogeyman. The dark, enclosed space behind the closet door, often filled with clothes, shoes, and toys, can become a breeding ground for shadows and strange shapes. For children, the closet represents a place of mystery—the door may be closed, but they know something could be lurking behind it.

The Boogeyman is attracted to closets for several reasons:

- **It's a space of unknown depth**: Unlike the space under the bed, which is somewhat limited, closets often extend into darkness, with clothes and objects hanging or sitting in the shadows. This creates a more complex environment where the Boogeyman can hide behind or within things.

- **It's often left closed, but not locked**: A closet door that is slightly ajar or can easily be opened gives the Boogeyman a sense of potential freedom. To the child, it feels as if the Boogeyman could emerge at any moment.
- **It's a place of transition**: Closets are spaces where items are put away and hidden. This sense of putting things out of sight also applies to fear—the Boogeyman represents the things we don't want to face.

How to Reclaim the Closet

To make the closet a safe space that no longer invites the Boogeyman:

- **Install a closet light**: A small light that automatically turns on when the closet door is opened can banish any lurking shadows. For children afraid of opening the closet, the light acts as an immediate reassurance that nothing is inside.
- **Keep the door securely closed**: Some children find comfort in knowing that the closet door is completely shut and latched before they go to sleep. This creates a boundary that the Boogeyman cannot cross.
- **Involve the child in a daily "inspection"**: Before bed, make a fun ritual of checking the closet together. This not only reassures the child that the space is safe but also gives them a sense of control over their environment.

3. In the Shadows: Where the Boogeyman Thrives

While under the bed and in the closet are the most classic places for the Boogeyman to hide, *shadows* themselves are where the Boogeyman truly thrives. He is a creature of darkness, and shadows provide the perfect camouflage for him to lurk, shift, and change form. Shadows are particularly unsettling because they are often ambiguous, allowing the Boogeyman to appear as something he's not—a flickering shape, a vague figure, or a movement just out of sight.

The Boogeyman is drawn to shadows because:

- **They are everywhere**: Unlike specific hiding spots like the bed or closet, shadows can appear anywhere in the room, making them harder to control or avoid.
- **They shift and change**: As light sources move or flicker, shadows can stretch, shrink, and distort, giving the Boogeyman a way to appear dynamic and unsettling.
- **They play on the imagination**: A child's mind can easily turn an ordinary shadow into something frightening. The Boogeyman exploits this by hiding in plain sight, using the shadows to create doubt and fear.

How to Reclaim the Shadows

Even though shadows can be tricky, there are ways to take control of them and banish the Boogeyman from the room:

- **Use multiple light sources**: Keeping the room well-lit with multiple sources of light reduces the number of deep shadows. Consider using nightlights, lamps, or even soft string lights to brighten all corners of the room.
- **Cast playful shadows**: Turn shadow play into a fun and empowering activity. Use a flashlight or a lamp to create playful shadow puppets on the walls. This helps the child see shadows as harmless and under their control, reducing the Boogeyman's ability to manipulate them.
- **Rearrange furniture**: Sometimes shadows are created by the way furniture is arranged in the room. By moving items or adding light, you can minimize dark areas where the Boogeyman might hide.

4. Behind Doors or Curtains: Lurking Just Out of Sight

Doors and curtains provide the Boogeyman with another ideal hiding spot. Like the closet, a closed door or curtain separates the child from the unknown. Anything could be behind it, and the Boogeyman uses this fear of the unseen to his advantage. Whether it's the door to another room or the thick curtains that cover a window, these barriers play into the fear of what lies beyond.

The Boogeyman hides behind doors and curtains because:

- **They create a barrier between the child and the unknown**: When a door or curtain is closed, the child has no way of knowing what's on the other side. This mystery feeds the Boogeyman's power.
- **They can move unexpectedly**: A breeze can cause a curtain to sway, or a door might creak open just a bit, creating unsettling movements that suggest the Boogeyman's presence.
- **They are associated with transition**: Doors and curtains represent boundaries between different spaces. For the Boogeyman, they are an ideal place to wait, lurking in the threshold between one world and another.

How to Reclaim Doors and Curtains

To make doors and curtains less appealing to the Boogeyman:

- **Securely close doors and curtains**: Make sure doors are properly latched and curtains are securely drawn. For some children, leaving the door open a crack may provide comfort, while others feel safer with everything closed.
- **Check behind them together**: Create a nightly routine where you and your child check behind the curtains or doors together. This shows the child that there is nothing to fear, and reinforces their control over the space.

- **Use doorstop alarms or clips**: If your child is especially afraid of doors opening unexpectedly, consider using doorstops or door clips to ensure the door stays securely closed throughout the night.

5. The Corners of the Room: Silent Watchers

Boogeymen love to lurk in the far corners of a room, where shadows collect and the light doesn't always reach. These corners, often empty or sparsely furnished, create a sense of isolation and distance from the rest of the space, making them an ideal hiding place for the Boogeyman. The presence of the Boogeyman in these corners can make a child feel like they are being watched, even when nothing is there.

How to Reclaim the Corners of the Room

To take control of the corners of a room:

- **Place objects in the corners**: By putting a comforting object—like a nightlight, a stuffed animal, or a piece of furniture—in the corner, you can disrupt the Boogeyman's hiding spot. This transforms the corner from a place of fear to a place of safety.
- **Illuminate the space**: A simple light directed into the corner can dissolve the shadows, leaving no place for the Boogeyman to hide.
- **Incorporate a nightly ritual**: Each night, walk with your child to the corner of the room, pointing out that the Boogeyman is not there. This habit reassures the child and breaks the illusion that the corners are a place of danger.

Conclusion: Taking Back the Space from the Boogeyman

The Boogeyman thrives in the hidden spaces of the room—under the bed, in the closet, behind doors, and within shadows. But by understanding where he hides and why, you can take proactive steps to reclaim those areas and turn them into spaces of safety and comfort for your child.

Using light, decluttering spaces, creating nightly rituals, and adding personal touches all help to weaken the Boogeyman's power, proving to children that they are in control of their environment. The Boogeyman may be skilled at lurking, but with these strategies, his favorite hiding spots will no longer be places of fear. Instead, they will become symbols of safety, security, and peace, where the Boogeyman has no power and no place.

Chapter 13: The Boogeyman's Weakness

The Boogeyman may seem like an all-powerful entity of darkness and fear, but like all creatures of the imagination, he has his weaknesses. In fact, the Boogeyman is far more vulnerable than he appears, relying heavily on fear, shadows, and uncertainty to maintain his strength. By understanding the Boogeyman's key vulnerabilities, children and parents can better protect themselves and turn the tables on this creature of the night. In this chapter, we explore the Boogeyman's most significant weaknesses, from mirrors that reflect his true nature to the cleansing power of sunlight, and how to use these to drive him away once and for all.

The Nature of the Boogeyman's Weaknesses

The Boogeyman's power is entirely derived from fear. He has no physical form that can harm or touch a child in reality, but he preys on a child's imagination, turning shadows and unknown spaces into sources of terror. This makes the Boogeyman both powerful and fragile. His strengths—darkness, fear, and uncertainty—are his greatest weaknesses when challenged. The more a child understands this, the less power the Boogeyman has.

Each of the Boogeyman's vulnerabilities targets a specific aspect of his existence. Whether it's through the use of light, objects like mirrors, or rituals that empower the child, these weaknesses can be exploited to keep the Boogeyman at bay and weaken his influence over time.

Key Vulnerabilities of the Boogeyman

1. Sunlight: The Ultimate Cleanser of Darkness

Sunlight is the most powerful and absolute weakness of the Boogeyman. As a creature that thrives in the dark, the Boogeyman cannot withstand the pure, unfiltered light of the sun. When the sun rises, his power is completely diminished, and he has no choice but to retreat. Sunlight represents clarity, truth, and safety—all things that counteract the fear and confusion the Boogeyman uses to gain strength.

- **How It Works**: The Boogeyman cannot exist in direct sunlight. As soon as the first rays of dawn touch a room, his presence is banished. This is why most Boogeyman encounters happen at night—once the sun rises, he is powerless.
- **How to Use It**: While you can't control the sun's schedule, you can use the power of sunlight to cleanse a room during the day. Encourage your child to open their curtains or blinds first thing in the morning, letting the sunlight flood their room. The more sunlight the room receives during the day, the less likely the Boogeyman will feel comfortable returning at night.
- **The Morning Ritual**: To empower your child, create a morning ritual of "banishing" the Boogeyman with sunlight. Every morning, as the sunlight enters the room, have your child say, "The light keeps me safe, and the Boogeyman cannot stay." This simple affirmation helps the child associate sunlight with safety and the end of nighttime fear.

2. Mirrors: Revealing the Boogeyman's True Nature

One of the Boogeyman's greatest weaknesses is his inability to face his true nature. While he thrives in darkness and ambiguity, a mirror forces him to confront what he really is—a shadowy figment of the imagination. Mirrors reflect not only light but also truth, and when the Boogeyman looks into one, he loses his ability to manipulate shadows and fear.

- **How It Works**: Mirrors expose the Boogeyman for what he truly is—nothing more than a trick of the imagination. When faced with his reflection, he loses the ability to hide in the darkness and must retreat.
- **How to Use It**: Place a mirror in key areas of your child's room, particularly near places where the Boogeyman might hide, like the closet, under the bed, or in dark corners. If your child feels the Boogeyman's presence, encourage them to hold up a small hand mirror and say, "Show yourself, Boogeyman!" The reflection will force the Boogeyman to face his own insubstantial nature, weakening his power.
- **Mirror Shield Ritual**: To give your child more confidence, turn the mirror into a shield. Explain to your child that when they hold up the mirror, it acts like a protective barrier, reflecting the Boogeyman's fear back at him. Teach them to say, "This mirror protects me and shows the Boogeyman what he really is."

3. Light of Any Kind: Chasing Away the Darkness

While sunlight is the Boogeyman's most potent enemy, any form of light can weaken him. Light disrupts the shadows where the Boogeyman hides and creates a barrier that he cannot cross. Whether it's the soft glow of a nightlight, the bright beam of a flashlight, or the flicker of a candle, light is a constant reminder that the Boogeyman has no place in a child's room.

- **How It Works**: Light exposes the Boogeyman's hiding spots and forces him to retreat into the few remaining shadows. The brighter and more consistent the light, the weaker he becomes.
- **How to Use It**: Equip your child's room with multiple light sources, such as nightlights, lamps, or string lights, especially in areas where shadows gather. If your child wakes up in the middle of the night feeling afraid, they can use a flashlight or bedside lamp to instantly weaken the Boogeyman's influence.
- **The Circle of Light**: Create a "Circle of Light" ritual by walking around the room with a flashlight or candle before bed, shining the light into every corner and dark space. As you do, have your child say, "This light keeps me safe, and the Boogeyman cannot hide."

4. Laughter: The Sound of Joy Weakens Fear

Laughter is another powerful weapon against the Boogeyman, as it is the complete opposite of fear. The Boogeyman thrives on a child's fear and uncertainty, but laughter breaks through those emotions, filling the room with joy and lightheartedness. When a child is laughing, the Boogeyman's hold on their imagination weakens, and he finds it difficult to maintain his presence.

- **How It Works**: Laughter disrupts the atmosphere of fear that the Boogeyman needs to survive. When a child laughs, they take control of their emotions, and the Boogeyman is forced to retreat.
- **How to Use It**: Encourage laughter and fun before bedtime. Whether it's reading a funny story, watching a silly video, or telling jokes, create an atmosphere of joy and positivity. This makes it harder for the Boogeyman to gain a foothold in the room.
- **Laughter Defense**: Teach your child to laugh in the face of fear. If they sense the Boogeyman, they can laugh loudly and say, "You're not scary, Boogeyman! You're silly!" This unexpected response throws the Boogeyman off balance, weakening his power over the child's imagination.

5. Positive Energy: Objects of Comfort and Love

The Boogeyman cannot thrive in an environment filled with positive energy. Objects that hold special meaning for the child—such as a favorite stuffed animal, a family photo, or a special blanket—carry with them a sense of comfort and love. These objects serve as a shield against the fear and darkness the Boogeyman tries to create.

- **How It Works**: Objects of comfort radiate positive energy, which weakens the Boogeyman's ability to instill fear. When a child feels loved and safe, the Boogeyman finds it difficult to maintain his influence.

- **How to Use It**: Help your child choose a "protector" object to keep near their bed—this could be a stuffed animal, a toy, or even a special pillow. Explain to your child that this object is filled with love and positivity, and as long as they hold onto it, the Boogeyman can't come near them.
- **Comfort Ritual**: Each night, have your child say goodnight to their protector object and place it near their bed. This small ritual reinforces the idea that they are surrounded by positive energy, which the Boogeyman cannot penetrate.

6. Sound: Bells, Chimes, and Music

Certain sounds, particularly those associated with peace and positivity, can weaken the Boogeyman. The clear, bright tones of bells and wind chimes, or the soothing melodies of music, create an environment where fear cannot take hold. The Boogeyman finds it difficult to thrive in a space filled with sound, as it disrupts his ability to manipulate silence and shadows.

- **How It Works**: Sound disrupts the quiet, shadowy spaces where the Boogeyman hides. Whether it's the ringing of a bell or the gentle melody of a lullaby, sound fills the room with positive energy, weakening the Boogeyman's influence.
- **How to Use It**: Place wind chimes near windows or keep a small bell near your child's bed. If your child feels afraid, they can ring the bell or listen to a favorite song to drive away the Boogeyman. Alternatively, play soft music or a white noise machine during the night to create a sound barrier that the Boogeyman cannot cross.
- **Sound Shield Ritual**: Each night, have your child ring a bell or listen to a calming song before bed. As they do, encourage them to say, "This sound keeps me safe, and no fear can stay." This ritual helps them take control of the space, pushing the Boogeyman out with positive sound waves.

7. Bravery and Confidence: The Boogeyman's Kryptonite

The Boogeyman's final and most potent weakness is a child's bravery and confidence. The Boogeyman preys on fear, doubt, and insecurity, but when a child faces him with courage, his power vanishes. Simply believing that the Boogeyman has no control over them is enough to weaken him significantly. The Boogeyman cannot withstand the force of a child who feels empowered, safe, and strong.

- **How It Works**: The Boogeyman thrives on fear. When a child believes in their own strength and courage, they deny the Boogeyman the fear he needs to survive, forcing him to retreat.
- **How to Use It**: Build up your child's confidence through positive affirmations and empowering rituals. Encourage them to say phrases like, "I am strong, and the Boogeyman can't hurt me," or "This is my room, and I'm not afraid." By reinforcing their belief in their own power, you take away the Boogeyman's greatest weapon.
- **The Courage Ritual**: Before bed, have your child stand tall and declare their bravery. Encourage them to say, "I am not afraid of the Boogeyman. I am strong, and I am safe." This affirmation serves as a powerful reminder that the Boogeyman has no real power over them.

Conclusion: Exploiting the Boogeyman's Weaknesses

The Boogeyman may seem like an unstoppable force of fear, but in reality, he is vulnerable to a variety of things—light, laughter, sound, and, most importantly, the confidence of a brave child. By understanding and using these weaknesses, children can take control of their environment and banish the Boogeyman from their lives. Whether it's through the warm rays of sunlight, the protective power of mirrors, or the courage that comes from within, the Boogeyman's hold can be broken.

This chapter empowers both parents and children with the knowledge and tools to turn the tide against the Boogeyman. Once his weaknesses are known and exploited, the Boogeyman is no longer a creature to be feared, but a shadow that can be driven away—leaving behind only peace, safety, and a restful night's sleep.

Chapter 14: Boogey Traps

While light, sound, and positive energy are excellent ways to repel the Boogeyman, there are times when a more direct approach is needed. That's where **Boogey Traps** come into play—simple but effective setups that either capture or repel the Boogeyman before he can cause fear. Setting these traps gives children a sense of control over their space, turning their bedroom into a fortified sanctuary where the Boogeyman has no chance to thrive. In this chapter, we'll explore how to create a variety of Boogey Traps using common household items, imagination, and a little creativity.

The Purpose of Boogey Traps

Boogey Traps serve two primary purposes:

1. **To capture** the Boogeyman and prevent him from lurking in the shadows or under the bed.
2. **To repel** the Boogeyman before he can approach or enter the room.

Boogey Traps are symbolic tools that empower children by allowing them to actively protect their space. These traps, while imaginative in nature, have a powerful psychological effect—helping the child believe they are in control of their environment and can keep the Boogeyman at bay.

Types of Boogey Traps

There are several types of Boogey Traps that can be set up around the room to either ensnare or repel the Boogeyman. The best part? They're easy to make and use items you likely already have at home. Below are some of the most effective Boogey Traps and how to set them up.

1. **The Mirror Trap: Exposing the Boogeyman's Form**

As discussed in the previous chapter, the Boogeyman cannot stand to see his own reflection. The Mirror Trap takes advantage of this weakness by "trapping" the Boogeyman in a reflective surface. When he is forced to look at his own distorted form, his power weakens, and he is driven back into the shadows.

- **Materials**: A handheld mirror, a small mirror placed on a stand, or even a mirrored surface like a shiny toy.
- **How to Set It**:
    - Place the mirror in areas where the Boogeyman is most likely to hide, such as under the bed, in the closet, or in dark corners.
    - Position the mirror so it reflects the entryway to the room or any shadowy areas. This way, if the Boogeyman tries to enter, he'll see himself in the reflection.
    - Encourage the child to say, "This mirror shows the Boogeyman's true face and sends him away," each night before bed.
    - If your child wakes up feeling frightened, they can use a handheld mirror to "catch" the Boogeyman by shining the reflection around the room, especially in shadowy areas.

The Mirror Trap is an easy and effective way to turn the Boogeyman's own weaknesses against him.

2. **The Salt Barrier: Sealing Off Entry Points**

Salt has been used in folklore and superstition for centuries to ward off evil spirits and protect homes from malevolent entities. The Boogeyman, who thrives on fear and darkness, is no match for a barrier of salt. Creating a **Salt Trap** is one of the simplest and most effective ways to keep him out of specific areas in the room.

- **Materials**: Table salt or coarse sea salt, a small container, and optionally, a spoon for precision.
- **How to Set It**:
    - Begin by sprinkling a thin line of salt along the threshold of the child's bedroom door or closet. This creates a barrier that the Boogeyman cannot cross.
    - If your child feels that the Boogeyman hides under the bed, sprinkle a line of salt around the bed's perimeter, focusing on any gaps or spaces beneath the bed frame.
    - As you sprinkle the salt, have your child say, "This salt keeps the Boogeyman away, he cannot pass through."
    - Once the salt is laid out, leave it undisturbed until morning. The salt forms an invisible shield, preventing the Boogeyman from entering the protected area.

For younger children, you can frame the salt as a "magic barrier" that the Boogeyman cannot break, giving them a sense of comfort knowing the trap is set and working throughout the night.

3. The Noise Trap: Startling the Boogeyman Away

Boogeymen love silence and thrive in the quiet, shadowy corners of a child's room. A **Noise Trap** works by creating sudden sounds that startle and repel the Boogeyman whenever he tries to approach. While Boogeymen may creep through darkness, they are easily scared away by unexpected noises, especially those that catch them off guard.

- **Materials**: A set of wind chimes, a bell, or even a noisemaker toy.
- **How to Set It**:
    - Hang a set of wind chimes or a small bell on the doorknob of your child's bedroom door or closet door. If the Boogeyman tries to enter, the movement of the door will cause the chimes to jingle, startling him away.
    - Alternatively, place a small noisemaker toy or bell on a chair or bookshelf near the bed. If your child senses the Boogeyman, they can shake the noisemaker or bell, filling the room with sound and forcing him to retreat.
    - Make it part of the bedtime routine for your child to ring the bell or chime before going to sleep, saying, "This noise keeps the Boogeyman away, and he cannot sneak in."

The Noise Trap uses sound to create a sudden disruption, forcing the Boogeyman to retreat from the room and seek quieter, less protected places.

4. The Flashlight Trap: Blinding the Boogeyman

Light is one of the Boogeyman's greatest weaknesses, and a **Flashlight Trap** allows children to wield this power directly. A bright flashlight can be used as a "weapon" of sorts, blinding the Boogeyman and forcing him to stay in the shadows or flee entirely.

- **Materials**: A powerful flashlight or headlamp, and optionally, glow-in-the-dark stickers or designs.
- **How to Set It**:
    - Keep a flashlight within easy reach of your child's bed, either on the nightstand or under the pillow. If they sense the Boogeyman, they can grab the flashlight and shine it toward any shadowy areas, including under the bed or in the closet.
    - For added effect, decorate the flashlight with glow-in-the-dark stickers or designs that make it feel like a magical tool.
    - Teach your child to turn on the flashlight and say, "This light makes you run away, Boogeyman. You can't stay here!" Shining the flashlight directly into the dark spaces forces the Boogeyman to retreat.

The Flashlight Trap is especially effective because it gives children direct control over their fear, allowing them to feel empowered as they shine the light into dark corners and banish the Boogeyman from their room.

5. The Dreamcatcher Trap: Filtering Out Nightmares

While traditionally used to catch bad dreams, a **Dreamcatcher Trap** can also be used to trap the Boogeyman in his attempts to enter a child's dreams. Dreamcatchers, often made with woven threads and feathers, are believed to filter out negative energies and nightmares, leaving only good dreams behind.

- **Materials**: A dreamcatcher, either purchased or homemade, and a piece of string for hanging.
- **How to Set It**:
    - Hang the dreamcatcher above your child's bed, making sure it is in a place where it can "catch" any negative energy or nightmares before they reach your child.
    - Explain to your child that the dreamcatcher is like a net that traps the Boogeyman and keeps him from entering their dreams.
    - As part of the nightly routine, have your child gently touch the dreamcatcher and say, "This dreamcatcher keeps all bad dreams and the Boogeyman away. I will sleep safely tonight."

Dreamcatchers can become a comforting symbol of protection, giving children the assurance that the Boogeyman will be trapped before he can cause any harm in their dreams.

6. The Blanket Trap: A Shield of Safety

Sometimes the simplest traps are the most effective. A **Blanket Trap** works by creating an impenetrable shield of safety around the child while they sleep. For many children, their blanket is a source of comfort and security. When empowered with the right words and imagination, this blanket becomes a protective barrier that the Boogeyman cannot cross.

- **Materials**: A favorite blanket or comforter.

- **How to Set It:**
  - Before bed, help your child tuck themselves in tightly with their blanket, explaining that the blanket acts like a shield that the Boogeyman cannot penetrate.
  - Encourage your child to say something like, "This blanket is my shield. The Boogeyman cannot get through."
  - If your child feels scared during the night, remind them to pull the blanket over themselves and repeat their protective phrase, imagining the Boogeyman being unable to approach.

The Blanket Trap uses the familiar comfort of a blanket to create a sense of safety and security, giving children the feeling of being fully protected while they sleep.

7. The Box Trap: Trapping the Boogeyman for Good

A **Box Trap** is designed to capture the Boogeyman and keep him locked away, preventing him from moving around the room or causing fear. This trap works by symbolically placing the Boogeyman inside a box where he can do no harm.

- **Materials:** A small cardboard box, some paper, crayons or markers, and tape.
- **How to Set It:**
  - Have your child decorate the box with drawings or symbols that represent safety and protection. Let them draw pictures of things that make them feel brave, like superheroes or protective animals.
  - Write "Boogeyman Trap" on the top of the box and place it in a corner of the room.
  - Explain to your child that the box is specially designed to trap the Boogeyman. If they feel his presence, they can imagine the Boogeyman being sucked into the box, where he is locked away.
  - Before bed, have your child say, "This box traps the Boogeyman, and he can't get out."

Once the box is set, the child will know that the Boogeyman is safely contained and unable to roam free in their room.

8. The Scent Trap: Using Smells to Repel the Boogeyman

Just as certain sounds and lights can repel the Boogeyman, so too can smells. The **Scent Trap** uses calming, pleasant scents like lavender or eucalyptus to create a peaceful atmosphere that the Boogeyman finds uncomfortable.

- **Materials**: A small spray bottle, water, a few drops of essential oils (lavender, eucalyptus, or chamomile), and optionally, a soft cloth.
- **How to Set It**:
    ◦ Fill the spray bottle with water and add a few drops of the essential oil. Shake the bottle to mix the scent.
    ◦ Before bed, let your child spray the air around their bed, closet, or under the bed, saying, "This smell keeps the Boogeyman far away."
    ◦ If they prefer, the child can use a cloth to lightly dab some of the scent on their pillow or blanket, creating a lasting fragrance that keeps the Boogeyman at bay throughout the night.

The Scent Trap not only helps calm and soothe your child but also creates a protective barrier that the Boogeyman cannot stand.

Conclusion: Mastering Boogey Traps for Peaceful Nights

Boogey Traps are an excellent way to empower children to take control of their space and their fears. By setting traps designed to capture or repel the Boogeyman, children feel more confident and less afraid, knowing they have direct tools at their disposal to protect themselves. These traps, while imaginative, serve as powerful psychological aids that help children overcome their fear of the Boogeyman and reclaim their bedrooms as spaces of safety and comfort.

From simple traps like the Blanket Shield to more elaborate setups like the Mirror Trap or Salt Barrier, there is a Boogey Trap for every type of fear. By encouraging your child to participate in setting these traps, you help them build confidence in their ability to face and conquer their fear of the Boogeyman, leading to more peaceful nights and a stronger sense of control over their environment.

Chapter 15: The Temporalfuge Device

In the realm of tools to combat the Boogeyman, few are as advanced and imaginative as the **Temporalfuge Device**—an invention that harnesses the power of time itself to age a Boogeyman rapidly, rendering him powerless and ineffective. By accelerating the Boogeyman's lifespan, the Temporalfuge weakens his abilities and causes him to "grow old" so quickly that he loses his strength, becomes frail, and eventually fades away. This chapter explores how the Temporalfuge Device works, how to build one, and how to use it to defeat even the most stubborn Boogeyman.

Understanding the Temporalfuge Device: How Time Defeats the Boogeyman

The Boogeyman is a creature born from fear, living in the shadows and thriving on a child's imagination. While he may seem ageless and eternal, the truth is that the Boogeyman has a limited lifespan, much like the fears that create him. The Temporalfuge Device exploits this vulnerability by speeding up the Boogeyman's aging process. Just as time weakens all living things, the Temporalfuge makes the Boogeyman grow older rapidly, causing him to lose his power, agility, and ability to scare.

In essence, the Temporalfuge forces the Boogeyman to experience years in just a few moments. He becomes slower, weaker, and eventually so old that he can no longer exist in the shadows he once thrived in. For children, the Temporalfuge is an exciting and empowering tool that gives them direct control over the Boogeyman's fate, turning him from a fearsome figure into a powerless shadow of his former self.

Building the Temporalfuge Device

While the Temporalfuge Device may sound like advanced technology from a science fiction novel, it can be constructed using simple household items combined with imagination and creativity. The true power of the Temporalfuge lies not in the materials but in the belief that it can rapidly age the Boogeyman and render him harmless. Below are the steps to build your very own Temporalfuge Device.

Materials Needed:

- **An empty cardboard box or plastic container**: This will serve as the main body of the device.
- **A small kitchen timer or stopwatch**: The "core" of the device that represents the flow of time.
- **Aluminum foil**: Used to wrap parts of the device, giving it a shiny, high-tech appearance.
- **Glow-in-the-dark stickers or paint**: To give the device a futuristic look and create the illusion of time manipulation.
- **A small fan or pinwheel**: This will act as the "temporal accelerator," visually representing the speeding up of time.
- **A flashlight or small LED light**: Used to "target" the Boogeyman and activate the aging process.
- **Colored buttons or stickers**: These serve as the controls for activating the device.
- **Tape or glue**: For assembling the components.
- **Markers or crayons**: To decorate the device and label the various parts.
- **Imagination**: The most important material, as belief in the Temporalfuge's power is key to making it work.

Step-by-Step Construction of the Temporalfuge Device:

Step 1: Construct the Body of the Device

Start by taking the empty cardboard box or plastic container, which will form the main body of the Temporalfuge. Decorate the outside using markers, crayons, or paint. Write the word "Temporalfuge" in bold letters across the front, and label the different parts, such as "Temporal Core," "Time Accelerator," and "Aging Beam."

Step 2: Attach the Time Core

Take the kitchen timer or stopwatch, which will represent the core of the device. This is the heart of the Temporalfuge and will control the flow of time. Secure the timer to the top of the box using tape or glue, making sure it is visible and easily accessible. You can decorate the timer with stickers or foil to make it look like a high-tech device.

Step 3: Add the Temporal Accelerator

The small fan or pinwheel will act as the "Temporal Accelerator," the part of the device that speeds up time. Attach the fan or pinwheel to the front of the box so that it spins when the device is activated. The spinning motion represents the rapid aging process that will affect the Boogeyman.

If using a pinwheel, make sure it can spin freely. If using a small fan, you may want to wire it to a battery pack so it can be turned on and off.

Step 4: Install the Aging Beam

The flashlight or small LED light serves as the "Aging Beam." This is the component that will directly target the Boogeyman and initiate the aging process. Attach the flashlight to the front or side of the box, positioning it so it can shine toward the Boogeyman's hiding spot. Decorate the flashlight with glow-in-the-dark paint or stickers to give it an extra futuristic effect.

Step 5: Add Control Buttons

Use colored buttons, stickers, or even small bottle caps to create the controls for the device. Glue them to the top or front of the box. These buttons are where your child will "program" the device, setting the time acceleration and activating the beam. Label each button with instructions like "Time Warp," "Aging On," and "Boogeyman Defeat."

Step 6: Final Touches and Decorations

Wrap parts of the box in aluminum foil to give it a shiny, metallic look. Add glow-in-the-dark stickers or paint for extra effect, and make sure the device looks as futuristic and powerful as possible. The more imaginative the decorations, the more your child will believe in the power of the Temporalfuge.

Once the device is fully assembled, it's time to test it out and learn how to use it against the Boogeyman.

How to Use the Temporalfuge Device

Now that your Temporalfuge Device is complete, it's time to learn how to use it to rapidly age the Boogeyman and render him powerless. The device works by targeting the Boogeyman's hiding spot, accelerating his time, and causing him to grow old in a matter of moments. Below is a step-by-step guide on how to activate and use the Temporalfuge.

Step 1: Identify the Boogeyman's Location

Before activating the device, help your child identify where the Boogeyman might be lurking. Whether he's hiding under the bed, in the closet, or in the shadows, your child should pinpoint the spot where the Boogeyman is most likely to be.

Step 2: Set the Timer

Once the Boogeyman's location has been identified, it's time to set the Temporalfuge's "Time Core." Have your child turn the kitchen timer or stopwatch to the desired setting—this represents how quickly time will pass for the Boogeyman. For example, setting the timer to one minute could represent 10 years of aging for the Boogeyman.

As they set the timer, encourage your child to say something like, "I'm speeding up time for you, Boogeyman. You're about to grow old and weak!"

Step 3: Activate the Temporal Accelerator

Next, have your child spin the pinwheel or turn on the small fan to activate the Temporal Accelerator. This represents the time warp that is now affecting the Boogeyman. As the fan spins, time is rapidly accelerating, and the Boogeyman is aging at a much faster rate than normal.

The spinning motion should be accompanied by your child saying, "Time is moving fast, Boogeyman! You can't keep up!"

Step 4: Target the Boogeyman with the Aging Beam

Now, it's time to activate the Aging Beam. Have your child point the flashlight or LED light toward the Boogeyman's hiding spot and turn it on. The beam of light represents the focused power of the Temporalfuge, causing the Boogeyman to age rapidly wherever he is hiding.

As they shine the light, encourage your child to say, "This beam makes you old, Boogeyman. You're getting weaker and weaker!"

Step 5: Complete the Time Cycle

As the timer counts down, the Boogeyman grows older and more powerless. When the timer rings or stops, it signifies that the Boogeyman has reached the end of his time—he is now too old and weak to continue lurking in the shadows.

Your child can declare, "Your time is up, Boogeyman! You're too old to scare me now!"

Step 6: Watch the Boogeyman Fade Away

Once the process is complete, explain to your child that the Boogeyman has aged so quickly that he has faded into nothingness. He is no longer a threat, and the Temporalfuge has rendered him powerless.

Your child can confidently say, "The Boogeyman is gone. The Temporalfuge worked!"

Maintenance of the Temporalfuge Device

While the Temporalfuge is highly effective, it's important to maintain it to ensure it's always ready for action:

- **Check the Timer**: Make sure the timer is still working properly and can be reset each night if necessary.
- **Replace Batteries**: If your flashlight or fan is battery-operated, be sure to replace the batteries regularly.
- **Reinforce the Belief**: The most important aspect of the Temporalfuge is the child's belief in its power. Regularly reinforce the idea that the device is effective and that it keeps the Boogeyman away for good.

Conclusion: Using Time as a Weapon Against the Boogeyman

The Temporalfuge Device is a unique and imaginative tool that allows children to take control of their fear by accelerating the Boogeyman's aging process. By harnessing the power of time, the Temporalfuge turns the tables on the Boogeyman, forcing him to experience the natural effects of aging in a matter of moments. As the Boogeyman grows older, weaker, and eventually powerless, the child gains confidence and control over their space.

Building and using the Temporalfuge is a fun and empowering activity that reinforces the idea that the Boogeyman is no match for a child's ingenuity and bravery. With the Temporalfuge at their side, children can face the night without fear, knowing that time itself is on their side and the Boogeyman has no place in their room.

Part 5: 150 Ways to "Bust Your Boogie"

Chapter 16: Introduction to Boogie Busting

Boogie Busting is the art and science of neutralizing the Boogeyman—turning fear into empowerment and reclaiming control over the night. In this chapter, we introduce a comprehensive set of techniques and strategies that every child (and parent) can use to defeat the Boogeyman. These methods range from psychological tools that reinforce bravery to practical tips for making the Boogeyman's hiding spots inhospitable. This chapter serves as an overview of Boogie Busting, offering a guide to building confidence, setting boundaries, and using creative traps and tools to make the Boogeyman powerless.

Understanding the Psychology of Boogey Busting

The Boogeyman exists primarily in the realm of the mind, thriving on the fear and uncertainty that many children feel in the dark. His power comes from fear, and as long as fear exists, the Boogeyman has room to grow. However, this also means that the Boogeyman is vulnerable to the opposite emotions—bravery, confidence, and empowerment. The foundation of Boogie Busting is built on transforming fear into strength, using a variety of imaginative techniques, environmental changes, and rituals to weaken the Boogeyman and keep him at bay.

The following strategies focus on key areas of Boogie Busting: **mental preparation, environmental control, practical tools**, and **imaginative defenses**.

Mental Preparation: Building Confidence and Courage

Before diving into the more hands-on strategies, it's important to recognize that mental preparation is a crucial first step in Boogie Busting. Helping children understand that they have the power to face and defeat the Boogeyman is the core of neutralizing his influence. By building a strong mental defense, children can reduce their fear and boost their sense of control over their surroundings.

1. Affirmations of Strength

One of the most effective mental tools in Boogie Busting is the use of **positive affirmations**. Teaching children to speak confidently about their power over the Boogeyman weakens his hold on their mind. Affirmations work by reinforcing the child's belief in their own abilities, helping them internalize the idea that the Boogeyman cannot harm them.

- **Examples of Affirmations**:
    - "I am strong, and the Boogeyman can't scare me."
    - "This is my room, and the Boogeyman is not allowed here."
    - "I have the power to keep the Boogeyman away."
    - "I'm brave, and I control what happens in my dreams."

Encourage your child to repeat these affirmations before bed, especially during moments when they feel afraid. Over time, these statements help build a mental barrier that makes it harder for the Boogeyman to invade their thoughts.

2. Visualizing Safety and Protection

Another key mental tool is the practice of **visualization**. By imagining themselves in a place of absolute safety, or surrounding themselves with protective energy, children can mentally "fortify" their bedroom against the Boogeyman's approach. Visualization turns the mind into a sanctuary where fear cannot enter.

- **How to Use Visualization**:
    - Encourage your child to close their eyes and imagine a powerful light surrounding their bed or their entire room, forming an impenetrable shield that the Boogeyman cannot cross.
    - They can also visualize their favorite superheroes, animals, or protectors standing guard at the door or in the corners of the room, ensuring that the Boogeyman stays far away.

Visualization gives children a sense of control over their space and reduces the fear of the unknown.

Environmental Control: Making the Room Inhospitable to the Boogeyman

Boogeymen thrive in environments filled with shadows, clutter, and hidden spaces. By changing the physical environment of the room, children can significantly reduce the Boogeyman's ability to hide or approach unnoticed. Environmental control is a cornerstone of Boogie Busting, as it turns the child's bedroom into a well-lit, organized, and protected space.

3. Lighting the Room

The Boogeyman is a creature of darkness, and one of the simplest yet most effective strategies is to fill the room with **light**. Whether it's a nightlight, a lamp, or strategically placed glow-in-the-dark objects, light is a powerful deterrent that weakens the Boogeyman's ability to lurk in the shadows.

- **How to Use Lighting**:
    - ○ Place nightlights in areas where shadows gather, such as the corner of the room, under the bed, or inside the closet.
    - ○ Use a string of fairy lights to create a soft glow across the room, ensuring that no area is left completely dark.
    - ○ Flashlights can be kept at the bedside for quick bursts of light if the child feels afraid in the middle of the night.

The key is to ensure that no space is left in complete darkness, leaving the Boogeyman with no place to hide.

4. Decluttering and Organizing the Space

A cluttered room with toys, clothes, or furniture scattered around provides plenty of opportunities for the Boogeyman to hide. By keeping the room clean and organized, children remove many of the dark corners and odd shadows that the Boogeyman uses to create fear.

- **How to Declutter**:
    - ○ Involve your child in a nightly cleanup routine, putting toys back in their place, folding clothes, and keeping the area around the bed clear.
    - ○ Make a habit of checking under the bed and in the closet to ensure there are no forgotten items that could cast strange shadows.

A tidy room not only reduces fear but also gives children a greater sense of control over their environment.

Practical Tools for Boogie Busting

Now that we've covered mental and environmental strategies, it's time to focus on practical tools that can be used to physically "neutralize" the Boogeyman. These tools are designed to give children a tangible sense of protection, allowing them to take immediate action if they feel the Boogeyman's presence.

5. The Flashlight Defense

One of the most reliable tools in Boogie Busting is the **flashlight**. The Boogeyman hates being exposed to light, and a flashlight allows children to "chase" the shadows away with the press of a button. It gives them an immediate sense of power and control, especially when they feel the Boogeyman is hiding in dark corners or under the bed.

- **How to Use**:
  - Keep the flashlight within easy reach on the bedside table or under the pillow.
  - If your child senses the Boogeyman, have them shine the light into the shadowy areas and say, "I see you, Boogeyman, and you have to go away!"

This simple act of shining a light into the darkness turns the child from a passive observer into an active defender, making the Boogeyman lose his strength.

6. Boogeyman Repellent Spray

The **Boogeyman Repellent Spray** is a powerful psychological tool that children can use to feel like they are physically driving the Boogeyman out of their room. Made from water mixed with a calming essential oil (like lavender), this spray is harmless but incredibly effective at creating the sense that the Boogeyman has been repelled.

- **How to Make It**:
  - Fill a small spray bottle with water and add a few drops of essential oil for a pleasant scent.
  - Label the bottle "Boogeyman Repellent" and explain to your child that it has special powers to keep the Boogeyman away.
- **How to Use**:
  - Before bed, let your child spray the repellent around the room, especially near the bed, closet, and under the bed.
  - As they spray, they can say something like, "This spray keeps the Boogeyman out. He can't come near me."

The act of spraying the room serves as both a comforting ritual and a symbolic act of protection.

7. The Dreamcatcher Trap

Dreamcatchers are traditional objects that are believed to trap bad dreams and negative energy, allowing only positive thoughts and good dreams to pass through. For Boogey Busting, the **Dreamcatcher Trap** works by catching the Boogeyman before he can reach the child's mind.

- **How to Use**:
    - Hang a dreamcatcher near the bed, preferably above it, where it can "trap" any bad dreams or Boogeyman attempts.
    - Before bed, encourage your child to say, "This dreamcatcher catches the Boogeyman and keeps him away from my dreams."

The dreamcatcher becomes a powerful symbol of protection, giving children peace of mind as they fall asleep.

Imaginative Defenses: Creative Tools for Boogey Busting

Imagination is a child's greatest strength when it comes to defeating the Boogeyman. By turning ordinary objects into magical tools of protection, children can engage their creativity and build confidence in their ability to repel the Boogeyman.

8. The Magic Blanket

The **Magic Blanket** is a simple but powerful concept—when a child is tucked in with their favorite blanket, it transforms into an impenetrable shield that the Boogeyman cannot cross. The child's imagination brings this blanket to life as a protective barrier, making them feel secure throughout the night.

- **How to Use**:
    - Before bed, tuck your child in with their blanket, explaining that it has the power to protect them from any harm.
    - Encourage them to say, "My magic blanket keeps the Boogeyman away. He can't touch me when I'm under here."

The idea of a magic blanket taps into the child's natural sense of wonder, making them feel like they have their own personal defense system against the Boogeyman.

9. The Mirror Shield

A **Mirror Shield** can be used to reflect the Boogeyman's fear back at him. Mirrors are powerful tools in Boogie Busting because they expose the Boogeyman's true nature. When a child holds up a mirror, they can "trap" the Boogeyman and force him to retreat.

- **How to Use**:

- Keep a small handheld mirror near the bed. If your child feels the Boogeyman is near, they can hold up the mirror and say, "I see you, Boogeyman! Go away!"
- The mirror "reflects" the Boogeyman's fear, making him weaker and forcing him to leave.

This creative tool gives children an active way to face their fears, literally reflecting the Boogeyman out of their room.

Conclusion: Mastering the Art of Boogie Busting

Boogie Busting is more than just a set of techniques—it's a mindset. By empowering children to face their fears with confidence, creativity, and practical tools, you help them realize that the Boogeyman has no real power over them. Whether through mental preparation, environmental control, practical defenses, or imaginative solutions, every child can become a master Boogie Buster.

The strategies outlined in this chapter provide a strong foundation for defeating the Boogeyman. With these techniques in hand, children can face the night with bravery and assurance, knowing that they have the tools, the mindset, and the power to keep the Boogeyman at bay—no matter where he hides.

Chapter 17: Psychological Tactics – Outsmarting the Boogeyman

Fear is the Boogeyman's greatest weapon, but it's also his biggest weakness. The more fear he can evoke, the more powerful he becomes. However, the human mind is far more powerful than the Boogeyman's influence, and with the right psychological tactics, children can learn to control their thoughts and emotions, ultimately outwitting him. This chapter introduces a variety of mental strategies that empower children to defeat the Boogeyman using nothing more than their imagination, bravery, and critical thinking.

1. Visualization Techniques: Creating Barriers Between You and the Boogeyman

Visualization is one of the most effective mental techniques for outwitting the Boogeyman. By imagining a protective barrier between themselves and the Boogeyman, children can reduce the Boogeyman's influence and feel more secure in their space. The key to this technique is to make the barrier feel real in the mind, transforming imagination into a protective shield.

- **How to Visualize a Barrier:**
  - Encourage your child to close their eyes and imagine a bright, glowing wall of light surrounding their bed or room. This light is impenetrable, and the Boogeyman cannot pass through it.
  - They can also visualize the barrier as a magical force field, reinforced with symbols of strength, like their favorite superhero or animal standing guard.

◦ As they imagine the barrier, they can repeat a phrase like, "This wall protects me, and the Boogeyman can't get through."

Visualization helps children mentally separate themselves from fear, giving them the space to feel safe and empowered.

2. Conquering Fear: Breaking Down Fear Into Manageable Parts

Fear often feels overwhelming because it's experienced as one large, intangible emotion. However, when broken down into smaller, manageable parts, fear becomes less daunting. Teaching children to deconstruct their fear into smaller pieces helps them approach the Boogeyman with confidence.

- **How to Break Down Fear**:
    ◦ Have your child identify specific parts of their fear. Is it the darkness under the bed? The shadows in the closet? The uncertainty of what's hiding behind the door?
    ◦ Once the fear is identified, focus on each part individually. For example, if the fear is of shadows, discuss how shadows are just areas where light doesn't reach—nothing more.
    ◦ Reassure the child that each part of the fear can be addressed with a solution (light, sound, or imagination). Over time, these small fears become manageable, and the larger fear of the Boogeyman diminishes.

3. Affirmation Shields: Using Positive Affirmations to Protect Yourself

Affirmations are powerful statements that reinforce a sense of confidence and control. Using affirmations, children can create a mental shield that protects them from the Boogeyman's influence. By repeating these positive statements, they build a mental defense that grows stronger with time.

- **Examples of Affirmations**:
    ◦ "I am brave, and nothing can scare me."
    ◦ "The Boogeyman is not real, and I control my room."
    ◦ "I am strong, and fear has no power over me."

Affirmation shields work by shifting the child's mindset from fear to empowerment, making the Boogeyman's influence fade as their confidence grows.

4. The Boogeyman's Name: Reducing His Power by Saying His Name

There is an old belief that saying a monster's name aloud diminishes its power, and this is true for the Boogeyman. The Boogeyman thrives on mystery and silence. By naming him, children take away his mystique and strip him of the unknown, which is one of his strongest weapons.

- **How to Use This Technique**:
    ◦ Teach your child to say the Boogeyman's name out loud if they feel afraid. It could be "Boogeyman" or even a funny, harmless name like "Boo" or "Shadowface." The sillier the name, the better.

- Once the name is said, they can follow up with, "You have no power here, Boogeyman. I'm not afraid of you!"

This tactic reduces the Boogeyman's power by turning him into something less mysterious and more manageable.

5. Laughing at Fear: Humor as a Defense Mechanism

Humor is a powerful tool for disarming fear. Laughing at something scary diminishes its power and makes it seem silly or less threatening. Teaching children to laugh at the Boogeyman, or even at their own fears, turns the situation from frightening to fun.

- **How to Laugh at Fear**:
    - Encourage your child to imagine the Boogeyman slipping on a banana peel or wearing funny clothes. This mental image turns the Boogeyman into a joke rather than a threat.
    - Laughing out loud at the Boogeyman can also reduce his power. Have your child giggle and say, "You're not scary, Boogeyman. You're just silly!"

Laughter shifts the emotional energy from fear to joy, making the Boogeyman weaker with every chuckle.

6. Imagination Power: Turning Imagination Into a Strength

Imagination is often the source of fear, but it can also be the Boogeyman's greatest weakness. By teaching children to reclaim their imagination and use it for positive purposes, they can transform fear into creative strength.

- **How to Use Imagination Power**:
    - Have your child imagine themselves as a hero or protector in their own story. They can picture themselves wielding a magical sword, shield, or power that drives the Boogeyman away.
    - They can also imagine the Boogeyman shrinking into a tiny, harmless creature, too small to scare anyone.

This technique puts the child in control of their imagination, using it as a source of strength instead of fear.

7. Familiar Objects Defense: Using Comfort Items to Ward Off Fear

Comfort items, such as a favorite stuffed animal, blanket, or toy, can serve as emotional anchors that ward off fear. These objects are associated with safety and love, making them powerful tools against the Boogeyman.

- **How to Use Familiar Objects**:

- Encourage your child to hold their favorite stuffed animal or blanket when they feel afraid. Explain that this object is their protector, and as long as they hold it, the Boogeyman cannot come near.
- Create a ritual where the child places the comfort item near their bed before sleeping, reinforcing its protective power.

Familiar objects provide emotional security and remind children that they are not alone, even in the dark.

8. Rationalizing the Boogeyman: Breaking the Myth

While the Boogeyman may feel real, he is ultimately an exaggerated imaginary threat. Helping children understand that the Boogeyman is a product of their imagination can reduce his power and turn fear into logic.

- **How to Rationalize the Boogeyman**:
  - Explain that the Boogeyman is like a character in a scary story—he isn't real, and he only exists in the imagination.
  - Point out that there's no evidence of the Boogeyman actually being there, and remind your child that nothing has ever happened.

Rationalizing the Boogeyman helps children separate fantasy from reality, reducing the grip that fear has on their mind.

9. Reverse Psychology: Confusing the Boogeyman

Reverse psychology can be a fun way to outsmart the Boogeyman. By acting like they aren't afraid—or even inviting the Boogeyman in—children can confuse the Boogeyman and take away his power.

- **How to Use Reverse Psychology**:
  - Have your child say, "Come on, Boogeyman, I'm not scared of you!" This unexpected response throws the Boogeyman off balance and reduces his influence.
  - They can also pretend to welcome the Boogeyman, saying, "Oh, hi, Boogeyman! Let's hang out!" This turns fear into curiosity and surprises the Boogeyman.

By acting in a way the Boogeyman doesn't expect, children take back control of the situation.

10. Daylight Thinking: Training Your Brain to See the Boogeyman's Weakness

During the day, the Boogeyman has no power. By training their brain to think about the Boogeyman in daylight terms, children can weaken his nighttime influence.

- **How to Use Daylight Thinking**:
  - Encourage your child to think about how silly the Boogeyman seems during the day. Ask them to imagine what the Boogeyman would look like in the bright sunshine.

◦ Teach them to say, "The Boogeyman is weak during the day, and I can remember that at night."

Daylight thinking helps children see the Boogeyman as a temporary, nighttime fear that can be conquered.

11. Fear Confrontation Practice: Building Resistance Through Exposure

Gradually confronting small fears helps children build resistance to the larger fear of the Boogeyman. This practice involves exposing children to minor fears in a safe environment, helping them gain confidence in their ability to handle fear.

- **How to Practice Fear Confrontation**:
  ◦ Start with small steps, like turning off the light for a few seconds or checking under the bed with a flashlight.
  ◦ Gradually increase the exposure as your child becomes more comfortable, eventually working up to spending time in the dark without fear.

This technique helps children build resilience and teaches them that they can handle fear in manageable doses.

12. Compartmentalizing Fear: Locking Fear Away

Compartmentalizing fear is a mental technique that teaches children to "lock" their fear away in a mental box, reducing its influence over them.

- **How to Compartmentalize Fear**:
  ◦ Have your child imagine their fear as a small object, like a ball or box, and mentally place it in a locked container.
  ◦ Once the fear is locked away, they can say, "I control this fear, and it can't hurt me while it's locked up."

This technique gives children a way to manage their fear by controlling when and how they feel it.

13. Boogeyman Alter Ego: Imagining the Boogeyman as Something Harmless

By giving the Boogeyman an alter ego—something harmless or even cute—children can transform fear into amusement.

- **How to Use This Technique**:

- ◦ Encourage your child to imagine the Boogeyman as a small puppy, a fluffy bunny, or even a harmless clown.
- ◦ Whenever they feel afraid, they can remind themselves that the Boogeyman is now something friendly and silly.

This reimagining takes away the Boogeyman's fear factor and turns him into a harmless character.

14. The Mirror Technique: Bouncing the Boogeyman's Power Back

Mentally "mirroring" the Boogeyman's power back at him is a tactic that turns his fear into weakness. When children imagine reflecting his power, they become the ones in control.

- • **How to Use the Mirror Technique**:
    - ◦ Teach your child to imagine holding up an invisible mirror whenever they feel afraid. The mirror reflects the Boogeyman's fear back at him, making him weaker.
    - ◦ They can say, "I'm reflecting your fear, Boogeyman. It goes back to you!"

This mental shield bounces the Boogeyman's fear back, weakening his influence.

15. Mind Over Matter: Training the Mind to Reshape Reality

At the heart of all these psychological tactics is the belief that **mind over matter** is the ultimate defense. Children can be taught that their mind is more powerful than fear, and by controlling their thoughts, they can control their reality.

- • **How to Train the Mind**:
    - ◦ Teach your child that fear is just an emotion, and they can control it by focusing on positive thoughts, breathing deeply, and using their imagination to reshape the situation.
    - ◦ They can say, "My mind is stronger than fear. I control what happens in my world."

By embracing mind over matter, children learn that they are the masters of their reality, and the Boogeyman is just a passing shadow.

Conclusion: Outsmarting the Boogeyman with the Power of the Mind

The most effective way to defeat the Boogeyman is by outsmarting him using the power of the mind. Through visualization, affirmations, humor, and critical thinking, children can take control of their thoughts and emotions, rendering the Boogeyman powerless. With these psychological tactics in hand, every child can face the night with confidence, knowing that their mind is stronger than any imaginary creature lurking in the shadows.

Chapter 18: Physical Defenses – Strengthening Your Boogeyman Guard

While psychological tactics are highly effective in outsmarting the Boogeyman, there are also many physical defenses that can be used to protect against him. These defenses create a physical boundary between the child and the Boogeyman, reinforcing safety and security in the room. In this chapter, we shift from mental strategies to practical, hands-on methods that you can use to keep the Boogeyman at bay. From classic techniques like salt lines to creative solutions like squeaky toys and stuffed animal soldiers, here are 15 ways to fortify your defenses against the Boogeyman.

1. Boogey Dust: A Magical Powder for Protection

Boogey Dust is a special powder that can be sprinkled around the bed to keep the Boogeyman away. The idea comes from ancient traditions where magical powders were used to ward off evil spirits. Boogey Dust works by creating a protective barrier that the Boogeyman cannot cross, keeping the area around the bed safe and secure.

- **How to Make Boogey Dust**:
  - You can make Boogey Dust by mixing simple household items like baking soda, glitter, or colored sand. Add a pinch of imagination to make it extra powerful.
  - Keep the Boogey Dust in a small jar or container near the bed.
- **How to Use It**:

- Before bedtime, sprinkle the Boogey Dust around the bed, focusing on the floor near the bedposts and the edges of the bed.
- As you sprinkle, say a protective phrase like, "Boogey Dust protects me, and no Boogeyman can cross this line."

This ritual helps children feel like they are actively participating in their protection, making the Boogeyman less likely to approach.

2. Light Traps: Using Strategic Lighting to Repel the Boogeyman

The Boogeyman thrives in darkness, and **Light Traps** are one of the best ways to take advantage of his weakness. By strategically placing nightlights or other light sources around the room, you can create zones where the Boogeyman cannot hide.

- **How to Set Up Light Traps**:
    - Place nightlights in areas where shadows typically form, such as under the bed, in the closet, and near corners. The soft glow will disrupt the Boogeyman's hiding places.
    - You can also use glow-in-the-dark stickers or string lights to brighten dark areas.
- **Tips**:
    - Use a mix of soft and bright lights to create layers of protection.
    - For an extra touch, choose nightlights shaped like animals or superheroes that can act as "guardians" in the room.

Light Traps ensure that the Boogeyman has nowhere to lurk, keeping the room brightly illuminated and safe.

3. Under-the-Bed Barriers: Blocking Boogeyman Entry Points

Many children fear that the Boogeyman hides under the bed. One effective solution is to create **Under-the-Bed Barriers** using toys, boxes, or furniture that block the Boogeyman's access to this space.

- **How to Create Barriers**:
    - Use large stuffed animals, toy boxes, or plastic bins to fill the space under the bed. This physically blocks the Boogeyman from getting underneath.
    - Make sure the items are arranged tightly so that no shadows are left where the Boogeyman can hide.
- **Fun Idea**:
    - Have your child choose their favorite toys to act as "guardians" under the bed. Explain that these toys are there to stop the Boogeyman from sneaking in.

Creating Under-the-Bed Barriers eliminates one of the Boogeyman's favorite hiding spots, giving children peace of mind.

4. Salt Lines: A Classic Defense Against the Boogeyman

Salt Lines are an ancient and powerful defense against dark forces, used in folklore to create protective boundaries that no evil spirit can cross. The Boogeyman, being a creature of darkness, cannot pass over a line of salt.

- **How to Use Salt Lines**:
    - Take table salt or sea salt and sprinkle it in a line around the bed. Focus on entry points like the doorway, window, and especially around the base of the bed.
    - As you sprinkle the salt, have your child say, "This salt keeps the Boogeyman out, and he cannot cross."

Salt Lines are a simple but effective way to create a protective boundary that the Boogeyman cannot breach.

5. Mirror Shields: Using Reflection to Weaken the Boogeyman

Mirrors are powerful tools for weakening the Boogeyman because they reflect light and force him to confront his own image. **Mirror Shields** can be placed around the room to reflect the Boogeyman's image, making him lose strength.

- **How to Create Mirror Shields**:
    - Place small mirrors in key locations, such as near the bed or facing dark corners. Mirrors can also be placed in closets or along walls to reflect light and dispel shadows.
    - If your child feels afraid, they can use a handheld mirror to "catch" the Boogeyman's reflection and drive him away.
- **Ritual**:
    - Have your child say, "This mirror reflects you, Boogeyman. You can't hide from me."

Mirror Shields not only repel the Boogeyman but also empower children by giving them a tool they can control.

6. Stuffed Animal Soldiers: An Army of Protection

Stuffed animals provide comfort and can also act as guardians. By positioning them strategically around the bed, you can create a force of **Stuffed Animal Soldiers** that protect the child from the Boogeyman.

- **How to Set Up Your Army**:
    - Choose your child's favorite stuffed animals and position them on the bed, near the door, or along the edges of the bed.
    - Explain that these stuffed animals are standing guard, keeping watch all night to make sure the Boogeyman stays away.
- **Fun Variation**:
    - Give each stuffed animal a special name or "rank" in the army, making the ritual more personal and engaging for your child.

This playful defense not only repels the Boogeyman but also provides emotional comfort, giving children the feeling of being surrounded by protective friends.

7. Talisman Crafting: Making Protective Charms

A **Talisman** is a small object believed to hold protective power. By crafting simple talismans from household items, children can carry a piece of protection with them wherever they go.

- **How to Make a Talisman**:
    - Use beads, string, feathers, or small stones to create a charm necklace or bracelet. Let your child choose items that make them feel safe.
    - As you make the talisman, explain that it has special powers to keep the Boogeyman away.
- **How to Use It**:
    - Your child can wear the talisman at night or keep it under their pillow to protect them while they sleep.

Talisman Crafting turns ordinary items into symbols of protection, helping children feel secure.

8. Sleep Patrol: Guarding the Bed with Strategic Sleeping Positions

Sometimes, the way a child sleeps can affect how safe they feel. **Sleep Patrol** involves changing sleeping positions or placing items under the bed to block the Boogeyman's access.

- **How to Conduct Sleep Patrol**:
    - Encourage your child to sleep facing the door or with their stuffed animals lined up along the bed as a "patrol."
    - You can also place a stuffed animal or toy under the bed to act as a sentinel guarding the space.
- **Tips**:
    - Teach your child to think of their stuffed animals as their "night patrol," keeping watch over them as they sleep.

Sleep Patrol creates a mental and physical sense of security, giving children more control over their environment.

9. Noise Distractors: Using Sound to Disrupt the Boogeyman

The Boogeyman prefers silence, as it allows him to move unnoticed. By creating **Noise Distractors**, such as white noise or soothing music, you can disrupt his ability to lurk.

- **How to Set Up Noise Distractors**:
    - Use a white noise machine, a fan, or a playlist of calming music to create a constant background noise that keeps the Boogeyman at bay.
    - Place the noise source near the bed, ensuring that it fills the room with a soft, soothing sound.

Noise Distractors make the environment less appealing to the Boogeyman and help children relax.

10. Temperature Control: Keeping the Room Cool

The Boogeyman is more active in warm, stuffy environments. Keeping the room at a cooler temperature weakens his presence. **Temperature Control** can be used as a defense strategy.

- **How to Control the Temperature**:
    - Use a fan or air conditioner to keep the room cool, especially at night.
    - Make sure the bedding is light and breathable to prevent the room from becoming too warm.

Cooler environments are less appealing to the Boogeyman, making it harder for him to linger.

11. Boogeyman Traps: Homemade Booby Traps

Creating **Boogeyman Traps** is a fun and creative way to deter the Boogeyman. Simple objects like string, bells, or flashlights can be used to make traps that alert you to his presence.

- **How to Make Boogeyman Traps**:
    - Tie a string with small bells across the door or along the edge of the bed. If the Boogeyman tries to enter, the bells will ring, alerting your child.
    - Place a flashlight on the floor or near the bed. If your child senses movement, they can quickly turn it on to scare the Boogeyman away.

These traps give children the feeling that they are actively protecting themselves from the Boogeyman.

12. Bed Guard Routines: Cleaning Under the Bed

A **Bed Guard Routine** ensures that the Boogeyman doesn't settle under the bed. By regularly cleaning and checking under the bed, you can remove any places where the Boogeyman might try to hide.

- **How to Perform Bed Guard Duty**:

- Make it a habit to clean under the bed once a week, removing any clutter or dust that could create shadows.
- Have your child help with the routine, turning it into a fun "inspection" where they check for Boogeyman activity.

A clean, clear space under the bed leaves no room for the Boogeyman to settle.

13. DIY Safe Zones: Creating Protective Spaces with Pillows

Safe Zones are areas in the room that the Boogeyman cannot enter. You can create these zones using pillows or blankets, giving children a space where they feel completely safe.

- **How to Create Safe Zones**:
    - Build a fortress of pillows or blankets around the bed, creating a soft, protective wall that the Boogeyman can't cross.
    - Let your child help arrange the pillows, turning it into a fun and empowering activity.

Safe Zones provide a physical and psychological barrier, making children feel protected.

14. Under the Bed Patrol: Using Long-Handled Objects to Check the Space

Under the Bed Patrol is a simple routine that involves checking under the bed with a long-handled object, such as a broomstick, to ensure the Boogeyman isn't hiding there.

- **How to Conduct Patrol**:
    - Use a broomstick or similar object to poke under the bed, moving it around to "clear" the space.
    - Have your child participate by holding a flashlight while you check, making it a team effort.

This routine helps reinforce the idea that the space is being actively guarded, reducing fear.

15. Squeaky Defense: Using Squeaky Toys to Detect Movement

Squeaky Toys can be placed around the room to detect the Boogeyman's movement. If he tries to sneak around, the squeaky toy will make noise, alerting your child.

- **How to Set Up the Squeaky Defense**:
    - Place squeaky toys near doors, windows, or the bed. If the Boogeyman moves, the toy will squeak, scaring him away.
    - Encourage your child to press the toy before bed, making sure it's "armed" and ready.

The Squeaky Defense is both fun and effective, giving children another tool to protect their space.

Conclusion: Fortifying Your Boogeyman Guard with Physical Defenses

Physical defenses are a crucial part of Boogie Busting, providing children with tangible ways to keep the Boogeyman at bay. From Light Traps to Salt Lines, these strategies help children feel in control of their environment, transforming fear into action. With these 15 techniques, your child can sleep soundly, knowing they are fully protected from the Boogeyman's tricks.

Chapter 19: Boogey Magic – Mystical Tactics to Fight Back

For centuries, humans have used magic, folklore, and the power of belief to protect themselves from dark forces, and the Boogeyman is no exception. **Boogey Magic** taps into ancient traditions, childlike wonder, and the imagination to create a powerful set of mystical tactics that can fend off the Boogeyman. From casting spells to enchanting objects, these magical methods empower children to take control of their environment, turning fear into strength through rituals, symbols, and charms. This chapter introduces 15 magical ways to fight back against the Boogeyman and reclaim peace and safety during the night.

1. The "Light of Imagination" Spell – Summoning Unbearable Light

The **Light of Imagination** spell is a simple but potent piece of magic that summons a brilliant, magical light no Boogeyman can withstand. This spell can be used at any moment when darkness feels too overwhelming or when the Boogeyman is near.

- **How to Cast the Spell**:

- Have your child close their eyes and visualize a glowing orb of light forming above their head. This light is powered by their imagination and glows brighter with every positive thought.
- As they visualize the light, have them chant, "Light of imagination, shine so bright, drive away the Boogeyman tonight!"
- Encourage them to imagine this light spreading throughout the room, banishing all shadows and leaving no space for the Boogeyman to hide.

This spell is quick to cast and works instantly, giving children control over the darkness by transforming their imagination into a beacon of protection.

2. Moonlight Blessings – Harnessing the Power of the Moon

In many ancient cultures, the moon was believed to have protective powers. **Moonlight Blessings** call upon the power of the moon to guard against the Boogeyman, especially during nights when the moon is visible from a window.

- **How to Perform Moonlight Blessings**:
  - On a night with a full or bright moon, have your child stand by the window, letting the moonlight touch their skin.
  - Encourage them to say, "Moon so bright, grant me your light, protect my dreams and guard the night."
  - If possible, position the bed near a window where the moonlight can shine in, creating a natural barrier against the Boogeyman.

Moonlight is a calming and protective force, perfect for those who find comfort in the night sky.

3. Boogeyman Binding Ritual – Immobilizing the Boogeyman

The **Boogeyman Binding Ritual** is a safe, easy-to-do spell that binds the Boogeyman's movements, preventing him from approaching the bed or moving freely around the room.

- **How to Perform the Ritual**:
  - Gather a piece of string or ribbon (preferably white or gold) to represent the binding force.
  - Tie the string in a circle around the bedposts or near the edges of the room while saying, "Boogeyman, I bind you tight, you cannot move, you cannot fight."
  - The string symbolizes a magical barrier that prevents the Boogeyman from entering the child's space.

This binding ritual is particularly useful when performed regularly, reinforcing the protective boundary.

4. Protection Symbols – Drawing Mystical Symbols for Safety

Symbols have long been used in magic for protection. Drawing **Protection Symbols** on paper or objects and placing them under the bed or around the room creates a mystical barrier that the Boogeyman cannot cross.

- **How to Draw Protection Symbols**:
    - Help your child draw simple protective symbols like stars, circles, or ancient symbols like the pentacle, which represents protection.
    - After drawing the symbols, place the paper under the bed or tape it to the back of the door.
    - Have your child say, "These symbols protect me from all harm. No Boogeyman can enter while they guard."

Protection symbols are both a creative activity and a magical shield, strengthening the room's defenses.

5. Dreamcatchers – Enchanting to Trap the Boogeyman

Dreamcatchers are traditionally used to filter out bad dreams, but they can also be enchanted to trap the Boogeyman before he enters a child's dreams.

- **How to Enchant a Dreamcatcher**:
    - Hang a dreamcatcher above the bed, near the window, or wherever the child feels most vulnerable.
    - Have the child chant, "Dreamcatcher bright, trap Boogeyman's fright, keep him away from my dreams tonight."
    - Let the child touch the dreamcatcher and visualize it glowing with protective energy.

Dreamcatchers not only guard dreams but also add a layer of enchantment to the child's room, keeping it safe from the Boogeyman's influence.

6. Boogeyman Repelling Crystals – Using Crystals to Block Negative Energy

Certain crystals, such as **amethyst** or **obsidian**, are known for their protective properties and ability to repel negative energy. Placing these crystals around the room can block the Boogeyman's presence.

- **How to Use Crystals**:
    - Place amethyst, obsidian, or black tourmaline stones near the bed, on the windowsill, or in the corners of the room.
    - Teach your child to hold the crystal and say, "Crystal bright, protect me from the Boogeyman tonight."

Crystals act as natural energy shields, absorbing negative forces and creating a calm, protective space.

7. Shadow Warding – Controlling Shadows to Block the Boogeyman

Shadows are the Boogeyman's favorite hiding place, but with the **Shadow Warding** method, children can manipulate and control shadows to prevent the Boogeyman from moving freely.

- **How to Perform Shadow Warding**:
  - Have your child stand in a room with dim lighting. Point out the shadows in the room, helping them understand that shadows are harmless when controlled.
  - Have them say, "I command the shadows, I am in charge. No Boogeyman can move without my permission."
  - Visualize the shadows shrinking, confining the Boogeyman so he cannot roam freely.

Shadow Warding teaches children to take control of their fear of the dark, turning shadows from something scary into something manageable.

8. Fairy Dust Defense – Finding or Making Fairy Dust

Fairy Dust is a magical substance believed to protect children from harm. By sprinkling fairy dust around the room, children can create an invisible shield that prevents the Boogeyman from entering.

- **How to Make Fairy Dust**:
  - Mix glitter with a pinch of sand or salt, placing it in a small jar or bag.
  - Encourage your child to sprinkle the fairy dust around the bed or windows while chanting, "Fairy dust strong, Boogeyman wrong, you cannot come where I belong."

Fairy Dust Defense is a fun, imaginative way to create a protective barrier, turning bedtime into a magical ritual.

9. Boogeyman Sigils – Creating Symbols to Seal the Boogeyman's Dimension

Sigils are symbols created with intention and power, used to seal the Boogeyman in his own dimension and prevent him from entering the child's world.

- **How to Create a Sigil**:
  - Help your child draw a unique symbol on a piece of paper, combining simple shapes or letters that represent protection.
  - Charge the sigil by holding it in your hands and visualizing it glowing with power.
  - Place the sigil under the bed, on the door, or near the windows to seal the Boogeyman's entry.

Sigils are powerful magical tools, empowering children to protect themselves by creating their own protective seals.

10. Sacred Candle Rituals – Creating a Protective Aura with Candlelight

Sacred Candle Rituals use the calming and protective power of candlelight to create a safe space that the Boogeyman cannot enter.

- **How to Perform a Candle Ritual**:
    - Light a small candle (with adult supervision) and place it near the bed or in the room before bedtime.
    - Have your child say, "By this flame, I am safe and sound. Boogeyman, you're not allowed around."

The warmth and light from the candle create a comforting aura of protection, perfect for calming the child before sleep.

11. Astral Projection Training – Attacking the Boogeyman in His Own Realm

For children who love imaginative exploration, **Astral Projection Training** offers a way to "visit" the Boogeyman's dimension in their dreams and surprise him by attacking first.

- **How to Train for Astral Projection**:
    - Before bed, have your child close their eyes and imagine themselves flying or traveling to the Boogeyman's world.
    - Teach them to say, "I'm coming for you, Boogeyman. You can't hide from me."

Astral Projection is a fun way to give children control over their imagination, turning them from the pursued into the pursuer.

12. Spells of Forgetting – Making the Boogeyman Forget About You

A **Spell of Forgetting** is a charm designed to make the Boogeyman forget about the child altogether, ensuring he never visits again.

- **How to Cast a Spell of Forgetting**:
    - Write the Boogeyman's name on a small piece of paper, then fold it up.
    - Have your child say, "Forget me, Boogeyman. You don't know my name, and you'll never come here again."
    - Burn the paper (with adult supervision) or bury it outside to seal the spell.

This charm creates a psychological barrier, making the Boogeyman forget that the child even exists.

13. Nighttime Guardians – Summoning Protectors for the Night

Nighttime Guardians are protective spirits or entities that can be summoned to watch over the child as they sleep, ensuring no harm comes their way.

- **How to Summon Guardians**:
  - ◦ Have your child imagine their favorite protector—this could be a mythical creature, an angel, or even a superhero.
  - ◦ Teach them to say, "Guardians of the night, protect me with your light, keep the Boogeyman out of sight."

These guardians serve as comforting figures that make the child feel protected and watched over during the night.

14. Herbal Warding – Using Herbs to Repel the Boogeyman

Herbal Warding uses protective herbs like **lavender**, **sage**, or **rosemary** to keep the Boogeyman away from the child's space.

- **How to Use Herbal Warding**:
  - ◦ Place dried lavender or sage in small pouches under the pillow or around the room.
  - ◦ Burn a small amount of sage (with adult supervision) to cleanse the space while saying, "Herbs so pure, Boogeyman, you're not welcome here."

Herbs have been used for centuries to ward off negative energy, making them perfect for repelling the Boogeyman.

15. The "Boogeyman's Curse" – A Last-Resort Spell

If all else fails, the **Boogeyman's Curse** is a powerful, last-resort spell that curses the Boogeyman, forcing him to retreat for good.

- **How to Cast the Curse**:
  - ◦ Write down the Boogeyman's name and draw an "X" over it.
  - ◦ Have your child chant, "Boogeyman, be gone from here. I curse you now, you disappear!"
  - ◦ Bury the paper or burn it to seal the curse.

The Boogeyman's Curse is a final, powerful spell that banishes the Boogeyman once and for all.

Conclusion: Harnessing the Power of Boogey Magic

With these mystical tactics, children can wield the power of magic to fend off the Boogeyman and protect their dreams. From casting spells of light to summoning protective guardians, **Boogey Magic** transforms fear into empowerment, giving children control over their nighttime world. With these 15 methods, they can create a magical fortress of protection, ensuring that the Boogeyman stays far, far away.

Chapter 20: Using Light as a Weapon

The Boogeyman, like many creatures of fear, thrives in darkness. He hides in shadows and moves undetected in the absence of light. This chapter explores how light can be transformed into a powerful weapon against the Boogeyman, keeping him at bay and protecting the child's space. By using various types of light—from sunlight to modern LED technology—children and parents can create a well-defended zone where the Boogeyman cannot hide. Each section delves into creative and practical ways to harness the power of light, turning it into a protective force.

1. Sunlight in a Jar – Trapping Daylight to Use at Night

One of the most imaginative defenses against the Boogeyman is the **Sunlight in a Jar** technique. The idea is simple: collect sunlight during the day and use it at night when the Boogeyman is most active. This tactic draws on the magical properties of sunlight, which can repel darkness and prevent the Boogeyman from approaching.

- **How to Trap Sunlight**:
  - Get a clear jar with a lid and take it outside during the day. Have your child hold the jar up to the sky, imagining it collecting the sun's rays.
  - As they hold the jar, have them say, "Sunlight bright, stay with me tonight. Keep the Boogeyman out of sight."
  - Once the jar is "full," bring it inside and place it by the bed. The jar will act as a magical protector, keeping the Boogeyman away.

While the sunlight in a jar is symbolic, the belief that it holds protective power can give your child a deep sense of security during the night.

2. LED Flashlight Defense – Using Modern Technology to Create a Barrier

LED Flashlights are powerful tools that can be used to shine bright, concentrated beams of light into dark corners and drive the Boogeyman away. Their long battery life and intense brightness make them ideal for creating a strong defense.

- **How to Use LED Flashlights**:
  - Keep a small LED flashlight by the bed or under the pillow. If your child feels scared or senses the Boogeyman nearby, they can quickly turn it on and point it toward the dark areas of the room.
  - Encourage your child to say, "This light makes you run, Boogeyman. You can't stay here!" as they shine the flashlight into shadowy spaces.
  - For extra protection, you can place multiple LED flashlights around the room, creating a perimeter of light.

The LED Flashlight Defense is a practical and easy-to-use method, giving children immediate access to a powerful light source whenever they need it.

3. Glow-in-the-Dark Stickers – Creating a Starry Defense

Glow-in-the-Dark Stickers are a fun and effective way to turn ordinary bedroom walls and ceilings into protective barriers. By strategically placing glow-in-the-dark stars, moons, and other shapes around the room, you can create a soothing, magical glow that keeps the Boogeyman away.

- **How to Set Up Glow-in-the-Dark Stickers**:
  - Place glow-in-the-dark stickers on the ceiling, walls, and even furniture. Focus on areas that might feel darker at night, like near the closet or under the bed.
  - You can explain to your child that each glowing star or shape is a tiny guardian, keeping watch over them while they sleep.
  - Before bed, have your child say, "The stars are shining bright, and the Boogeyman can't come near tonight."

These stickers offer a comforting glow that lasts throughout the night, providing a gentle but effective light defense.

4. The Power of the Nightlight – Choosing the Right One to Repel Boogeymen

Nightlights are essential in keeping the room softly lit and the Boogeyman at bay. Choosing the right **Nightlight** can make all the difference in creating a safe, peaceful environment for your child.

- **How to Choose the Right Nightlight**:
  - Look for a nightlight that emits a soft but steady glow, preferably in colors like blue or white, which are calming and known to dispel fear.
  - Nightlights with motion sensors or dimming features are also great, as they can adjust to the child's needs throughout the night.
  - Place the nightlight near areas that tend to have shadows, such as the closet, corners, or under the bed.

The right nightlight provides constant reassurance, gently lighting the room and preventing the Boogeyman from hiding in the darkness.

5. Laser Pointer Tactics – Trapping and Disorienting the Boogeyman

A **Laser Pointer** can be an unexpected but highly effective weapon against the Boogeyman. By flashing the laser into dark areas or directly toward imagined Boogeyman movements, you can disorient him and trap him in the beam of light.

- **How to Use a Laser Pointer**:
  - Keep a small laser pointer near the bed. If your child hears or senses the Boogeyman, they can point the laser into shadowy areas and "trap" him in the red or green light.
  - Teach your child to say, "Boogeyman, you're caught in my laser! You can't move!" This creates the feeling that the Boogeyman is immobilized.

Laser Pointer Tactics are fun and interactive, giving children a direct way to fight back and feel in control of their space.

6. Light Reflection Methods – Amplifying Light with Mirrors

Light Reflection involves using mirrors and other reflective surfaces to bounce and amplify light around the room. This technique can create a more powerful light defense by covering more areas that might otherwise be in shadow.

- **How to Use Mirrors to Amplify Light**:
  - Place mirrors in strategic locations around the room, such as opposite windows or near nightlights. The mirrors will reflect light into darker areas, keeping the entire room illuminated.
  - If your child feels scared, they can use a handheld mirror to "catch" light from a flashlight or nightlight and shine it into the Boogeyman's hiding spots.

Light Reflection Methods are a clever way to ensure that even the darkest corners of the room are covered in protective light.

7. Strobe Light Defense – Disorienting the Boogeyman with Flashing Lights

Strobe Lights can be used to disorient and confuse the Boogeyman, making it harder for him to move or hide in the room. While strobe lights are typically associated with parties or events, they can be repurposed as a powerful tool against nighttime fears.

- **How to Use Strobe Lights**:
  - Keep a small, battery-powered strobe light near the bed. If your child feels like the Boogeyman is approaching, they can activate the strobe light, filling the room with flashing lights.
  - Teach your child to say, "These lights confuse you, Boogeyman! You can't come any closer."

The rapid flashing of the strobe light creates a chaotic environment for the Boogeyman, preventing him from advancing toward the child.

8. The UV Light Strategy – Weakening the Boogeyman with Ultraviolet Light

Ultraviolet (UV) Light has a unique effect on the Boogeyman's form, causing him to weaken and become less substantial. UV light can be used to expose and repel him, especially in areas where he might be hiding.

- **How to Use UV Light**:
  - Purchase a small UV light or blacklight and shine it into the corners of the room, under the bed, or in the closet. The UV light will reveal anything hiding in the shadows and make the Boogeyman's form fade.
  - Have your child say, "You can't hide from the UV light, Boogeyman. You're getting weaker!"

The UV Light Strategy offers a high-tech way to expose the Boogeyman's presence and drive him away.

9. Lantern Circles – Creating a Protective Barrier of Lanterns

A **Lantern Circle** is a circle of lights placed around the bed or room to create a strong, protective barrier that the Boogeyman cannot cross.

- **How to Create a Lantern Circle**:
  - Place battery-powered lanterns, candles (real or LED), or lamps in a circle around the bed or along the floor. This creates a literal circle of light that surrounds and protects the child.
  - Teach your child to say, "This circle of light keeps me safe and strong. No Boogeyman can cross."

Lantern Circles are a visual and symbolic form of defense, giving children a clear boundary of safety that the Boogeyman cannot enter.

10. Candlelight Spells – Confusing the Boogeyman with Flickering Flames

The flickering flame of a **Candlelight Spell** can confuse and scare the Boogeyman, making it difficult for him to focus or approach the bed. Candlelight, whether real or LED, offers a calming and magical atmosphere that doubles as a defense.

- **How to Use Candlelight Spells**:
    - Light a small candle (with adult supervision) and place it near the bed or on a windowsill. The flickering light will create a dance of shadows that keeps the Boogeyman disoriented.
    - Teach your child to say, "Candle's flame, flicker bright, keep the Boogeyman out of sight."

Candlelight Spells work by creating movement in the shadows, making it harder for the Boogeyman to find a place to hide.

11. Laser Light Circles – Creating a Barrier of Laser Beams

Laser Light Circles are an advanced defense that involves creating a "web" of laser beams around the bed, making it impossible for the Boogeyman to get through.

- **How to Set Up Laser Light Circles**:
    - Use several laser pointers or laser light projectors to create beams of light that cross around the bed. Place them in corners or on the floor to ensure full coverage.
    - Have your child say, "This laser circle stops you, Boogeyman. You can't cross these beams of light."

Laser Light Circles are a futuristic and effective way to create a physical barrier that the Boogeyman cannot penetrate.

12. Firefly Lanterns – Using Nature to Ward Off the Boogeyman

Firefly Lanterns use the natural light of fireflies or mimic their glow to create a soft, protective barrier of light.

- **How to Create Firefly Lanterns**:
    - If possible, collect fireflies in a jar and place them by the window or bed. Their natural glow will create a calming and protective light.
    - Alternatively, use LED lights or glowsticks to mimic the effect of fireflies, creating a similar gentle glow.

Firefly Lanterns offer a natural, magical light that keeps the Boogeyman away while adding a soothing atmosphere to the room.

13. Glowstick Barricades – Blocking Entry Points with Glowsticks

Glowstick Barricades can be set up around doorways, windows, or the bed to block the Boogeyman's entry points.

- **How to Set Up Glowstick Barricades**:
  - Activate several glowsticks and place them along the floor near doors, windows, and the edges of the bed.
  - Have your child say, "These glowsticks form a barrier you can't cross, Boogeyman!"

Glowstick Barricades are easy to set up and create a vibrant, glowing defense that clearly marks safe zones in the room.

14. Solar-Powered Lamps – Harnessing the Sun to Keep the Boogeyman Away

Solar-Powered Lamps store sunlight during the day and use it to keep the room lit at night, creating a constant source of light that repels the Boogeyman.

- **How to Use Solar-Powered Lamps**:
  - Place solar-powered lamps on windowsills during the day to charge. At night, bring them into the room and use them to create a steady light source.
  - Encourage your child to say, "This light is powered by the sun, and it keeps the Boogeyman on the run."

Solar-Powered Lamps are an eco-friendly way to keep the room illuminated, ensuring that no shadows remain for the Boogeyman to hide in.

15. Creating a Beacon – Building a Large, Magical Light Beacon for Protection

If the Boogeyman ever becomes too strong, building a **Beacon of Light** can summon help and protection, creating a powerful defense that reaches far beyond the bedroom.

- **How to Build a Light Beacon**:
  - Create a large lantern or lamp and place it in the center of the room. Surround it with smaller lights or candles to amplify its power.
  - Have your child say, "This beacon shines bright, summoning help to keep me safe all night."

The Beacon of Light acts as a powerful magical force, calling on protective energies to keep the Boogeyman away for good.

Conclusion: Light as the Ultimate Weapon Against the Boogeyman

Light, in all its forms, is the Boogeyman's greatest weakness. By using the strategies in this chapter—whether it's trapping sunlight in a jar, setting up glowstick barricades, or creating a powerful beacon—children can harness the power of light to protect themselves. Each method not only banishes darkness but also gives children a tangible way to take control of their fears and create a safe, secure environment where the Boogeyman cannot survive.

Chapter 21: The Power of Sound – Sonic Boogeyman Busting

Boogeymen thrive in silence, using the quiet of night to sneak, hide, and create fear. But sound can be their greatest weakness. By introducing noise—whether it's a loud whistle, rhythmic clapping, or the calming resonance of a Tibetan singing bowl—children can disrupt the Boogeyman's ability to move and create a safe, noisy environment. In this chapter, we explore how sound-based methods can be used as powerful tools to repel and confuse the Boogeyman, creating a sound defense that keeps nighttime fears at bay.

1. Whistle Alarm – Instant Boogeyman Defense with a Loud Whistle

A **Whistle Alarm** is a quick and effective defense against the Boogeyman. The sudden, sharp sound of a whistle can startle and disorient the Boogeyman, causing him to flee from the room.

- **How to Use a Whistle Alarm**:
    - Keep a whistle within easy reach, such as on the bedside table or attached to a necklace for your child.

- If your child senses the Boogeyman nearby, they can blow the whistle as hard as they can, producing a loud, piercing sound that will drive the Boogeyman away.
- Have your child say, "This whistle sends you away, Boogeyman. You can't stay here!"

The Whistle Alarm creates an immediate sound barrier that disrupts the Boogeyman's silence, making it harder for him to hide or move around the room.

2. Clapping Defense – Repelling the Boogeyman with Rhythm

Clapping Defense uses a rhythmic sequence of claps to create confusion and drive the Boogeyman out of the room. The repetitive, echoing sound of clapping interrupts the Boogeyman's sense of stealth, making him vulnerable.

- **How to Perform the Clapping Defense**:
    - Teach your child a simple clapping sequence, such as "clap-clap-pause-clap." This rhythm creates a pattern that echoes around the room.
    - When your child feels the Boogeyman's presence, they can start the clapping sequence, making the sound bounce off the walls and disrupt the Boogeyman's movements.
    - As they clap, encourage them to say, "This rhythm keeps you out, Boogeyman. You can't handle the sound."

The Clapping Defense is not only effective but also a fun, interactive way for children to actively repel the Boogeyman.

3. Tibetan Singing Bowls – Disrupting the Boogeyman with Sound Vibrations

Tibetan Singing Bowls produce sound vibrations that can disrupt a Boogeyman's form, making it difficult for him to maintain his presence in the room. The calming, resonant tones also create a peaceful atmosphere that reduces fear.

- **How to Use Tibetan Singing Bowls**:
    - Place a singing bowl near the bed. When your child feels scared, they can gently strike or rub the bowl's edge to create a long, resonating sound.
    - Teach your child to say, "This sound breaks your form, Boogeyman. You can't stay here."
    - Let the bowl's vibrations fill the room, creating a protective wave of sound that makes it harder for the Boogeyman to remain.

Tibetan Singing Bowls not only repel the Boogeyman but also help calm and soothe children before sleep.

4. Musical Instruments – Using Drums and Flutes to Drive the Boogeyman Away

Musical instruments, such as **drums** or **flutes**, can be powerful tools to disrupt the Boogeyman's presence. The loud, continuous sound created by these instruments keeps the Boogeyman from moving freely.

- **How to Use Musical Instruments**:
    - If your child plays an instrument, encourage them to keep it near the bed. When they feel frightened, they can play a few notes or beats to send the Boogeyman away.
    - Drums work well for creating a strong, grounding sound, while flutes can produce high-pitched notes that confuse and repel the Boogeyman.
    - Encourage your child to say, "This music drives you away, Boogeyman. You can't stand this sound!"

Musical instruments turn a child's talent into a defense mechanism, making them feel powerful and in control of their space.

5. Sound Barriers – Using White Noise or Ambient Sound to Block the Boogeyman

Sound Barriers are created by filling the room with constant, ambient noise, such as white noise, nature sounds, or soft music. These sounds prevent the Boogeyman from moving undetected and block his ability to lurk in silence.

- **How to Set Up a Sound Barrier**:
    - Use a white noise machine, a fan, or a nature sound playlist to create a constant stream of sound throughout the night.
    - Position the sound source near the bed or in a corner of the room where the Boogeyman might hide.
    - Teach your child to say, "This sound protects me, Boogeyman. You can't sneak through it."

Sound Barriers are a simple but effective way to create a peaceful atmosphere that keeps the Boogeyman at bay while helping children fall asleep.

6. Sound Waves of Imagination – Using Imaginary Sounds to Disrupt the Boogeyman

Children have powerful imaginations, and **Sound Waves of Imagination** tap into this strength to create "imaginary sounds" that disrupt the Boogeyman's senses. This method requires no physical noise but relies on the child's ability to visualize and "hear" sounds that can scare the Boogeyman away.

- **How to Use Sound Waves of Imagination**:
  - Encourage your child to close their eyes and imagine a loud, disruptive sound, such as a lion's roar or a blaring siren, filling the room.
  - Have them say, "I'm creating a sound you can't stand, Boogeyman. You have to leave!"
  - As they imagine the sound getting louder, they can visualize the Boogeyman retreating.

This method allows children to use their imagination as a tool for defense, turning fear into creative power.

7. Sound Traps – Simple Noise Triggers to Detect the Boogeyman

Sound Traps are easy-to-make devices that release sound when activated, alerting children to the Boogeyman's movements and scaring him away. These traps can be as simple as wind chimes or bells placed near entry points.

- **How to Set Up Sound Traps**:
  - Hang wind chimes near the window or attach small bells to the door handle. If the Boogeyman tries to enter, the sound will alert your child to his presence.
  - You can also place marbles or pebbles in a cup near the bed. If the Boogeyman knocks it over, the noise will act as an alarm.
  - Teach your child to say, "If you try to move, Boogeyman, my trap will catch you!"

Sound Traps add an extra layer of security, giving children confidence that they'll hear the Boogeyman before he gets close.

8. Sonic Boogeyman Detectors – Using Sound Alarms to Detect Movement

A more advanced sound-based defense involves using **Sonic Boogeyman Detectors**—small devices that produce a noise when they detect movement. These alarms can be placed under the bed or near the closet to detect any lurking Boogeyman.

- **How to Set Up Sonic Detectors**:
  - Place motion-sensitive sound alarms under the bed or in areas where the Boogeyman might hide.
  - If the Boogeyman moves, the detector will emit a sound, alerting your child and scaring the Boogeyman away.
  - Encourage your child to say, "This detector knows where you are, Boogeyman. You can't hide!"

Sonic Boogeyman Detectors give children the reassurance that they will be alerted to any movement, making them feel safe throughout the night.

9. Musical Playlists – Targeting Boogeyman Vulnerabilities with Music

Certain types of music can target the Boogeyman's weaknesses, especially songs that are joyful, loud, or calming. Creating a **Musical Playlist** can keep the Boogeyman away by surrounding the room with positive energy and sound.

- **How to Create a Musical Playlist**:
  - Work with your child to create a playlist of their favorite songs, especially upbeat, cheerful, or calming tunes.
  - Play the playlist softly in the background during the night to keep the room filled with sound.
  - Teach your child to say, "This music is too strong for you, Boogeyman. You can't stay here."

Music has the power to shift the emotional energy of a room, turning fear into comfort and joy while repelling the Boogeyman.

10. Frequency Defense – Using Specific Sound Frequencies to Neutralize the Boogeyman

Certain **sound frequencies** can disrupt the Boogeyman's energy, neutralizing his presence. High-frequency tones, in particular, are known to disorient and repel him.

- **How to Use Frequency Defense:**
    - Use a sound generator or an app that produces high-pitched frequencies, and play it in the room for a few minutes before bed.
    - Focus the sound near areas where the Boogeyman might be hiding, such as the closet or under the bed.
    - Have your child say, "This frequency drives you out, Boogeyman. You can't handle this sound."

Frequency Defense is a modern, scientific method that harnesses the power of sound waves to block the Boogeyman from entering the room.

11. Tuning Fork Defense – Disorienting the Boogeyman with Resonating Sounds

Tuning Forks produce a pure, resonant tone that can disorient and repel the Boogeyman. The vibration of a tuning fork disrupts the Boogeyman's energy, making it harder for him to stay in the room.

- **How to Use Tuning Forks:**
    - Strike the tuning fork to produce a clear tone and move it around the room, focusing on dark corners or hiding spots.
    - Teach your child to say, "This sound confuses you, Boogeyman. You can't stay here."
    - The resonating vibration will fill the space, making the room less hospitable for the Boogeyman.

Tuning Fork Defense is a unique and effective way to harness the power of sound vibrations to repel the Boogeyman.

12. Echo Chamber Strategy – Confusing the Boogeyman with Echoes

Rooms with natural echoes can be used to confuse the Boogeyman. The **Echo Chamber Strategy** involves using the natural acoustics of the room to bounce sound around, making it difficult for the Boogeyman to locate himself.

- **How to Use the Echo Chamber Strategy**:
  - Teach your child to shout or clap loudly, creating echoes in the room.
  - As the sound bounces around, encourage your child to say, "These echoes confuse you, Boogeyman. You don't know where to go."
  - The shifting sound will make it hard for the Boogeyman to move or hide.

The Echo Chamber Strategy uses the room's own acoustics to disorient the Boogeyman, creating a shifting, confusing environment that he cannot navigate.

13. Sonic Boom – Combining Clapping and Shouting for a Powerful Burst

A **Sonic Boom** combines loud clapping and shouting to create a powerful burst of sound that drives the Boogeyman away instantly.

- **How to Perform a Sonic Boom**:
  - Have your child clap their hands loudly while shouting a phrase like, "Go away, Boogeyman! You're not welcome here!"
  - The combined sound creates a sudden, overwhelming burst that scares the Boogeyman away.

Sonic Boom is an energetic and empowering method that allows children to confront their fear head-on with a loud, confident defense.

14. Audio Projection – Projecting Powerful Noises to Scare the Boogeyman

Audio Projection involves imagining or playing powerful sounds, such as animal roars or sirens, to scare off the Boogeyman. The noise projects strength and fearlessness, causing the Boogeyman to retreat.

- **How to Use Audio Projection**:
  - Use a speaker or phone to play loud, intimidating sounds like a lion's roar or a loud siren.
  - Teach your child to say, "This sound is stronger than you, Boogeyman. You have to go away!"
  - The powerful noise will project authority, making the Boogeyman feel unwelcome.

Audio Projection is a dramatic, confidence-boosting method that gives children a direct way to push the Boogeyman out of their space.

15. Silent Sounds – Using Vibrations to Detect Boogeymen Without Noise

For children who prefer silence but still want protection, **Silent Sounds**—such as vibrations from silent alarms or vibrating toys—can detect Boogeyman movement without making noise.

- **How to Use Silent Sounds**:
  - Place a vibration-sensitive device under the bed or near the closet. If the Boogeyman moves, the vibration will be felt but not heard, alerting your child to his presence.
  - Teach your child to say, "Even without noise, I can detect you, Boogeyman. You can't sneak by."

Silent Sounds offer a discreet method of Boogeyman detection, perfect for children who prefer a quieter environment but still want to feel secure.

Conclusion: Sonic Boogeyman Busting with the Power of Sound

Sound is an incredibly powerful weapon against the Boogeyman. By introducing noise—whether it's through clapping, musical instruments, or sound traps—children can disrupt the Boogeyman's movements and take control of their environment. Each of the methods in this chapter provides a unique way to repel and confuse the Boogeyman using the power of sound, giving children confidence and peace of mind during the night.

Chapter 22: Collaborative Defense Strategies – Strength in Numbers

Fighting the Boogeyman alone can be a daunting task, but working as a team can make all the difference. **Collaborative Defense Strategies** focus on how to join forces with friends, family, and even imaginary companions to increase the chances of defeating the Boogeyman. By combining multiple minds, imaginations, and skills, you can create a coordinated and powerful defense. This chapter covers a range of team-based methods to repel the Boogeyman and reclaim the night.

1. Partner Patrols – Pairing Up for Stronger Defense

Partner Patrols involve teaming up with a sibling or friend to create a more effective defense against the Boogeyman. By working in pairs, you can cover more ground and keep a closer watch on potential Boogeyman hiding spots.

- **How to Run Partner Patrols:**
  - Assign each partner a specific area of the room to patrol, such as the closet or under the bed. One partner can guard the bed, while the other patrols the shadows.
  - Check in with each other throughout the night, ensuring all areas are safe.
  - Encourage each partner to say, "We're stronger together. Boogeyman, you don't stand a chance!"

Partner Patrols create a sense of teamwork and shared responsibility, making the Boogeyman less likely to approach a well-guarded room.

2. Parent Reinforcements – Involving Adults in the Defense

Sometimes, calling in **Parent Reinforcements** or an older sibling can bolster your defense. With their experience and authority, parents can add an extra layer of protection to the team.

- **How to Involve Parent Reinforcements:**
  - Ask a parent or older sibling to participate in setting up traps, checking dark corners, or standing guard while you fall asleep.
  - Have them help with protective rituals, such as placing nightlights, drawing protection symbols, or using Boogeyman-repelling sprays.
  - Encourage them to say, "I'm here to protect you, and the Boogeyman won't get past me."

Parent Reinforcements give children a reassuring presence, reminding them that they're not alone in the fight against the Boogeyman.

3. Boogey Watch Teams – Rotating Watch Duty for Continuous Protection

Forming **Boogey Watch Teams** with siblings or friends allows for continuous surveillance throughout the night. By rotating watch duties, the team ensures that someone is always keeping an eye out for the Boogeyman.

- **How to Form Boogey Watch Teams:**
  - Divide the night into shifts, with each team member responsible for keeping watch during a specific period.

- Create a schedule where one person stays awake for a set amount of time before waking the next teammate to take over.
- Have each person say, "It's my turn to keep you safe. Boogeyman, you don't have a chance."

Boogey Watch Teams provide round-the-clock protection, preventing the Boogeyman from sneaking in when everyone is asleep.

4. Team Traps – Setting Complex Traps That Require Teamwork

Team Traps are more elaborate than regular traps, requiring multiple people to set up and manage. By working together, you can create intricate traps that catch or repel the Boogeyman with greater efficiency.

- **How to Set Up Team Traps**:
  - Assign different tasks to each teammate: one person can set up string traps, while another sets up sound alarms or mirrors.
  - Create a chain reaction where one trap triggers another, confusing the Boogeyman and driving him into the next trap.
  - Encourage your team to say, "This trap needs all of us to work. Together, we'll stop the Boogeyman!"

Team Traps not only require collaboration but also give each team member a specific role in the Boogeyman defense.

5. Boogeyman Hide-and-Seek – Outmaneuvering the Boogeyman with a Twist on a Classic Game

Boogeyman Hide-and-Seek is a playful yet strategic way to outmaneuver the Boogeyman. By turning the classic game into a defense tactic, you can learn to track and evade the Boogeyman's movements.

- **How to Play Boogeyman Hide-and-Seek**:
  - One team member pretends to be the Boogeyman and hides in the room, while the others search for them. This practice helps you learn where the real Boogeyman might hide.

- Rotate who plays the Boogeyman, helping everyone on the team become skilled at identifying hiding spots and movement patterns.
- Encourage the team to say, "We're finding you first, Boogeyman. You can't hide from us!"

This game improves the team's ability to detect and outmaneuver the Boogeyman, making it harder for him to surprise anyone.

6. Boogey Defense Council – Strategizing Together to Formulate a Plan

Creating a **Boogey Defense Council** with friends or siblings allows everyone to share ideas and strategize the best defense methods. Working together to brainstorm new tactics makes your team more creative and prepared.

- **How to Form a Boogey Defense Council**:
  - Gather your team for a council meeting before bedtime to discuss the best defense strategies for the night.
  - Each member can suggest a new idea, such as setting up new traps, using sound-based defenses, or creating a protective circle.
  - Have the council say, "Together, we're stronger. Boogeyman, you won't get past our plans."

The Boogey Defense Council promotes teamwork, creativity, and problem-solving, ensuring everyone feels involved in the defense process.

7. Imagination Link – Connecting Imaginations for Greater Defense Power

Imagination Link involves linking your imagination with that of your teammates, creating a shared mental space where you can summon greater power to fight the Boogeyman.

- **How to Use Imagination Link**:
  - Sit in a circle with your teammates and close your eyes. Imagine that you're linking your minds together, forming a protective shield that surrounds the entire group.

- ○ Visualize the Boogeyman being pushed away by the combined power of everyone's imagination.
- ○ Say together, "Our imaginations are linked, and we're unstoppable. Boogeyman, you can't break through."

The Imagination Link strengthens each teammate's power by combining their mental energy, making the Boogeyman's presence weaker.

8. Family Defense Rituals – Performing Protective Routines Together

Family Defense Rituals involve performing nightly protective routines as a family, creating a shared ritual that strengthens everyone's belief in their ability to keep the Boogeyman away.

- **How to Perform Family Defense Rituals:**
  - ○ Set a specific time each night to perform rituals like drawing protection symbols, placing nightlights, or sprinkling Boogey Dust around the bed.
  - ○ Each family member can take a different role, whether it's setting traps, lighting candles, or saying protective affirmations.
  - ○ Say together, "As a family, we're stronger than the Boogeyman. He can't come near us."

Family Defense Rituals create a comforting and unifying experience, showing children that they have a strong support system behind them.

9. Boogeyman Busters Club – Sharing Tips and Coordinating Defenses with Friends

Forming a **Boogeyman Busters Club** with friends or classmates allows you to share defense tips, plan strategies, and coordinate your efforts to keep the Boogeyman away from everyone's room.

- **How to Start a Boogeyman Busters Club:**
  - ○ Gather a group of friends and create a club dedicated to sharing Boogeyman defense strategies. Each member can contribute new ideas or gadgets that work for them.
  - ○ Plan group activities like trap-building workshops, defense drills, or brainstorming sessions to come up with new ways to outsmart the Boogeyman.

◦ Encourage club members to say, "Together, we're the Boogeyman Busters. No Boogeyman stands a chance!"

The Boogeyman Busters Club creates a sense of community, helping everyone feel supported in their defense efforts.

10. Boogey Battle Drills – Practicing Defense with Your Team

Boogey Battle Drills are practice sessions where your team runs through different defense scenarios to ensure everyone is prepared for a Boogeyman encounter.

- **How to Run Boogey Battle Drills**:
    ◦ Create different scenarios, such as "Boogeyman under the bed" or "Boogeyman in the closet," and assign each team member a role in responding to the threat.
    ◦ Practice setting traps, turning on lights, and using sound-based defenses in a coordinated manner.
    ◦ Say as a team, "We're ready for anything, Boogeyman. You don't stand a chance!"

Boogey Battle Drills keep your team sharp and ready, making sure everyone knows their role in the defense.

11. The Buddy System – Never Investigating the Boogeyman Alone

The **Buddy System** ensures that no one investigates Boogeyman activity alone, making it safer to check suspicious areas or set traps. Having a buddy nearby increases confidence and keeps fear in check.

- **How to Use the Buddy System**:
    ◦ Always pair up when investigating dark corners, under the bed, or in the closet. One person can hold the flashlight while the other checks the area.
    ◦ Buddies can also take turns standing watch while the other sleeps, providing constant support.

- Say to each other, "We're in this together, Boogeyman. You can't take us by surprise."

The Buddy System reinforces the idea that teamwork makes defense easier and more effective.

12. Synchronized Defenses – Attacking the Boogeyman from Multiple Angles

Synchronized Defenses involve coordinating with your teammates to attack the Boogeyman from different directions at the same time, making it harder for him to escape or regroup.

- **How to Use Synchronized Defenses:**
  - Assign each team member a specific task: one person can shine a flashlight while another claps or uses sound-based traps.
  - On a signal, all team members activate their defenses simultaneously, surrounding the Boogeyman with light, sound, and movement.
  - Say together, "We've got you surrounded, Boogeyman. You can't escape our defenses!"

Synchronized Defenses are highly effective because they overwhelm the Boogeyman from all angles, leaving him with nowhere to hide.

13. Tag Team Tactics – Switching Roles to Keep the Boogeyman Off Guard

Tag Team Tactics involve switching roles with your teammates during a Boogeyman encounter, keeping him off guard and unable to predict the next move.

- **How to Use Tag Team Tactics:**
  - Start by assigning roles: one person distracts the Boogeyman while the other sets up a trap. At a specific moment, switch roles to confuse the Boogeyman.
  - Each teammate should be prepared to take over the other's task at a moment's notice, keeping the Boogeyman guessing.
  - Say to each other, "We're switching roles, Boogeyman. You'll never see it coming!"

Tag Team Tactics create unpredictability, making it harder for the Boogeyman to plan his moves or avoid being caught.

14. Team Distraction Strategies – Dividing the Boogeyman's Focus

Team Distraction Strategies involve one teammate distracting the Boogeyman while the others set up defenses or prepare an attack. Dividing the Boogeyman's focus weakens his ability to defend himself.

- **How to Use Team Distraction Strategies:**
  - Have one teammate make noise, use a flashlight, or move around the room to draw the Boogeyman's attention.
  - Meanwhile, the other teammates can quietly set up traps, prepare defense tools, or position themselves for a surprise attack.

◦ Say as a team, "We're dividing your attention, Boogeyman. You can't focus on all of us at once."

Team Distraction Strategies create confusion, giving your team the upper hand while the Boogeyman is distracted.

15. Joint Imaginary Friend Power – Combining Imaginary Friends for a Stronger Defense

Joint Imaginary Friend Power involves combining the strength of multiple imaginary friends to create a powerful team of protectors who can fight the Boogeyman together.

- **How to Use Joint Imaginary Friend Power**:
    ◦ Each teammate introduces their imaginary friend, explaining what powers or abilities they have.
    ◦ Work together to create a scenario where all the imaginary friends combine their abilities to form a strong defense against the Boogeyman.
    ◦ Say together, "Our imaginary friends are here to protect us, Boogeyman. You can't stand against them!"

Joint Imaginary Friend Power strengthens each child's sense of protection, making them feel supported by an entire team of guardians.

Conclusion: Collaborative Defense Strategies – Defeating the Boogeyman Together

Working together increases the chances of outsmarting and defeating the Boogeyman. Whether it's through Partner Patrols, Boogey Defense Councils, or Team Distraction Strategies, collaborative defense strategies create a sense of unity and strength. By combining imaginations, coordinating actions, and sharing responsibilities, children can form an unbeatable team that the Boogeyman simply cannot overcome. With these team-based methods, no one has to face the Boogeyman alone, and together, you can reclaim the night.

Chapter 23: Imagination-Based Defenses – Defeating the Boogeyman with Creativity

The Boogeyman originates from the imagination, which means that imagination is also the key to his defeat. Harnessing creativity allows you to bend the rules of reality, creating powerful defenses that can repel the Boogeyman. **Imagination-Based Defenses** teach you how to use mental imagery, creative thinking, and story-building to fight back and take control. In this chapter, we'll explore a range of techniques for using your imagination to summon protectors, create barriers, and reshape the Boogeyman into something you can easily defeat.

1. Summoning Imaginary Heroes – Calling Upon Protectors from Your Mind

Imagination is a boundless source of strength, and **Summoning Imaginary Heroes** allows you to bring fictional or heroic figures to life who can protect you from the Boogeyman.

- **How to Summon Imaginary Heroes**:
  - Close your eyes and imagine your favorite hero—this could be a superhero, a knight, or even an animal with magical powers.
  - Picture this hero standing tall beside you, guarding your bed and facing off against the Boogeyman.
  - Say, "My hero is here to protect me. Boogeyman, you're no match for them!"

Whether it's a superhero with laser eyes or a knight with an indestructible shield, Imaginary Heroes stand as powerful defenders, giving you confidence and a sense of security.

2. Imagination Weapons – Creating Magic Swords and Shields to Fight

Your mind is capable of creating powerful **Imagination Weapons**—from magic swords to force-field shields—designed to defeat the Boogeyman in an instant. These weapons are as strong as your belief in them.

- **How to Create Imagination Weapons**:
  - Close your eyes and picture a glowing sword in your hand, a shield on your arm, or even a magical staff. Imagine it radiating with protective energy.
  - If the Boogeyman approaches, imagine swinging your sword or raising your shield, deflecting his attacks or scaring him away.
  - Say, "This sword cuts through fear, and this shield protects me. Boogeyman, you can't harm me!"

Imagination Weapons allow you to take direct action, giving you the mental tools to fight back and push the Boogeyman away.

3. Fictional Armor – Visualizing Armor that Repels the Boogeyman

In the world of imagination, you can create powerful **Fictional Armor** that deflects any of the Boogeyman's attempts to scare or harm you. This armor makes you invincible to his tricks.

- **How to Wear Fictional Armor**:
  - Imagine yourself putting on a suit of armor. It can be made of glowing metal, shimmering light, or even scales from a dragon.

- ◦ Visualize this armor forming an impenetrable barrier that protects you from anything the Boogeyman tries.
- ◦ Say, "I am covered in armor. Boogeyman, you can't touch me!"

With Fictional Armor, you create an extra layer of mental defense, boosting your confidence and making it impossible for the Boogeyman to affect you.

4. Imagination Transformation – Becoming a Powerful Creature to Overpower the Boogeyman

Imagination Transformation allows you to temporarily transform into a powerful creature, like a dragon, superhero, or warrior, giving you the strength to overpower the Boogeyman in your mind.

- **How to Perform an Imagination Transformation:**
  - ◦ Close your eyes and imagine yourself transforming into a powerful creature—wings growing from your back, claws forming in your hands, or armor enveloping you.
  - ◦ Picture yourself towering over the Boogeyman, ready to defeat him with your new-found strength.
  - ◦ Say, "I am now a dragon (or superhero, or warrior). Boogeyman, you can't win against me!"

This transformation makes you the most powerful figure in the room, turning the tables and making the Boogeyman afraid of you.

5. Storybook Defense – Using the Plot of a Favorite Story to Fight

Drawing inspiration from a favorite book or story, **Storybook Defense** involves imagining yourself as the main character who defeats the Boogeyman using the lessons and powers from that story.

- **How to Use Storybook Defense:**
  - ◦ Choose a favorite story where the hero defeats an evil villain or overcomes a powerful enemy.
  - ◦ Imagine yourself as the hero of the story, using the same tactics or powers to fight the Boogeyman.

- Say, "I am the hero of this story, and like in the book, I will defeat the Boogeyman."

Storybook Defense taps into the lessons of bravery and resourcefulness from your favorite tales, helping you craft a mental strategy for victory.

6. Turning Fear into Fun – Making the Boogeyman Harmless or Goofy

One of the simplest yet most effective methods is **Turning Fear into Fun** by reshaping the Boogeyman into something silly, harmless, or goofy. This takes away his power to scare you.

- **How to Turn Fear into Fun**:
  - Picture the Boogeyman in a goofy outfit, like wearing clown shoes or a giant chicken costume.
  - Imagine him tripping over his own feet or trying to scare you but failing miserably because he's so ridiculous.
  - Say, "You're not scary, Boogeyman. You're just silly!"

Turning Fear into Fun helps neutralize the Boogeyman by taking away his intimidating presence and turning him into a joke.

7. Imaginary Fortresses – Building a Fortress the Boogeyman Cannot Enter

An **Imaginary Fortress** is a mental stronghold that you can construct to protect yourself from the Boogeyman. Inside this fortress, you are completely safe and untouchable.

- **How to Build an Imaginary Fortress**:
  - Close your eyes and imagine a giant fortress surrounding your bed. It can be made of stone, light, or even crystal—anything you feel is strong.
  - Picture high walls, thick doors, and guards protecting the entrances. The Boogeyman cannot enter.
  - Say, "This fortress keeps me safe. Boogeyman, you can't get inside."

Imaginary Fortresses create a safe mental space where no threat can reach you, giving you peace of mind throughout the night.

8. Dream Crafting – Controlling Dreams to Create Safe Environments

Dream Crafting involves learning to control your dreams so that you can create safe environments or even turn the tables on the Boogeyman while you're asleep.

- **How to Craft Your Dreams**:
  - Before bed, think about the kind of dream you want to have. Picture a safe place, like a sunny beach or a magical castle.
  - If the Boogeyman appears in your dream, imagine that you can control the dream and change the environment to make him disappear or shrink.

◦ Say to yourself, "I control my dreams. I can make the Boogeyman go away."

Dream Crafting empowers you to take control of your subconscious, ensuring that the Boogeyman has no power over you while you sleep.

9. Imagination Barriers – Blocking the Boogeyman from Your Mind

Using **Imagination Barriers**, you can create mental blocks that prevent the Boogeyman from entering your mind or causing fear. These barriers are invisible but impenetrable.

- **How to Create Imagination Barriers**:
  ◦ Imagine a strong wall or shield surrounding your mind, keeping it safe from any negative thoughts or fears the Boogeyman might try to create.
  ◦ Visualize the Boogeyman trying to approach but bouncing off the barrier, unable to get through.
  ◦ Say, "My mind is protected by this barrier. Boogeyman, you can't enter."

Imagination Barriers give you control over your thoughts, blocking out any influence the Boogeyman might try to have.

10. Reshaping Reality – Bending the Rules of the Boogeyman's Dimension

Reshaping Reality involves using your imagination to bend or rewrite the rules of the Boogeyman's world. In this method, you take control of his dimension and make it work in your favor.

- **How to Reshape Reality**:
  ◦ Imagine that you can control the Boogeyman's world, changing the way it works. For example, you can make gravity disappear so the Boogeyman floats away, or turn everything into jelly so he can't move.
  ◦ Visualize yourself as the master of his dimension, rewriting the rules however you like.
  ◦ Say, "I control your world now, Boogeyman. You have no power here."

Reshaping Reality gives you ultimate control, turning the Boogeyman's threats into powerless illusions.

11. Imaginary Friend Callbacks – Bringing Back Your Imaginary Friend to Defend You

If you've ever had an imaginary friend, **Imaginary Friend Callbacks** allow you to summon them back to defend you from the Boogeyman.

- **How to Call Back Your Imaginary Friend**:
  ◦ Close your eyes and picture your old imaginary friend, whether it's a talking animal, a superhero, or a magical creature.
  ◦ Ask them to stand by your side and protect you from the Boogeyman, just like they did when you were younger.

- Say, "My imaginary friend is back, and they're here to help me. Boogeyman, you can't win!"

Imaginary friends provide a sense of comfort and nostalgia, turning them into powerful allies against the Boogeyman.

12. Cartoon World Defense – Trapping the Boogeyman in a Cartoon World

With **Cartoon World Defense**, you can trap the Boogeyman in a world where his powers are ineffective, turning him into a harmless cartoon character.

- **How to Use Cartoon World Defense**:
  - Imagine that the Boogeyman has entered a cartoon world where he can't do anything serious—every time he tries to scare you, something silly happens instead.
  - Picture him slipping on banana peels, getting squished by anvils, or falling through trapdoors.
  - Say, "You're in a cartoon world now, Boogeyman. You can't hurt anyone here!"

Cartoon World Defense turns the Boogeyman into a comedic character, stripping away his ability to be frightening.

13. Shape-Shifting Mindset – Shifting Your Form to Confuse the Boogeyman

In the **Shape-Shifting Mindset**, you imagine yourself constantly changing forms—becoming different animals, creatures, or objects—so the Boogeyman can never catch or harm you.

- **How to Use Shape-Shifting**:
  - Imagine yourself turning into different shapes: a bird that flies away, a tiger that roars, or even a cloud that the Boogeyman can't touch.
  - Keep changing shapes in your mind, making it impossible for the Boogeyman to know where you'll be next.
  - Say, "You can't catch me, Boogeyman. I'm always changing!"

Shape-Shifting Mindset creates a feeling of agility and power, making you feel invincible and unpredictable.

14. Dream Guardians – Summoning Creatures to Protect You While You Sleep

Dream Guardians are powerful protectors you summon in your dreams to watch over you and fend off the Boogeyman while you sleep.

- **How to Summon Dream Guardians**:
  - Before bed, imagine powerful guardians like dragons, knights, or wizards standing guard at the edges of your dreams.

- Picture them keeping watch and fighting off the Boogeyman if he tries to enter your dreams.
- Say, "My Dream Guardians are here to protect me. Boogeyman, you can't get past them."

Dream Guardians create a mental army of protectors, giving you peace of mind as you drift into sleep.

15. Story Control – Rewriting the Story of Your Boogeyman Encounter

Story Control allows you to rewrite the story of your Boogeyman encounter, making yourself the hero who defeats him.

- **How to Use Story Control**:
  - Imagine your night as a storybook, with yourself as the main character. Rewrite the ending where you stand up to the Boogeyman and defeat him with your bravery and cleverness.
  - Picture the Boogeyman shrinking, disappearing, or running away as you take control of the story.
  - Say, "I'm the hero of this story, and I win every time."

Story Control gives you the power to reshape your fears into a narrative where you are always victorious.

Conclusion: Imagination-Based Defenses – Unlocking Your Creative Power

Imagination is the Boogeyman's origin, and it's also the key to his defeat. By harnessing the power of creativity, you can summon protectors, build fortresses, and reshape reality to keep the Boogeyman at bay. These **Imagination-Based Defenses** give you the ultimate control over your mind, turning fear into strength and making the Boogeyman powerless against your creative force. With these techniques, your imagination becomes your greatest weapon, ensuring that you always win the battle against the Boogeyman.

Chapter 24: Science and Tech – Futuristic Boogeyman Busting

While the Boogeyman is often seen as a creature of myth and imagination, modern science and technology offer powerful new ways to defend against, weaken, or even destroy him. **Futuristic Boogeyman Busting** combines cutting-edge gadgets, experimental devices, and high-tech solutions to provide a full range of defenses. This chapter delves into advanced technological tools that can detect, trap, or neutralize the Boogeyman using energy, light, sound, and even quantum mechanics.

Armed with these futuristic tools, you'll turn the fight against the Boogeyman into a battle of science and strategy.

1. The Temporalfuge Device – Aging the Boogeyman Rapidly

The **Temporalfuge Device** is an advanced machine designed to manipulate time and rapidly age the Boogeyman. By accelerating his aging process, the Boogeyman becomes too old and weak to pose a threat.

- **How the Temporalfuge Device Works**:
  - The device emits a temporal field that targets the Boogeyman's molecular structure, speeding up time around him while leaving the rest of the room unaffected.
  - Once activated, the Boogeyman begins to age rapidly, weakening him to the point where he can no longer move or cause fear.
  - To use the device, simply point it toward the area where the Boogeyman is lurking and press the activation button. The aging process begins immediately, and the Boogeyman will disappear soon after.

The Temporalfuge Device is a high-tech solution for quickly neutralizing the Boogeyman, reducing him to a powerless, aged form in seconds.

2. Anti-Boogey Lasers – Destabilizing the Boogeyman's Form

Anti-Boogey Lasers are cutting-edge tools designed to destabilize the Boogeyman's form, making it impossible for him to maintain his presence. These lasers target the dark energy that holds the Boogeyman together.

- **How Anti-Boogey Lasers Work**:

- The laser emits a high-energy beam that disrupts the molecular bonds holding the Boogeyman together, causing him to disintegrate.
- Aim the laser at the Boogeyman, focusing on areas where his form is most solid, such as under the bed or in the closet.
- Once hit by the laser, the Boogeyman will begin to lose shape and dissolve into nothingness.

Anti-Boogey Lasers are highly effective for quick, direct attacks, breaking down the Boogeyman's form at the molecular level.

3. Boogeyman Energy Detectors – Sensing Boogeyman Energy Signatures

Boogeyman Energy Detectors are specialized devices that can detect the unique energy signature of a Boogeyman. These detectors help you locate and track the Boogeyman, even if he's hiding in the shadows.

- **How Boogeyman Energy Detectors Work:**
  - The device scans the room for abnormal energy fluctuations, which are typical of Boogeyman activity. These fluctuations appear as dark energy signatures.
  - If the detector senses Boogeyman energy, it will beep or flash, giving you a clear indication of his presence and location.
  - Use the detector to sweep the room, paying particular attention to high-risk areas like under the bed or in dark corners.

Boogeyman Energy Detectors make it easier to find and neutralize the Boogeyman before he has a chance to strike.

4. Electromagnetic Shields – Creating an Impenetrable Barrier

Electromagnetic Shields are energy fields that create an impenetrable barrier around you, preventing the Boogeyman from coming close. This high-tech shield uses electromagnetic energy to repel the Boogeyman's dark essence.

- **How Electromagnetic Shields Work:**

- The shield generator creates a bubble of electromagnetic energy around your bed or the entire room. The Boogeyman cannot pass through this field without being repelled.
- Activate the shield by placing the generator near your bed and turning it on before sleep. The shield will form immediately, keeping you safe all night.
- The shield's energy disrupts the Boogeyman's presence, making it impossible for him to come near you.

Electromagnetic Shields offer 24/7 protection, ensuring that the Boogeyman can't penetrate your defenses.

5. Boogeyman Disruptor Guns – Interfering with the Boogeyman's Structure

Boogeyman Disruptor Guns are experimental weapons that interfere with the Boogeyman's molecular structure, causing him to lose cohesion and vanish.

- **How to Use Boogeyman Disruptor Guns:**
  - Aim the disruptor gun at the Boogeyman and fire. The gun emits a pulse that scrambles the Boogeyman's molecular makeup, breaking apart the dark energy that holds him together.
  - Once hit, the Boogeyman will begin to flicker and fade, unable to hold his shape.
  - This weapon is highly effective for targeting Boogeymen hiding in confined spaces, such as closets or under beds.

Boogeyman Disruptor Guns are powerful tools that can quickly take down a Boogeyman, making him lose form and disappear.

6. Thermal Imaging – Spotting the Boogeyman with Heat Sensors

Thermal Imaging cameras are advanced tools that detect the Boogeyman's cold trail, making it easier to spot him even in complete darkness.

- **How Thermal Imaging Works**:
  - The Boogeyman often leaves a cold trail behind him, as his presence lowers the temperature in the areas he occupies.
  - Use a thermal imaging camera to scan the room. Cold spots will appear as blue or dark areas on the camera's display, indicating where the Boogeyman has been or is currently hiding.
  - Once you identify his location, you can take further action using other defense tools.

Thermal Imaging allows you to see the Boogeyman even when he's invisible to the naked eye, making it an essential tool for tracking and capturing him.

7. Boogeyman Neural Scramblers – Confusing the Boogeyman's Mind

Boogeyman Neural Scramblers are devices that disrupt the Boogeyman's brainwaves, confusing him and making him slow and disoriented.

- **How Boogeyman Neural Scramblers Work**:
  - The scrambler emits a signal that interferes with the Boogeyman's neural patterns, causing him to become confused and lose focus.
  - Place the scrambler in the room and activate it when you sense the Boogeyman's presence. The signal will cause him to stumble, making it easier to trap or scare him away.
  - Use this device to buy time while you prepare other defenses or escape.

Neural Scramblers are excellent for creating confusion and disorientation, weakening the Boogeyman's ability to focus on his targets.

8. Holographic Boogeyman Decoys – Distracting the Boogeyman with High-Tech Decoys

Holographic Boogeyman Decoys use advanced holographic technology to create realistic decoys that distract the Boogeyman, giving you time to prepare an attack or escape.

- **How to Use Holographic Boogeyman Decoys**:
  - Activate the decoy in the Boogeyman's hiding spot. The hologram will look and move like a real person, drawing the Boogeyman's attention.

- While the Boogeyman is focused on the decoy, you can set up traps or activate other defenses.
- The hologram will keep the Boogeyman occupied for several minutes, giving you a tactical advantage.

Holographic Decoys are ideal for distracting the Boogeyman, making it easier to outsmart him with other defenses.

9. Virtual Reality Traps – Trapping the Boogeyman in a Digital World
Virtual Reality Traps use VR technology to lure the Boogeyman into a digital world where he can be trapped indefinitely.

- **How Virtual Reality Traps Work**:
    - The VR trap creates a digital environment that looks and feels real to the Boogeyman. Once he enters, he is unable to escape back into the real world.
    - Activate the VR trap by placing it near the Boogeyman's hiding spot. The device will project a virtual space that draws the Boogeyman inside.
    - Once trapped, the Boogeyman cannot affect you in the real world.

Virtual Reality Traps are a futuristic way to completely isolate the Boogeyman in a digital environment, where he can no longer pose a threat.

10. Sonic Blasters – Incapacitating the Boogeyman with High-Pitched Sounds
Sonic Blasters emit high-pitched sound waves that are unbearable to the Boogeyman, incapacitating him and forcing him to retreat.

- **How to Use Sonic Blasters**:
    - Point the blaster in the direction of the Boogeyman and activate it. The device emits a sonic frequency that disrupts the Boogeyman's senses, rendering him unable to move or concentrate.

- The sound waves can travel through walls and under beds, making them perfect for flushing out hidden Boogeymen.
- Once the Boogeyman is incapacitated, you can use other tools to neutralize him.

Sonic Blasters are fast-acting and effective for stopping the Boogeyman in his tracks.

11. Anti-Boogey Drones – Hunting Down the Boogeyman with High-Tech Drones

Anti-Boogey Drones are small, agile drones equipped with lights, sound generators, and sensors to hunt down and weaken the Boogeyman.

- **How to Use Anti-Boogey Drones:**
    - Launch the drone into the room and use its camera and sensors to search for the Boogeyman's hiding spot.
    - The drone emits a bright light and loud sound, both of which weaken the Boogeyman and make him easier to catch.
    - Once located, the drone can guide you to the Boogeyman's position so you can take further action.

Anti-Boogey Drones provide a high-tech, hands-free method of hunting down and disabling the Boogeyman.

12. Stasis Fields – Freezing the Boogeyman in Place

Stasis Fields are energy-based technologies that can temporarily freeze the Boogeyman in place, preventing him from moving or escaping.

- **How to Activate a Stasis Field:**
    - Place the stasis field generator in the Boogeyman's vicinity and activate it. The field will instantly freeze the Boogeyman, trapping him in place.
    - The field can hold the Boogeyman for several minutes, giving you time to prepare additional defenses or remove him from the room.
    - Stasis Fields are ideal for stopping the Boogeyman's movement without causing permanent harm.

Stasis Fields are highly effective for immobilizing the Boogeyman and preventing him from escaping or retaliating.

13. Time Loop Traps – Trapping the Boogeyman in a Repeating Time Loop

Time Loop Traps are advanced devices that trap the Boogeyman in a repeating loop of time, preventing him from advancing or escaping.

- **How Time Loop Traps Work:**
    - Activate the time loop trap when the Boogeyman is in a confined space. The trap creates a bubble where time repeats itself, trapping the Boogeyman in an endless cycle.

- Once in the loop, the Boogeyman will be stuck in the same moment over and over, unable to continue his attack or escape.
- Use this time to remove the Boogeyman from your space or set up additional defenses.

Time Loop Traps offer a unique way to neutralize the Boogeyman by trapping him in an inescapable loop.

14. Boogey Energy Drainers – Draining the Boogeyman's Dark Energy

Boogey Energy Drainers are machines that extract the Boogeyman's dark energy, leaving him powerless and unable to maintain his form.

- **How to Use Boogey Energy Drainers**:
    - Place the energy drainers in the room and activate them. The devices will begin to draw the dark energy from the Boogeyman, weakening him with every passing second.
    - Once enough energy is drained, the Boogeyman will collapse and fade away, unable to regenerate his strength.
    - These machines work best in enclosed spaces where the Boogeyman has little room to escape.

Boogey Energy Drainers are an efficient way to sap the Boogeyman's strength, making him powerless in your presence.

15. Quantum Cage – Trapping the Boogeyman Across Multiple Dimensions

The **Quantum Cage** is an advanced containment system that exists in multiple dimensions, preventing the Boogeyman from escaping no matter where he tries to go.

- **How the Quantum Cage Works**:
    - Once the Boogeyman is detected, activate the Quantum Cage around him. The cage operates across several dimensions, ensuring that the Boogeyman cannot slip into another realm to escape.
    - The cage holds the Boogeyman indefinitely, keeping him isolated and harmless.
    - Use this device for Boogeymen that are particularly tricky or capable of shifting between dimensions.

The Quantum Cage offers the ultimate in Boogeyman containment, trapping him across all known dimensions and ensuring he can never return.

Conclusion: Science and Tech – Futuristic Tools for Boogeyman Busting

With the advancements of modern technology and scientific innovation, the fight against the Boogeyman has entered a new era. From devices that scramble the Boogeyman's mind to quantum cages that trap him across dimensions, these futuristic tools provide cutting-edge defenses that make the Boogeyman's old tricks obsolete. Using science and tech, you can neutralize, capture, or destroy the Boogeyman with precision, ensuring that he never haunts your nights again.

Bottom of Form

Chapter 25: Traditional and Folklore Defenses – Ancient Methods for Fighting the Boogeyman

For centuries, people around the world have used folklore and traditional methods to protect themselves from dark creatures, including the Boogeyman. These defenses have stood the test of time, rooted in cultural beliefs and practices passed down through generations. **Traditional and Folklore Defenses** offer a rich variety of techniques for warding off the Boogeyman, using symbols, natural objects, and spiritual rituals that draw on ancient wisdom. In this chapter, we explore how iron horseshoes, garlic wreaths, sacred fire, and other timeless practices can help protect you and keep the Boogeyman away.

1. Iron Horseshoes – Using Iron to Repel the Boogeyman

In many cultures, iron is believed to have protective properties, capable of warding off evil spirits, including the Boogeyman. **Iron Horseshoes** are a popular symbol of protection, often hung above doors or windows to keep malevolent beings out.

- **How to Use Iron Horseshoes**:
    - Hang an iron horseshoe above your bedroom door or near a window. The iron will act as a barrier, preventing the Boogeyman from entering your space.
    - Make sure the horseshoe is placed with the open end facing upward to "catch" good luck and keep the Boogeyman at bay.
    - Say, "Iron protects me, Boogeyman, you can't pass through."

Iron objects, especially horseshoes, have been used for centuries to provide protection from dark forces, making them an essential part of any Boogeyman defense.

2. Garlic Wreaths – Repelling the Boogeyman with Garlic

Although **Garlic Wreaths** are most commonly associated with repelling vampires, folklore suggests that garlic's powerful scent also keeps the Boogeyman away. The strong odor is believed to be unpleasant to malevolent creatures, driving them away from your room.

- **How to Use Garlic Wreaths**:
    - Hang a garlic wreath near the entrance to your room or above your bed to create a protective barrier.
    - You can also place individual cloves of garlic around the bed or in the corners of the room where the Boogeyman might hide.
    - Say, "Garlic strong, keep the Boogeyman from coming along."

Garlic's protective reputation spans multiple cultures, making it a potent and simple defense against the Boogeyman.

3. Silver Coins – Warding Off Dark Creatures with Silver

In many traditions, silver is known to repel evil entities, including werewolves and dark spirits. **Silver Coins** placed under the pillow or around the bed are said to protect against the Boogeyman by disrupting his ability to enter your space.

- **How to Use Silver Coins**:
    - Place a few silver coins under your pillow or in a circle around your bed. The presence of silver will create a barrier that the Boogeyman cannot cross.

- You can also wear a silver necklace or bracelet while you sleep to add an extra layer of protection.
- Say, "Silver pure, keep me safe and sure. Boogeyman, stay away."

Silver has long been associated with purity and protection, making it a valuable tool in the fight against the Boogeyman. Silver has been known to harm all sorts of mythical creatures such as vampires, werewolves, ghosts. if you are interested in getting real silver, I personally recommend AP-MEX.com, JMbullion.com, WholesaleCoinDirect.com. these are the main ones that have Silver Coins, bars and other precious metals.

4. Protective Oils – Using Scent to Repel the Boogeyman

Certain **Protective Oils**, like lavender and cedarwood, have been used in folklore to create a calming, protective atmosphere that keeps dark entities at bay. These oils can be applied around the room to prevent the Boogeyman from entering.

- **How to Use Protective Oils**:
  - Place a few drops of lavender, cedarwood, or another protective oil in a diffuser to fill the room with a protective scent.
  - You can also rub a small amount of oil on the bedframe, windowsill, or doors to create an invisible shield of protection.
  - Say, "This oil's scent keeps danger away. Boogeyman, you're not welcome to stay."

The calming properties of protective oils not only repel the Boogeyman but also help you feel more relaxed and safe during the night.

5. Ancestor Spirits – Calling Upon the Spirits of Ancestors for Protection

Many cultures believe that **Ancestor Spirits** can be called upon to protect their descendants from harm. By invoking the spirits of your ancestors, you can create a spiritual shield that keeps the Boogeyman away.

- **How to Call Upon Ancestor Spirits**:
    - Before bed, close your eyes and imagine the spirits of your ancestors surrounding you, standing guard against the Boogeyman.
    - Light a small candle or incense in their honor, asking them to watch over you while you sleep.
    - Say, "Ancestors wise, protect me from the Boogeyman's eyes."

Calling on the protective power of ancestors brings comfort and strength, helping you feel watched over and safe from harm.

6. Protective Tattoos – Wearing Symbols that Ward Off Evil

Temporary **Protective Tattoos** of ancient symbols can be worn on the body to provide protection from the Boogeyman. These tattoos, based on folklore and spiritual beliefs, act as protective shields that keep dark forces at bay.

- **How to Use Protective Tattoos**:
    - Apply temporary tattoos of protective symbols, such as the eye of Horus, pentacles, or ancient runes, to your body before going to bed.
    - These tattoos will act as personal shields, protecting you from the Boogeyman's influence.
    - Say, "With these symbols on my skin, the Boogeyman cannot come in."

Wearing protective symbols creates a personal barrier, ensuring that the Boogeyman can't touch or scare you during the night.

7. Sacred Fire – Honoring Protective Spirits with Light

Sacred Fire in the form of a small candle or incense is used in many traditions to honor protective spirits and create a safe, sacred space. The light from the fire acts as a beacon of protection, keeping the Boogeyman at bay.

- **How to Use Sacred Fire**:
  - Light a small candle or incense before bed, dedicating it to the protective spirits or ancestors you wish to honor.
  - Allow the flame to burn in a safe place, such as a bedside table or a windowsill, until it naturally goes out or you extinguish it.
  - Say, "By this sacred flame, no harm can come near. Boogeyman, you are not welcome here."

Sacred Fire rituals create a calming, protective atmosphere that drives away the Boogeyman and brings peace to your space.

Please have parental supervision when having a candle lit.

8. Holy Water Sprays – Using Blessed Water to Create a Shield

Holy Water is a powerful protective tool in many spiritual traditions, believed to ward off evil entities. By sprinkling or spraying holy water around the room, you can create a spiritual shield that keeps the Boogeyman from entering.

- **How to Use Holy Water**:
  - Fill a spray bottle with holy water and lightly mist the room, focusing on windows, doors, and the bed.
  - You can also dip your fingers in the holy water and sprinkle it in the corners of the room or directly on the bed.
  - Say, "With this holy water, I cleanse and protect. Boogeyman, you are rejected."

Holy Water Sprays create a sacred barrier, ensuring that the Boogeyman cannot cross into your protected space.

9. Chalk Circles – Drawing Circles of Protection Around the Bed

Chalk Circles are a simple yet powerful traditional method for creating a boundary that the Boogeyman cannot cross. In many cultures, drawing a circle is believed to trap or repel evil spirits.

- **How to Use Chalk Circles**:

- Use white chalk to draw a circle around your bed, creating a protective barrier that the Boogeyman cannot penetrate.
- Make sure the circle is continuous and unbroken, as this will strengthen the protection.
- Say, "This circle keeps me safe and sound. Boogeyman, you're not allowed around."

Chalk Circles are easy to create and act as an effective boundary that prevents the Boogeyman from getting too close.

10. Ancient Prayers – Reciting Protective Prayers or Chants

Many cultures have passed down **Ancient Prayers** or chants designed to protect against evil forces. Reciting these prayers before bed can invoke protective spirits and create a sacred shield around you.

- **How to Use Ancient Prayers:**
  - Choose a protective prayer or chant that resonates with you. It could be a traditional prayer from your own culture or a simple protective phrase.
  - Recite the prayer slowly and deliberately before bed, visualizing a shield of light forming around you.
  - Say, "With these words, I call protection near. Boogeyman, you have no power here."

Ancient Prayers connect you to centuries of wisdom and spiritual protection, keeping you safe from the Boogeyman's tricks.

11. Boogeyman Totems – Creating or Finding Totems to Ward Off Evil

Boogeyman Totems are objects or figures created to ward off dark spirits, including the Boogeyman. These totems can be handcrafted from natural materials or found objects that hold personal significance.

- **How to Create or Use Boogeyman Totems:**
  - Create a totem using natural materials like wood, stones, or feathers, carving or drawing protective symbols into the totem's surface.
  - Place the totem near your bed or in the room's corners to create a shield of protection.
  - Say, "This totem stands strong, and with it, the Boogeyman is gone."

Totems are physical symbols of protection, believed to scare away malevolent beings through their spiritual or symbolic power.

12. Feathers of Protection – Hanging Feathers to Keep the Boogeyman Away

In some cultures, **Feathers** are seen as symbols of protection, believed to carry the power of the air and spirit. Hanging feathers near the bed can create a protective barrier that keeps the Boogeyman at bay.

- **How to Use Feathers of Protection**:
  - Hang feathers above your bed or near a window to prevent the Boogeyman from entering.
  - You can also place feathers around the bed, creating a circle of protection.
  - Say, "With these feathers, I am safe and light. Boogeyman, you cannot come near tonight."

Feathers of Protection are simple, natural tools that connect you to spiritual protection and guard against the Boogeyman.

13. Runes and Symbols – Drawing Ancient Symbols for Protection

Runes and Symbols from ancient traditions are believed to carry protective power. By drawing these symbols on paper or directly on the bedframe, you can create a ward that repels the Boogeyman.

- **How to Use Runes and Symbols**:
  - Choose a protective rune or symbol, such as the Algiz rune (representing protection) or the Ankh (symbolizing life).
  - Draw the symbol on a piece of paper and place it under your pillow, or draw it directly on the bedframe or window.
  - Say, "This symbol stands between me and harm. Boogeyman, you cannot come near."

Ancient symbols and runes carry spiritual power, creating a strong defense against dark forces like the Boogeyman.

14. Traditional Wards – Building Protective Wards from Natural Materials

Traditional Wards made from sticks, stones, or other natural materials are used in many cultures to protect homes from evil spirits. These wards can be placed at the bedroom entrance to prevent the Boogeyman from entering.

- **How to Build Traditional Wards**:

- Collect small sticks, stones, or leaves and arrange them in a pattern near the door or window.
- The arrangement acts as a barrier that the Boogeyman cannot pass.
- Say, "This ward keeps danger outside. Boogeyman, you can't come inside."

Building Traditional Wards brings the protection of nature into your room, creating a natural defense against the Boogeyman.

15. Protective Masks – Confusing the Boogeyman with Masks

Protective Masks are worn or placed around the room to confuse or scare the Boogeyman. Masks are believed to hide the wearer's identity or frighten dark spirits, preventing them from coming closer.

- **How to Use Protective Masks**:
    - Wear a mask when you feel the Boogeyman's presence, or place masks around the room facing the bed or door.
    - The Boogeyman will be confused by the masks, unable to identify his target.
    - Say, "These masks protect and confuse. Boogeyman, you will lose."

Protective Masks have been used for centuries to ward off spirits, adding an extra layer of defense against the Boogeyman.

Conclusion: Traditional and Folklore Defenses – Timeless Protection Against the Boogeyman

From iron horseshoes to protective oils and chalk circles, **Traditional and Folklore Defenses** offer ancient wisdom for fighting the Boogeyman. These time-tested methods draw on cultural beliefs and spiritual practices that have been used for centuries to protect against dark forces. By incorporating these defenses into your nightly routine, you can ward off the Boogeyman with the power of tradition and ensure a safe, peaceful night's sleep.

Chapter 26: Special Boogeyman Busting Challenges – Advanced Techniques for the Brave

This chapter is dedicated to those who have faced the Boogeyman, stared into the darkness, and come out the other side. **Special Boogeyman Busting Challenges** are for those who want to take their defenses to the next level. These advanced methods push the boundaries of imagination, bravery, and strategy. Whether you're confronting the Boogeyman head-on or battling him in his own dimension, these techniques will equip you with the knowledge and courage to stand your ground and, perhaps, even eliminate the Boogeyman for good.

1. Face Your Fear Challenge – Confronting the Boogeyman Head-On

The **Face Your Fear Challenge** is not for the faint of heart. It involves confronting the Boogeyman directly, in a controlled and empowered way. The goal is to take the fear out of the encounter and demonstrate your strength.

- **How to Face Your Fear**:
  - Find a moment when you feel the Boogeyman's presence, but rather than using light or other defenses, stand your ground.
  - Speak directly to the Boogeyman, saying, "I am not afraid of you, Boogeyman. I confront you, and I am stronger than you."
  - Visualize yourself surrounded by a protective shield of light, but remain calm and assertive as you face the Boogeyman.

By facing your fear head-on, you take away the Boogeyman's greatest weapon: your fear. This challenge is about reclaiming control and standing firm in the face of darkness.

2. Boogeyman Duel – A Mental Duel of Willpower

The **Boogeyman Duel** is a mental battle between you and the Boogeyman, where the strength of your willpower is tested. In this duel, you must resist the Boogeyman's attempts to invade your mind and overpower him with your mental strength.

- **How to Initiate a Boogeyman Duel**:
  - Sit quietly in your room and invite the Boogeyman to show himself, not physically, but mentally.
  - As you feel his presence, focus your mind on positive, strong thoughts. Picture a mental battlefield where you are equipped with powerful armor and weapons of the mind.
  - Say, "Boogeyman, I challenge you to a duel of wills. My mind is stronger, and I will win."
  - Mentally push back against any fear or negative thoughts the Boogeyman tries to plant in your mind.

The Boogeyman Duel is a test of inner strength, where you must outwit and overpower the Boogeyman with sheer will.

3. Ultimate Light Bomb – Creating a Massive Explosion of Light

The **Ultimate Light Bomb** combines all light-based defenses to create a massive explosion of protective energy that obliterates the Boogeyman. This is a one-time, powerful technique for when you need to eliminate the Boogeyman in a single, decisive blow.

- **How to Create the Ultimate Light Bomb**:
  - Gather all your light-based tools: flashlights, glowsticks, candles, and nightlights. Place them around the room, forming a circle of light.
  - Stand in the center and imagine a brilliant sphere of light growing larger and brighter, absorbing the energy from all the lights around you.
  - When the sphere is at its peak, say, "With this light, I banish all darkness! Boogeyman, be gone!" and visualize the light exploding outward, filling the room and beyond.
  - The light bomb will overwhelm the Boogeyman, forcing him to flee or vanish entirely.

The Ultimate Light Bomb is an advanced, last-resort technique designed to wipe out the Boogeyman's influence in an instant.

4. The Mirror Confrontation – Trapping the Boogeyman in a Mirror

The **Mirror Confrontation** uses a mirror to trap the Boogeyman, forcing him to face himself and interrogating him about his motives. Mirrors are known to reflect both physical and spiritual entities, making them a powerful tool in the fight against the Boogeyman.

- **How to Perform the Mirror Confrontation**:
    - Place a mirror in front of you, ideally a small handheld one.
    - When you sense the Boogeyman's presence, hold the mirror up and say, "Boogeyman, show yourself in the mirror. You cannot escape this reflection."
    - Watch as the Boogeyman's image appears in the mirror. Speak to him directly, asking why he haunts you and demanding that he leave.
    - Trap him in the mirror by focusing your energy on keeping him within the reflection, then cover the mirror with a cloth or turn it face down to seal him inside.

The Mirror Confrontation forces the Boogeyman to confront his own darkness, trapping him in the reflection and giving you control over the encounter.

5. Total Darkness Strategy – Defending Against the Boogeyman Without Light

The **Total Darkness Strategy** is an advanced challenge where you face the Boogeyman in complete darkness, relying solely on mental defenses. This technique requires intense focus and confidence in your mental strength.

- **How to Use the Total Darkness Strategy**:
    - Turn off all lights and sit or lie still in complete darkness.
    - Focus on your inner strength, building mental barriers that protect you from the Boogeyman's attempts to scare you.
    - Say, "Even in total darkness, I am not afraid. I create my own light within, and you cannot harm me."
    - Visualize a powerful light inside yourself that grows brighter with every breath, creating an invisible barrier that the Boogeyman cannot cross.

This strategy is about trusting your mental and emotional defenses, proving that the Boogeyman has no power over you, even in his preferred environment of darkness.

6. Advanced Boogey Traps – Complex Traps Requiring Strategic Placement

Advanced Boogey Traps are more intricate than standard traps and require precise placement and timing to catch or repel the Boogeyman. These traps involve multiple components, such as light, sound, and physical barriers.

- **How to Set Up Advanced Boogey Traps:**
  - Combine multiple trap elements: place a nightlight near the bed, string bells across the doorway, and use chalk to create a protective circle around the room.
  - Time each trap to activate in sequence, ensuring that the Boogeyman is lured into one area before triggering another.
  - Say, "These traps are set, and the Boogeyman cannot escape. Step into my trap, and you will be caught."

Advanced Boogey Traps are a strategic way to outsmart the Boogeyman, using his own movements against him to ensure he is caught and neutralized.

7. Boogeyman Eradication Spell – A Powerful Spell to Eliminate the Boogeyman

The **Boogeyman Eradication Spell** is a high-level spell designed to completely eliminate the Boogeyman from your life. This spell is complex and requires careful preparation.

- **How to Cast the Boogeyman Eradication Spell:**
  - Gather the following items: a black candle, salt, and a piece of paper with the Boogeyman's name or image.
  - Place the candle in the center of a salt circle and light it. Write the Boogeyman's name or draw his form on the paper.
  - Say, "By the power of this flame, I eradicate you, Boogeyman. You will never return." Burn the paper and watch as the Boogeyman's influence is destroyed.
  - Once the paper is reduced to ash, scatter the ashes outside to finalize the spell.

The Boogeyman Eradication Spell is a potent method for permanently eliminating the Boogeyman's presence.

8. The Great Boogey Banishment – A Multi-Step Ritual for Permanent Removal

The **Great Boogey Banishment** is a multi-step ritual that requires the help of friends or family to permanently banish the Boogeyman from your home.

- **How to Perform the Great Boogey Banishment**:
    - Gather your friends or family in a circle around the room. Each person should hold a candle or flashlight.
    - Recite a protective chant together, such as, "Boogeyman, we banish you. You have no power here. Leave this place and never return."
    - As you chant, move clockwise around the room, using the candles or flashlights to drive the Boogeyman out.
    - Seal the room by placing salt at each doorway and window, completing the ritual with a final, "This space is now protected."

The Great Boogey Banishment uses collective power to ensure the Boogeyman is permanently removed from your life.

9. Astral Battle – Battling the Boogeyman in His Dimension

The **Astral Battle** takes place in the Boogeyman's dimension. By learning to astrally project, you can enter his world and fight him on his own turf.

- **How to Engage in an Astral Battle**:
    - Practice meditation until you can project your consciousness into the astral plane.
    - Once in the astral realm, seek out the Boogeyman's lair. You will recognize it by the dark, eerie atmosphere.
    - Equip yourself mentally with light-based weapons and protective armor, and confront the Boogeyman directly.
    - Say, "I've come to defeat you in your world, Boogeyman. I will end your terror."

Astral Battles require advanced meditation skills but allow you to directly weaken the Boogeyman by fighting him in his own dimension.

10. Time Loop Escape – Breaking Free of a Boogeyman-Induced Time Loop

Sometimes, the Boogeyman traps his victims in **Time Loops**, forcing them to repeat the same events over and over. This challenge teaches you how to break free.

- **How to Escape a Time Loop**:
  - Recognize the signs of a time loop, such as repeating events or strange occurrences.
  - Find a way to disrupt the loop, such as changing your actions or saying something unexpected to break the pattern.
  - Say, "I recognize this loop, Boogeyman, and I will not be trapped. I break free from your cycle."

Breaking free from a time loop requires quick thinking and the ability to disrupt the Boogeyman's control over time.

11. Dual Dimension Strategy – Fighting in Two Worlds at Once

The **Dual Dimension Strategy** involves learning how to fight the Boogeyman in both the real world and his dimension simultaneously. This requires mental dexterity and quick decision-making.

- **How to Use the Dual Dimension Strategy**:
  - Train your mind to remain present in the real world while also projecting part of your consciousness into the Boogeyman's dimension.
  - Fight the Boogeyman on both fronts, using physical defenses in the real world and mental or astral defenses in his realm.
  - Say, "I am here in both worlds, and I defeat you in both places."

This advanced strategy allows you to weaken the Boogeyman on multiple fronts, ensuring he has no escape.

12. Boogeyman-Slaying Artifacts – Collecting Rare Items to Defeat the Boogeyman

Boogeyman-Slaying Artifacts are rare and powerful items that can be collected to permanently defeat the Boogeyman. These artifacts may be found in mystical shops, inherited, or created using special materials.

- **How to Find or Create Boogeyman-Slaying Artifacts**:
  - Seek out items made of iron, silver, or other materials known to repel dark creatures. Ancient weapons, enchanted stones, or special charms can all act as artifacts.
  - Keep the artifact close when facing the Boogeyman, using it to weaken or defeat him.
  - Say, "With this artifact, I destroy you, Boogeyman. You have no power over me."

Boogeyman-Slaying Artifacts are valuable tools that give you a tangible advantage in your battle.

13. Nightmare Infiltration – Entering the Boogeyman's Nightmares

Nightmare Infiltration involves entering the Boogeyman's own nightmares to weaken him from within. By confronting him in his own fears, you gain control over him.

- **How to Infiltrate the Boogeyman's Nightmares**:

- Before bed, visualize yourself entering the Boogeyman's mind. Picture his worst fears and nightmares.
- Confront him in this vulnerable state, turning his fears against him.
- Say, "I have entered your nightmares, Boogeyman. You cannot escape me here."

Infiltrating the Boogeyman's nightmares is a daring tactic that gives you a psychological advantage.

14. Ultimate Boogey Light – Eradicating All Traces of the Boogeyman

The **Ultimate Boogey Light** is a powerful source of light that can eradicate all traces of the Boogeyman from your home. This light is created by combining all your light-based tools into one ultimate defense.

- **How to Create the Ultimate Boogey Light**:
  - Gather every light-based defense you have: nightlights, flashlights, glowsticks, and more.
  - Focus their energy into a single source, imagining the light growing stronger and brighter until it fills the entire room.
  - Say, "With this ultimate light, I destroy every trace of you, Boogeyman. You are no more."

The Ultimate Boogey Light is the final solution for eliminating the Boogeyman once and for all.

15. The Final Showdown – Preparing for the Ultimate Confrontation

The **Final Showdown** is the ultimate confrontation between you and the Boogeyman. Armed with every defense technique you've learned throughout the book, you are fully prepared to face him one last time.

- **How to Prepare for the Final Showdown**:
  - Review all the defenses you've mastered, from light-based strategies to mental tactics and advanced traps.
  - Gather any protective items, artifacts, or tools you have and position them strategically around the room.
  - Stand tall and say, "Boogeyman, this is our final battle. I am ready, and I will win."

The Final Showdown is the culmination of everything you've learned, where you face the Boogeyman with full confidence and mastery of your defenses.

Conclusion: Special Boogeyman Busting Challenges – For the Brave and Fearless

These advanced techniques push the limits of what it means to defend yourself from the Boogeyman. From mental duels to astral battles, these challenges are for those who have faced the Boogeyman and come out stronger. Whether you choose to confront the Boogeyman in total darkness or engage him in a final showdown, these methods will empower you to overcome your fears and emerge victorious in your fight against the Boogeyman.

Part 6: The Boogeyman's Return

Chapter 27: When the Boogeyman Comes Back – Dealing with a Resurgent Threat

Defeating the Boogeyman is a great victory, but sometimes the darkness returns, and so does the Boogeyman. Whether it's the same Boogeyman you've fought before or a new incarnation, knowing how to handle a returning Boogeyman is crucial. **When the Boogeyman Comes Back** offers strategies for identifying the warning signs, reinforcing your defenses, and using new techniques to confront and defeat the Boogeyman again. This chapter also explores why the Boogeyman might return and how to prevent future encounters.

1. Understanding Why the Boogeyman Returns – Unfinished Business

One of the most important questions to ask when the Boogeyman returns is **why**. Often, a defeated Boogeyman reappears because the fear or vulnerability that originally attracted him has resurfaced. Sometimes, there may be unfinished business that wasn't fully resolved in your initial battle.

- **Common Reasons for the Boogeyman's Return**:
  - **Lingering Fear**: If your fear of the Boogeyman has returned or grown stronger, he may sense it and come back to feed on that fear.
  - **New Stress or Changes**: Life changes, such as moving to a new home, starting a new school, or dealing with personal challenges, can reignite the Boogeyman's interest.
  - **New Vulnerabilities**: A new source of fear or insecurity may have opened the door for the Boogeyman to reappear.
  - **Strengthened Boogeyman**: In rare cases, the Boogeyman may have learned from his previous defeat and returned stronger, hoping to regain control.

Understanding why the Boogeyman has come back is the first step in effectively dealing with him again.

2. Recognizing the Warning Signs – Knowing When the Boogeyman is Near

Before the Boogeyman fully reveals himself, he often leaves behind subtle **warning signs** that signal his return. Being able to recognize these signs early will allow you to take action before the situation escalates.

- **Common Warning Signs of a Returning Boogeyman**:
  - **Shadows Seem Thicker**: Shadows in your room may seem darker or more oppressive than usual, even when you turn on lights.
  - **Sudden Chills**: The temperature in your room may drop unexpectedly, especially around your bed or closet.
  - **Strange Noises**: Creaks, whispers, or unexplained sounds in the night may signal the Boogeyman's return.
  - **Unsettling Dreams**: Recurring nightmares about the Boogeyman or dark figures could indicate that he's working his way back into your life.
  - **Sense of Dread**: A general feeling of unease or fear, even during the day, might suggest that the Boogeyman is lurking nearby.

By staying alert to these warning signs, you can prepare your defenses before the Boogeyman has a chance to fully manifest.

3. Reinforcing Your Defenses – Strengthening Your Protection

Once you recognize the signs that the Boogeyman has returned, it's time to **reinforce your defenses**. The key to successfully fending him off again lies in adapting and strengthening the protective strategies you've used before.

- **How to Reinforce Your Defenses**:
  - **Double the Light**: If you've used light to defeat the Boogeyman before, consider adding more light sources. Use stronger flashlights, additional nightlights, or even LED strips to eliminate any potential hiding places.
  - **Refresh Protective Symbols**: If you've drawn protective symbols, such as chalk circles or rune drawings, redraw them with fresh energy. Make sure the lines are unbroken and the symbols are clearly visible.
  - **Reapply Protective Oils**: Oils like lavender or cedarwood may have weakened over time. Reapply them around windows, doors, and bedframes to maintain their protective properties.
  - **Reset Traps**: Review any Boogeyman traps you've set. Reset them or create new ones, combining techniques like string traps, sound alarms, and mirror shields to catch the Boogeyman off guard.
  - **Call for Reinforcements**: Consider involving others in your defense. Bring in a sibling, friend, or parent to help strengthen your strategies. You can also perform family rituals or partner patrols to ensure all areas of the room are protected.

Reinforcing your defenses ensures that the Boogeyman won't catch you off guard if he attempts to return.

4. Facing the Boogeyman Again – Using Past Lessons to Win

If the Boogeyman does manage to return despite your defenses, you'll need to face him directly again. Fortunately, you've already defeated him once, which gives you a valuable advantage: **experience**. Use the lessons you've learned from your previous encounter to face him with confidence and determination.

- **How to Confront a Returning Boogeyman**:
    - **Stay Calm and Confident**: The Boogeyman thrives on fear, so it's essential to stay calm. Remind yourself that you've faced him before and know how to win.
    - **Speak with Authority**: Address the Boogeyman directly, using assertive language like, "I've beaten you before, Boogeyman, and I'll do it again. You have no power over me."
    - **Use Improved Defenses**: If you successfully used a certain tactic last time—such as light or sound-based defenses—rely on that technique again, but with added strength or intensity.
    - **Adopt New Strategies**: If the Boogeyman seems stronger or more resistant this time, it's time to try new strategies. Use advanced methods from earlier chapters, such as the Ultimate Light Bomb or Boogeyman Disruptor Guns, to catch him off guard.

Facing the Boogeyman again isn't about starting from scratch—it's about using everything you've learned to win faster and with greater confidence.

5. Creating Long-Term Protections – Keeping the Boogeyman from Returning

Once you've defeated the Boogeyman a second time, it's important to put long-term protections in place to **prevent him from coming back** in the future. By creating a stronger, more permanent barrier, you can live in peace knowing the Boogeyman won't return.

- **Long-Term Protection Techniques**:
    - **Permanent Protective Symbols**: Instead of using temporary chalk or paper symbols, consider creating more permanent protection. For example, you can paint protective runes on wooden objects or carve symbols into a special talisman that stays near your bed.
    - **Crystals and Amulets**: Place protective crystals, such as amethyst or black tourmaline, around your room to absorb negative energy and prevent the Boogeyman from re-entering. Carrying a small amulet can also keep you protected at all times.
    - **Blessings and Rituals**: Perform a long-term protection ritual, such as the Great Boogey Banishment or a family defense ritual, to seal off your home and room from future attacks.
    - **Boogeyman Totems**: Create or find a powerful Boogeyman totem that can serve as a guardian. Place it in your room or carry it with you to keep dark spirits at bay.
    - **Daily Affirmations**: Repeat daily affirmations such as, "I am safe. I am strong. No Boogeyman can enter my space," to reinforce your mental defenses and prevent fear from taking root again.

Long-term protections ensure that the Boogeyman doesn't get a chance to return, giving you peace of mind and a safe, secure environment.

6. Learning to Let Go of Fear – Overcoming the Root Cause of the Boogeyman's Power

In many cases, the Boogeyman's return is tied to unresolved fear. Learning to confront and **let go of that fear** is one of the most powerful ways to stop the Boogeyman from coming back. When you release fear, you also release the Boogeyman's hold over you.

- **How to Let Go of Fear**:
  - **Acknowledge Your Fear**: It's okay to admit that you're afraid. Recognizing your fear is the first step to letting it go.
  - **Break Fear into Parts**: Identify what exactly scares you about the Boogeyman. Is it the darkness, the unknown, or something specific he represents? By breaking fear into smaller parts, it becomes less overwhelming.
  - **Use Positive Affirmations**: Replace fear-based thoughts with positive affirmations like, "I am brave. I am in control. Nothing can harm me."
  - **Practice Visualization**: Visualize yourself as powerful, protected, and surrounded by light. Picture the Boogeyman shrinking and disappearing as your strength grows.
  - **Seek Support**: Don't hesitate to seek support from others. Talk to a trusted friend, family member, or mentor who can help you work through any lingering fears.

By addressing the root cause of your fear, you weaken the Boogeyman's ability to return and regain control of your mind.

7. Seeking Professional Help – When the Boogeyman Becomes Persistent

In rare cases, the Boogeyman may persist despite your best efforts to keep him away. If this happens, it's okay to **seek outside help**. A professional, such as a counselor, therapist, or spiritual guide, can help you navigate persistent fears and find deeper solutions.

- **When to Seek Help**:
    - If the Boogeyman returns repeatedly, despite using multiple defenses.
    - If fear of the Boogeyman begins to interfere with daily life, sleep, or mental well-being.
    - If you feel overwhelmed or unable to cope with the fear on your own.

Professionals can offer strategies and insights to help you regain control, addressing any underlying fears that might be keeping the Boogeyman alive.

Conclusion: When the Boogeyman Comes Back – Taking Control of the Situation

When the Boogeyman returns, it can feel frustrating or even terrifying, but you're not powerless. By recognizing the warning signs, reinforcing your defenses, and applying new techniques, you can confront the Boogeyman with confidence. Each encounter with the Boogeyman makes you stronger and more prepared. Whether through light-based methods, mental defenses, or long-term protective measures, you'll be able to keep the Boogeyman from returning again. And, most importantly, by learning to let go of fear, you'll find that the Boogeyman loses his power over you completely, allowing you to live in peace, free from his influence.

Chapter 28: Advanced Boogeyman Tactics – Fighting Smarter Against Evolving Threats

As you've learned throughout this book, the Boogeyman is not a static force. He can adapt, change, and even evolve, becoming more dangerous and difficult to defeat. When faced with an evolving Boogeyman, you need to go beyond basic defenses and employ **Advanced Boogeyman Tactics**. This chapter focuses on how to fight smarter, not harder, using a combination of strategy, technology, creativity, and psychological warfare to outwit even the most cunning Boogeyman.

1. Recognizing an Evolving Boogeyman – When the Rules Change

An **evolving Boogeyman** is one who has learned from your past encounters and adapted to become stronger, more elusive, or more terrifying. Recognizing the signs that your Boogeyman is evolving is the first step to employing more advanced tactics.

- **Signs of an Evolving Boogeyman**:
  - **Immunity to Previous Defenses**: The Boogeyman may no longer be affected by simple light or sound defenses that once worked.
  - **Increased Aggressiveness**: He might appear more frequently or with greater intensity, pushing your defenses to their limits.
  - **New Powers or Tricks**: An evolving Boogeyman might develop new abilities, such as creating illusions, manipulating shadows, or even interfering with technology.
  - **Adaptive Behavior**: The Boogeyman may start avoiding your traps, becoming smarter and more strategic in his attacks.

If you notice any of these signs, it's time to change your approach and start thinking strategically.

2. Tactical Observation – Learning the Boogeyman's Patterns

Before you can defeat an evolved Boogeyman, you need to **observe his behavior** closely. By understanding his patterns, you'll gain insight into his weaknesses and the best times to strike.

- **How to Observe the Boogeyman's Behavior**:
  - Keep a **Boogeyman Journal**: Write down each time you sense the Boogeyman's presence, including the time of day, the location, and any specific actions he takes. Over time, you'll notice patterns in his behavior.
  - Use **Technology to Monitor**: Set up cameras or motion sensors to detect the Boogeyman's movements. If he can manipulate shadows, use thermal imaging or night vision to track his presence.
  - Analyze **His Weak Spots**: Does the Boogeyman avoid certain areas of the room? Does he react to certain objects or sounds? Identify the things that make him hesitate or retreat.
  - Pay Attention to **Timing**: Does the Boogeyman appear at the same time every night? Knowing when he's most likely to strike allows you to be prepared in advance.

By learning his behavior, you can anticipate the Boogeyman's next move and set up countermeasures before he has a chance to act.

3. Psychological Warfare – Turning the Boogeyman's Fear Against Him

While the Boogeyman feeds on fear, he is not immune to it himself. **Psychological warfare** involves using the Boogeyman's own tactics against him, making him doubt his power and fear your strength.

- **How to Use Psychological Warfare Against the Boogeyman**:
    - **Reverse the Fear Dynamic**: When the Boogeyman appears, instead of reacting with fear, laugh or mock him. Say things like, "You're not scary, Boogeyman. You're just a shadow. You don't frighten me!" This will undermine his confidence.
    - **Use His Name**: If you've discovered the Boogeyman's name through research or past encounters, saying it aloud reduces his power. Names have power in the realm of fear, and using his name puts you in control.
    - **Create Fear for the Boogeyman**: Tell the Boogeyman that you've prepared a new defense that he's never faced before, even if you haven't. Bluffing can make him hesitate. Say, "Boogeyman, I've got something new for you tonight. You won't like it."
    - **Mirror His Tactics**: If the Boogeyman creates illusions or manipulates shadows, mentally reflect those tricks back at him. Picture the Boogeyman trapped in a loop of his own illusions, unable to distinguish what's real.

Psychological warfare is about shifting the balance of power, making the Boogeyman fear you rather than the other way around.

4. Adapting Your Defenses – Evolving with the Boogeyman

As the Boogeyman evolves, so must your defenses. **Adapting your defenses** means combining old methods with new ones, experimenting with different approaches, and using tools in creative ways.

- **How to Adapt Your Defenses**:
    - **Upgrade Your Light Sources**: If regular nightlights and flashlights aren't enough anymore, consider using stronger light sources like **LED floodlights** or **UV light**. UV light can destabilize the Boogeyman's form by breaking down his energy.
    - **Multi-Layered Defenses**: Combine multiple types of defenses. For example, set up a chalk circle around your bed, place crystals at the corners of the room, and position a mirror at the entrance. Each layer of defense adds to the overall protection.
    - **Mobile Defenses**: Create mobile defense tools like **light wands** or **sonic blasters** that you can carry with you. These allow you to respond to the Boogeyman's movements no matter where he appears.
    - **Boogeyman-Specific Traps**: If the Boogeyman has developed new powers, create traps tailored to his abilities. For example, if he manipulates shadows, use reflective surfaces like mirrors or glass to bounce light and disrupt his movements.

By constantly evolving your defenses, you ensure that the Boogeyman can't gain the upper hand.

5. Strategic Retreats – Knowing When to Fall Back

While it's important to stand your ground, sometimes the best tactic is a **strategic retreat**. This doesn't mean surrendering—it means buying time to prepare for a more effective counterattack.

- **When to Use a Strategic Retreat**:
    - If the Boogeyman is overwhelming your defenses or if he's revealed new powers you weren't expecting, retreat to a safer space to reassess the situation.
    - Move to a room with more natural light or fewer shadows, where the Boogeyman has fewer places to hide.
    - Call in reinforcements, such as family members, or use advanced tech to gather more data about the Boogeyman's new abilities while you regroup.

A strategic retreat is about being smart and not wasting energy on a losing battle. Use the time to gather strength and plan a new strategy.

6. The Power of Distraction – Redirecting the Boogeyman's Attention

One of the most effective advanced tactics is using **distractions** to redirect the Boogeyman's attention. This gives you time to prepare your next move or attack when he's not expecting it.

- **How to Use Distraction Tactics**:
    - **Holographic Decoys**: Use **holographic images** or reflective objects to create the illusion of movement in another part of the room. The Boogeyman may focus on the decoy, allowing you to set a trap.
    - **Sound-Based Distractions**: Play sounds that confuse or disorient the Boogeyman. This could be as simple as a rhythmic clap or as advanced as using a **Tibetan singing bowl** to disrupt his energy.
    - **Light Flashes**: Use strobe lights or intermittent bursts of light to confuse the Boogeyman's senses. The sudden shifts in brightness will make it harder for him to focus.
    - **Move Between Spaces**: If you have multiple safe spaces set up in your home, move between them quickly. This forces the Boogeyman to follow you, stretching his presence thin and making him easier to trap.

Distraction tactics are all about keeping the Boogeyman off balance, giving you more control over the encounter.

7. Advanced Boogeyman Technologies – High-Tech Defenses

As the Boogeyman becomes more advanced, you can use **high-tech defenses** to stay ahead. These technologies are designed to neutralize or contain the Boogeyman in ways that traditional methods can't.

- **Cutting-Edge Tools for Advanced Boogeyman Defense**:
    - **Boogeyman Neural Scramblers**: These devices emit low-frequency waves that scramble the Boogeyman's neural energy, making it impossible for him to concentrate or manifest.
    - **Quantum Cages**: High-tech cages that trap the Boogeyman in multiple dimensions, preventing him from escaping no matter how strong he becomes.
    - **Temporal Freezers**: Devices that can temporarily freeze time in a specific area, trapping the Boogeyman in place and giving you time to prepare your attack.
    - **Energy Drainers**: Machines that drain the Boogeyman's dark energy, weakening him to the point where he can no longer manifest.

These advanced tools offer a high-tech edge, allowing you to combat the Boogeyman even as he evolves and becomes more dangerous.

8. Collaboration with Others – Joining Forces

Sometimes the best tactic is to **join forces** with others. The Boogeyman might become too strong for one person to handle alone, but a team of defenders can overwhelm him.

- **How to Collaborate for Maximum Defense**:
    - **Boogeyman Watch Teams**: Form a team with friends or family members to take turns keeping watch at night. With more eyes on the lookout, the Boogeyman has fewer opportunities to strike.
    - **Synchronized Defenses**: Coordinate your defenses with others, timing your traps and light-based strategies to create a multi-pronged attack that overwhelms the Boogeyman.
    - **Shared Knowledge**: Exchange information about the Boogeyman's new powers or tactics with others who have faced him. Learning from each other's experiences strengthens your defenses.

Collaboration amplifies your strength, making it harder for the Boogeyman to adapt or find new ways to attack.

9. The Element of Surprise – Outthinking the Boogeyman

The **element of surprise** is one of the most powerful tactics you can use. The Boogeyman may expect certain defenses based on your past encounters, but if you surprise him with new, unexpected methods, you'll catch him off guard.

- **How to Use the Element of Surprise**:
  - **Switch Up Your Routine**: If you've been using the same defenses every night, change things up. Move your light sources to different areas, set traps in new places, or introduce a completely new defense, such as sound or scent-based barriers.
  - **Deploy a Sudden Attack**: Don't always wait for the Boogeyman to make the first move. Preemptively shine a flashlight into the dark corners where he usually hides or activate a Boogeyman Scrambler before he fully manifests.
  - **Use Decoys**: Set up objects or devices that distract the Boogeyman, such as a decoy figure under the bed or a glowing crystal that draws his attention. While he focuses on the decoy, you can prepare your next attack.

Surprising the Boogeyman keeps him off balance and prevents him from adapting to your defenses.

Conclusion: Advanced Boogeyman Tactics – Outsmarting and Overcoming Evolving Threats

As the Boogeyman evolves and becomes more dangerous, you must adapt your tactics and outthink him at every turn. By learning his patterns, using psychological warfare, employing high-tech defenses, and collaborating with others, you can stay one step ahead. The key to defeating an evolving Boogeyman is to fight smarter, not harder. With these **Advanced Boogeyman Tactics**, you'll be fully equipped to take on even the most cunning version of the Boogeyman, ensuring that no matter how he changes, you will always emerge victorious.

Part 7: Recipes for Boogeyman Baits

Chapter 29: How to Lure a Boogeyman – Using Bait for Boogeyman Traps

One of the most effective strategies for dealing with the Boogeyman is turning the tables and luring him into your traps. By using bait, you can draw the Boogeyman out of hiding and into a position where you can either trap or neutralize him. **How to Lure a Boogeyman** explores the art of setting up bait and using psychological tricks to make the Boogeyman come to you, rather than waiting for him to strike. This chapter introduces a variety of baiting techniques, traps, and strategies designed to make your defenses more proactive and effective.

1. Understanding the Boogeyman's Weaknesses – What Attracts Him?

Before you can successfully lure the Boogeyman, it's essential to understand what **attracts him**. The Boogeyman feeds on fear and negative emotions, but there are other things that may also draw him in, depending on his nature. Identifying what lures your specific Boogeyman is the first step to setting an effective trap.

- **Common Triggers for the Boogeyman**:
    - **Fear and Anxiety**: The Boogeyman is attracted to emotional energy, especially fear, insecurity, or feelings of helplessness.
    - **Dark Spaces**: Shadows, closets, and under-the-bed areas naturally draw the Boogeyman, as these are his preferred hiding spots.
    - **Isolation**: The Boogeyman often targets individuals who feel isolated, alone, or vulnerable.
    - **Toys or Familiar Objects**: Some Boogeymen are attracted to specific items in a child's room, such as a favorite toy, blanket, or stuffed animal, which may hold sentimental energy.

By identifying what attracts your Boogeyman, you can use these elements to create effective bait that lures him out of hiding.

2. Using Emotional Bait – Luring the Boogeyman with Fear and Vulnerability

One of the most powerful forms of bait is **emotional energy**, specifically fear. The Boogeyman thrives on fear, so creating a situation that mimics fear can draw him in.

- **How to Set Emotional Bait**:
    - **Pretend Vulnerability**: Act as if you are afraid, even if you aren't. The Boogeyman senses vulnerability, so pretending to be scared, hiding under the blankets, or sitting in the dark may attract him.
    - **Fake Nightmares**: Tell a story of a terrifying nightmare or create a fake diary entry about a scary encounter with the Boogeyman. Leave it in a visible spot where the Boogeyman can "find" it, luring him into your trap.
    - **Imitate Fearful Situations**: Create the illusion of being scared by leaving the lights off or making it appear as though you've left your defenses down, all while being fully prepared.

Important Note: It's crucial to only *pretend* to be vulnerable. Always ensure your defenses are ready before setting emotional bait to avoid falling into your own trap.

3. Object-Based Bait – Using Familiar Items to Lure the Boogeyman

The Boogeyman is often drawn to **objects** with emotional energy or personal significance. Using these items as bait can help you lure him out.

- **How to Use Object-Based Bait**:
    - **Toys and Blankets**: Place a favorite stuffed animal, doll, or blanket in an open, dark space—such as the middle of the room or at the edge of the bed—where the Boogeyman is likely to approach.
    - **Old Clothing**: Items like old jackets, shoes, or hats, which carry your scent or emotional connection, can also be used as bait. Leave these items near the closet or under the bed.
    - **Open Closets or Drawers**: Leave a closet door slightly ajar, or pull open a drawer to invite the Boogeyman's curiosity. These dark, partially open spaces are natural lures for him.

When using object-based bait, make sure the items are placed strategically, near areas where you've set traps or defenses.

4. Light and Shadow Manipulation – Using Darkness as a Lure

While light is often used to repel the Boogeyman, you can manipulate **darkness and shadows** to lure him out. The Boogeyman thrives in the dark, so setting up areas of shadow can draw him toward your traps.

- **How to Manipulate Light and Shadows as Bait**:
    - **Create Pockets of Darkness**: Dim the lights in certain parts of the room, especially near a closet, under the bed, or in a corner. These dark zones will attract the Boogeyman's attention, making him feel safe enough to approach.
    - **Use Reflective Surfaces**: Place mirrors or shiny objects around the dark areas to confuse the Boogeyman. He'll be drawn to the dark space but distracted by the reflections, making it easier to trap him.
    - **Switch Between Light and Dark**: Flick the lights off for a moment, then back on. The sudden change will attract the Boogeyman, giving you the chance to catch him off guard.

Using darkness as a lure allows you to take advantage of the Boogeyman's comfort zone, drawing him into a space where you have the upper hand.

5. Scent-Based Bait – Using Smells to Attract the Boogeyman

Just like certain creatures are drawn to specific smells, the Boogeyman can also be lured by **scents** that either represent fear or are linked to human presence. Setting up scent-based bait can draw him into your trap.

- **How to Use Scent-Based Bait**:
    - **Fear Scents**: Fear releases certain pheromones that can attract the Boogeyman. You can simulate this effect by placing a few drops of **scented oils** associated with fear, such as myrrh or dark musk, in areas where the Boogeyman is likely to hide.
    - **Human Scents**: The smell of skin oils, worn clothing, or even sweat can attract the Boogeyman. Leave a piece of recently worn clothing in a strategic location to lure him in.
    - **Contradictory Scents**: Alternatively, use pleasant scents like lavender or cedar to confuse the Boogeyman. He may be drawn in by curiosity, only to be caught in your trap.

Scent-based bait is subtle but effective, especially when paired with other forms of bait, such as light manipulation or emotional vulnerability.

6. Sound-Based Bait – Using Noise to Draw the Boogeyman

Sound is another powerful tool to attract the Boogeyman. Whether it's soft whispers, creaks, or sudden loud noises, certain sounds will pique the Boogeyman's interest and draw him toward your traps.

- **How to Set Sound-Based Bait**:
  - **Soft Whispers or Calls**: Record or simulate the sound of quiet whispers, like someone talking in their sleep or muttering in fear. These noises will attract the Boogeyman's attention, pulling him closer.
  - **Creaking Doors or Floors**: Create noises that mimic someone moving in the dark—creaky floorboards, a door opening slowly, or even the sound of footsteps. The Boogeyman will be drawn to the idea of someone being alone or vulnerable.
  - **Sudden Noises**: Use a sound that starts suddenly, like a loud thud or knock, to catch the Boogeyman off guard and lure him into investigating the source.

Sound-based bait is especially effective when paired with dark spaces or object-based bait, as it simulates the environment where the Boogeyman feels most comfortable.

7. Setting the Trap – Using Bait to Lure the Boogeyman into a Snare

Once you've chosen your bait, the next step is to set up a **trap** that will capture the Boogeyman when he approaches. Depending on the type of Boogeyman you're dealing with, the trap can range from simple to complex.

- **Basic Trap Setup**:
    - **Mirror Traps**: Place mirrors around the bait so that when the Boogeyman approaches, his reflection will be caught, weakening his form. You can then use light or sound to further disorient him.
    - **Light Traps**: Set up a circle of glowsticks, flashlights, or candles around the bait. When the Boogeyman steps into the circle, activate the lights all at once, trapping him in the center.
    - **Chalk or Salt Circles**: Draw a protective circle of chalk or salt around the bait. When the Boogeyman approaches, he will be unable to leave the circle, giving you time to act.
- **Advanced Trap Setup**:
    - **Energy Fields**: If you have access to high-tech tools, use **electromagnetic shields** or **quantum cages** to trap the Boogeyman once he steps into the bait zone.
    - **Sound and Light Combination**: Combine strobe lights with sudden loud noises to disorient the Boogeyman once he takes the bait. The lights will confuse his senses, while the noise will keep him off balance.
    - **Timed Traps**: Set traps that trigger after the Boogeyman has interacted with the bait, such as a door slamming shut or a flash of light from an unexpected direction. These traps work well in confined spaces like closets or under the bed.

Once the Boogeyman is trapped, you can neutralize him using light, sound, or other advanced methods covered earlier in the book.

8. Combining Multiple Baits – Making the Trap Irresistible

For the most effective results, it's best to **combine different types of bait** to make the trap irresistible. The more senses you engage, the more likely the Boogeyman is to fall into your trap.

- **How to Combine Baits**:
    - Use **emotional bait** by creating an atmosphere of vulnerability, combined with **sound-based bait** like soft whispers.
    - Set **object-based bait** (such as a favorite toy) in a **pocket of darkness**, manipulating light and shadow to make the area appear inviting to the Boogeyman.
    - Add a **scent-based lure** by placing a familiar scent, like worn clothing, near the bait, while using **sound cues** like creaking floorboards to draw him closer.

By engaging multiple senses—fear, sight, sound, and scent—you make the trap more convincing and more likely to attract the Boogeyman.

9. Using the Boogeyman's Curiosity Against Him

The Boogeyman is a creature of **curiosity**. He thrives on exploring dark places, scaring those who are vulnerable, and feeding on fear. By exploiting his natural curiosity, you can draw him directly into your trap.

- **How to Exploit the Boogeyman's Curiosity**:
    - **Leave a Journal or Diary**: Write a fake journal entry detailing your fears or plans to protect yourself, then leave it out where the Boogeyman will "find" it. His curiosity will draw him toward the trap.
    - **Create False Defenses**: Make it appear as though you've set weak or ineffective defenses, leaving gaps or vulnerabilities that invite the Boogeyman to investigate. When he approaches, your real trap will activate.
    - **Simulate Activity**: Make it seem like someone is moving in the dark by using sound cues or objects that mimic human activity. The Boogeyman's curiosity will lead him to investigate, giving you the upper hand.

Curiosity can be one of the Boogeyman's biggest weaknesses, making him more susceptible to well-set traps.

Conclusion: How to Lure a Boogeyman – Setting the Perfect Trap

Luring the Boogeyman into a trap requires a combination of patience, strategy, and an understanding of what draws him in. By using emotional bait, manipulating light and shadows, and exploiting his natural curiosity, you can create an irresistible setup that forces the Boogeyman into your trap. Whether you use simple toys or advanced high-tech defenses, the key is to think like the Boogeyman and turn his instincts against him. With these **baiting techniques**, you'll no longer wait for the Boogeyman to strike—you'll take the fight to him, ensuring that he's caught in a snare of your making.

Chapter 30: Recipe for Boogie Goo – A Sticky Trap for Boogeymen

If you're looking for a fun and creative way to trap the Boogeyman, there's nothing quite like **Boogie Goo**—a sticky, slimy substance that you can make at home to catch and contain the Boogeyman in his tracks. This chapter will teach you how to create your very own Boogie Goo using simple ingredients, making it a great activity for kids and adults to do together. Boogie Goo is not only a playful craft, but it's also an effective Boogeyman trap, helping you defend your space from any sneaky creatures lurking in the shadows.

What is Boogie Goo?

Boogie Goo is a homemade, sticky slime designed to trap Boogeymen. When placed around key areas of your room—like under the bed, near the closet, or around windows—Boogie Goo can stop the Boogeyman in his tracks. It's incredibly sticky, so once the Boogeyman steps in it, he'll be stuck long enough for you to reinforce your defenses or scare him away. Best of all, making Boogie Goo is fun, simple, and safe, with ingredients that you can find in your kitchen or at a craft store.

Ingredients for Boogie Goo

Here's what you'll need to make your very own **Boogie Goo**:

- **1 cup of white school glue** (such as Elmer's Glue) – The base for your Boogie Goo, this gives it the perfect sticky texture.
- **½ cup of warm water** – To thin out the glue and help it mix smoothly.
- **1 teaspoon of baking soda** – This adds structure and thickness to the goo.
- **2 tablespoons of contact lens solution** – The magical ingredient that activates the goo, making it stretchy and sticky.
- **Optional: Food coloring** – Add a drop or two of green or purple food coloring to give your Boogie Goo that signature "monster" look.
- **Optional: Glitter or glow-in-the-dark powder** – For extra fun, you can add glitter or glow-in-the-dark powder to make your Boogie Goo even more magical and appealing to Boogeymen.

How to Make Boogie Goo – Step-by-Step Instructions

Follow these easy steps to make your own Boogie Goo. It's a fun project for families, and kids will love being part of the process!

Step 1: Prepare Your Work Area

Before you start, set up your workspace. You'll want to cover your table with newspaper or a plastic sheet to make cleanup easier. Make sure you have all your ingredients and mixing tools ready, including a bowl, spoon, and measuring cups.

Step 2: Mix the Glue and Water

In a large bowl, pour **1 cup of white school glue**. Slowly add **½ cup of warm water** to the glue, stirring continuously. This will help thin out the glue and make it easier to mix. Stir until the glue and water are fully combined and smooth.

Step 3: Add Color and Fun

If you want your Boogie Goo to look extra spooky, now's the time to add your **food coloring** and any fun extras like **glitter** or **glow-in-the-dark powder**. Just add a few drops of food coloring—green, purple, or even orange work well—and mix it in until the color is evenly distributed.

For a glow-in-the-dark effect, sprinkle in a small amount of glow powder and stir. If you're using glitter, add it in and mix thoroughly to give your Boogie Goo a magical, sparkly look.

Step 4: Add the Baking Soda

Next, add **1 teaspoon of baking soda** to the mixture. Baking soda helps thicken the Boogie Goo and gives it more structure. Stir well until the baking soda is fully incorporated into the glue mixture. You'll start to notice the mixture becoming slightly thicker.

Step 5: Add the Contact Lens Solution

Now comes the fun part—activating the Boogie Goo! Slowly add **2 tablespoons of contact lens solution** while stirring. As you mix, you'll see the glue start to come together and form a slime-like consistency. Keep stirring until the goo pulls away from the sides of the bowl and becomes stretchy and sticky.

If the Boogie Goo is too sticky, you can add a tiny bit more contact lens solution (about ½ teaspoon at a time), but be careful not to add too much, or your goo will become too rubbery.

Step 6: Knead the Boogie Goo

Once the Boogie Goo has formed, take it out of the bowl and start **kneading** it with your hands. This helps fully combine the ingredients and makes the goo extra stretchy and fun to play with. Knead for about 2-3 minutes until the texture is just right—sticky enough to trap a Boogeyman, but stretchy enough to handle easily.

How to Use Boogie Goo to Trap the Boogeyman

Now that you've made your Boogie Goo, it's time to use it as a Boogeyman trap! Here are a few ways to set your goo and catch the Boogeyman:

1. Under-the-Bed Goo Trap

The Boogeyman loves hiding under the bed, so one of the best places to lay your Boogie Goo is right along the edges of the bed. Roll the goo into long, sticky strips and press it down on the floor where the Boogeyman might try to sneak out. When he steps into the goo, he'll get stuck, giving you time to turn on the lights or activate another defense!

2. Closet Door Goo Barrier

If the Boogeyman likes to hide in the closet, you can create a **goo barrier** along the bottom of the closet door. Roll your Boogie Goo into a snake-like shape and place it across the floor where the closet door meets the ground. This sticky barrier will trap the Boogeyman as soon as he tries to slink out of the closet, keeping him contained.

3. Window Sill Goo Defense

Sometimes, the Boogeyman might try to enter through a dark window. To prevent this, spread Boogie Goo along the window sill or frame. Any attempt to crawl in will leave the Boogeyman stuck in a web of goo. Plus, if you've added glow-in-the-dark powder, the goo will light up at night, helping you spot any Boogeyman activity.

4. Goo Circle Trap

Create a **circle of Boogie Goo** around key areas of your room, like your bed, closet, or even a favorite stuffed animal. This circle acts as a protective barrier—the Boogeyman won't be able to cross it without getting stuck. To make this even more fun, you can shape the goo into spirals, stars, or other designs!

How to Store Your Boogie Goo

When you're not using your Boogie Goo to trap the Boogeyman, make sure you store it properly so it stays fresh and sticky.

- **Air-Tight Container**: Place the Boogie Goo in an air-tight container or resealable plastic bag to keep it from drying out.
- **Reactivating the Goo**: If the goo starts to get a little stiff, simply add a few drops of contact lens solution and knead it again to bring it back to life.

Your Boogie Goo should stay fresh for several weeks if stored properly, making it a reusable tool for multiple Boogeyman encounters!

Safety Tips for Boogie Goo

Boogie Goo is safe to handle and play with, but here are a few tips to ensure everyone stays safe and has fun:

- **Avoid Contact with Eyes**: While Boogie Goo is non-toxic, avoid getting it in your eyes. If it does, rinse thoroughly with water.
- **Wash Hands After Use**: Always wash your hands after handling Boogie Goo to prevent any residue from sticking.
- **Parental Supervision**: For younger children, it's best to have a parent or adult supervise the goo-making process, especially when using food coloring or glitter.

Making Boogie Goo a Fun Family Tradition

Creating and using **Boogie Goo** can become a fun family tradition! Not only does it help ward off the Boogeyman, but it also provides a creative bonding activity that everyone can enjoy. Here are some ways to make the experience even more fun:

- **Boogie Goo Decorating**: Let kids decorate their goo with googly eyes, glitter, or tiny figurines to create their own "Boogeymen" to trap.
- **Goo Art**: Spread the Boogie Goo on wax paper and create fun shapes like monsters, stars, or protective symbols to enhance the experience.
- **Boogie Stories**: While making the goo, tell stories about past Boogeyman encounters and how this special goo has helped trap them over the years.

Conclusion: Recipe for Boogie Goo – A Sticky Solution for Boogeyman Defense

Boogie Goo is more than just a fun craft—it's a powerful tool for trapping the Boogeyman and keeping your room safe. By combining creativity, strategy, and a little bit of science, you can make an effective Boogeyman trap that's both enjoyable to create and practical to use. Whether you're placing goo under the bed, at the closet door, or along the windowsill, this sticky solution ensures that the Boogeyman won't stand a chance. Plus, it's a fantastic activity for kids and adults alike, making Boogeyman defense a fun, family-friendly affair!

Safety Note to Parents:

While **Boogie Goo** is a fun and imaginative way to engage with your child's creativity and explore the world of Boogeyman defense, it is **not intended for consumption**. The ingredients used, while non-toxic, should not be ingested. Please ensure that this activity is done under **adult supervision**, particularly for younger children.

As with any crafting activity, accidents can happen. By participating in the creation and use of Boogie Goo, parents and guardians accept responsibility for ensuring a safe environment. The author and publisher are not liable for any injuries, allergic reactions, or accidents that may occur during the making or use of Boogie Goo. Please use this activity to encourage your child's **creativity and imagination** in a safe and enjoyable manner.

Key Safety Reminders:

- Boogie Goo is **not edible**.
- **Avoid contact with eyes.** If Boogie Goo gets in the eyes, rinse thoroughly with water.
- Always **wash hands after use**.
- Store Boogie Goo in a safe place, away from small children and pets.
- **Adult supervision** is recommended, especially for children under 8.

Have fun, stay safe, and let your child's imagination run wild!

Chapter 31: Sugar Trap Sweets – Sweet Treats to Attract and Immobilize Boogeymen

Boogeymen may thrive on fear, but like many creatures, they have a weakness for the sweet and tempting allure of **candy**. In this chapter, you'll learn how to create **Sugar Trap Sweets**—special candies that attract Boogeymen and then immobilize them. These sweets act like bait, luring the Boogeyman out of hiding with their irresistible sugary scent and flavor. Once he takes the bait, the sugary trap kicks in, freezing the Boogeyman in place long enough for you to activate your defenses or escape. Creating these treats is a fun activity that the whole family can enjoy together, combining creativity with effective Boogeyman-busting techniques.

What Are Sugar Trap Sweets?

Sugar Trap Sweets are no ordinary candies. Infused with a special blend of sticky ingredients, these candies are designed to do more than just look and taste delicious—they trap Boogeymen when they try to eat them. Once a Boogeyman bites into one of these sweet treats, the candy becomes incredibly sticky, immobilizing him and preventing him from moving or hiding.

These sweets can be scattered around key areas where the Boogeyman tends to appear—like under the bed, near the closet, or by a window—luring him in with their sugary smell. Once he takes the bait, the trap is set!

Ingredients for Sugar Trap Sweets

To make your own **Sugar Trap Sweets**, you'll need a few basic ingredients commonly found in your kitchen, along with some special additions to give the candy its immobilizing properties. Here's what you'll need:

- **1 cup of sugar** – The sweet base that will attract the Boogeyman with its scent and flavor.
- **½ cup of corn syrup** – Provides the stickiness that will trap the Boogeyman once he bites into the candy.
- **¼ cup of water** – To help dissolve the sugar and create the candy mixture.
- **1 teaspoon of gelatin** – Adds an extra layer of thickness and strength to the candy, making it harder for the Boogeyman to escape.
- **Food coloring (optional)** – Add a few drops of red, green, or purple food coloring to give the candies a spooky look.
- **Flavor extracts (optional)** – Choose from flavors like vanilla, mint, or cherry to make the candy even more tempting.
- **Powdered sugar** – Used for dusting the candies once they're set, making them look more like real sweets.

These ingredients are safe to handle and fun to work with, making the activity enjoyable for kids and parents alike.

How to Make Sugar Trap Sweets – Step-by-Step Instructions

Here's how you can make your own **Sugar Trap Sweets** at home, with easy-to-follow steps that make the process fun and engaging for the whole family.

Step 1: Prepare Your Workspace

Before starting, make sure your kitchen or crafting area is clean and ready. Lay out your ingredients and tools (a medium saucepan, a spoon for stirring, candy molds or a baking sheet, and parchment paper). Cover your workspace with parchment or wax paper to make cleanup easier.

Step 2: Heat the Sugar Mixture

In a medium saucepan, combine **1 cup of sugar**, **½ cup of corn syrup**, and **¼ cup of water**. Place the saucepan over medium heat and stir continuously until the sugar dissolves completely. This will create the sticky base of your Sugar Trap Sweets.

Keep stirring until the mixture comes to a boil. Once it starts bubbling, stop stirring and let it cook for about 5-7 minutes, or until the mixture reaches **300°F** on a candy thermometer (the hard-crack stage). If you don't have a candy thermometer, you'll know it's ready when the mixture turns a golden color and thickens.

Step 3: Add Gelatin for Stickiness

Once the sugar mixture has reached the right temperature, remove the saucepan from the heat and stir in **1 teaspoon of gelatin**. The gelatin will give the candy extra stickiness, making it harder for the Boogeyman to break free once he bites into the candy. Stir quickly to fully dissolve the gelatin.

Step 4: Add Color and Flavor

At this stage, you can add **food coloring** and **flavor extracts** to make your Sugar Trap Sweets more appealing (and to make them look even more tempting to the Boogeyman). A few drops of green or purple food coloring will give the candies a spooky, eerie look. Add 1-2 teaspoons of your chosen flavor extract, such as cherry or vanilla, to make the candy smell delicious.

Stir the mixture until the color and flavor are fully incorporated.

Step 5: Shape the Candies

Now it's time to shape your **Sugar Trap Sweets**. You can pour the hot candy mixture into **candy molds** to create fun shapes, like circles, stars, or even spooky ghosts. If you don't have candy molds, you can pour the mixture onto a **parchment-lined baking sheet** and spread it out evenly.

Let the candy sit for a few minutes to cool slightly. Once it's cool enough to touch but still soft, use a knife or cookie cutter to cut it into small, bite-sized pieces.

Step 6: Dust with Powdered Sugar

To make the candies look like real sweets (and prevent them from sticking to everything), lightly dust them with **powdered sugar** once they've cooled and set. The powdered sugar gives the candy a smooth finish while hiding the sticky core that will trap the Boogeyman.

How to Use Sugar Trap Sweets to Catch the Boogeyman

Once you've made your Sugar Trap Sweets, it's time to put them to use! Here are a few fun and effective ways to use these candies to lure and trap the Boogeyman:

1. Candy Trail Trap

One of the best ways to lure the Boogeyman is by setting a **candy trail** that leads directly into your trap. Here's how to set up a candy trail that's impossible for the Boogeyman to resist:

- Place small pieces of Sugar Trap Sweets in a trail leading from a dark corner of the room (like under the bed or from the closet) toward a more open area where you've set up your main defenses.
- The Boogeyman will be attracted to the candy and follow the trail, getting closer to your trap with each step.
- At the end of the trail, set a circle of light or another defense mechanism that will immobilize the Boogeyman once he's lured in by the sweets.

2. Candy Bait in Dark Spaces

Boogeymen love to hide in dark spaces, so using Sugar Trap Sweets as **bait** near these areas is a great strategy.

- Place a few candies in areas where the Boogeyman likes to hide, such as the closet, under the bed, or near a window.
- As the Boogeyman approaches the candy, the sticky gelatin will immobilize him, allowing you to shine a flashlight or activate another defense to weaken him further.
- If you've made glow-in-the-dark candies, they will also act as a visual deterrent, helping you spot any Boogeyman activity around the candy.

3. Boogeyman Candy Box

Create a **Boogeyman Candy Box** by placing your Sugar Trap Sweets inside a decorative tin or jar, and leave it in a strategic location in your room.

- The Boogeyman, drawn by the sweet scent of the candy, will be tempted to open the box and eat the sweets inside.
- Once he does, the sticky candy will glue his mouth and hands, making it impossible for him to escape or cause mischief.
- You can place this candy box near a known entry point, such as a door or window, or in a location where the Boogeyman frequently appears.

4. Bedside Boogey Trap

Place a small plate or bowl of **Sugar Trap Sweets** near your bed at night. This way, if the Boogeyman tries to sneak up on you while you're asleep, he'll be distracted by the candy.

- The candy's sweet scent will attract the Boogeyman before he can get too close to you.
- As soon as he touches or bites into the candy, the gelatin will trap him, preventing him from moving.
- Keep a flashlight or other defense tool by your bed to quickly deal with the immobilized Boogeyman.

Customizing Your Sugar Trap Sweets

One of the best things about making Sugar Trap Sweets is that you can **customize** them to suit your Boogeyman-busting needs. Here are a few ideas to make your candies even more special:

- **Glow-in-the-Dark Candy**: Add a small amount of glow-in-the-dark powder to your sugar mixture to create candies that glow in the dark. This will attract the Boogeyman and help you spot him once he takes the bait.
- **Edible Glitter**: Add edible glitter to make your candies sparkle, making them even more tempting for the Boogeyman to eat.
- **Flavored Syrups**: Experiment with different flavors, like strawberry, caramel, or peppermint, to change the scent of the candy and appeal to different Boogeymen.

Safety Note for Sugar Trap Sweets

Sugar Trap Sweets are designed as an imaginative way to trap the Boogeyman, but they are not meant for human consumption. Although the ingredients are safe to handle, these candies should only be used for trapping Boogeymen.

Key Safety Tips:

- **Not for Eating**: Make sure children understand that Sugar Trap Sweets are for Boogeyman traps only and should not be eaten.
- **Clean Up Carefully**: After using Sugar Trap Sweets, make sure to clean up any leftover candy or sticky residue to prevent it from being tracked through the house.
- **Supervision**: Always supervise younger children during the candy-making process to ensure safety.

Conclusion: Sugar Trap Sweets – A Sweet Way to Catch the Boogeyman

Sugar Trap Sweets are a fun, creative, and effective way to lure and immobilize the Boogeyman. By turning simple kitchen ingredients into sticky, irresistible candy traps, you can outsmart the Boogeyman and protect your home from his nighttime mischief. Whether you set up a candy trail, a candy box trap, or place sweets near dark spaces, these sugary delights will keep the Boogeyman stuck long enough for you to take action. Plus, the process of making and setting these traps is a great bonding activity for kids and adults, encouraging imagination while keeping the Boogeyman at bay!

Chapter 32: Moonlight Dust – A Glowing Powder to Reveal Boogeyman Tracks

In the dark and shadowy realms where Boogeymen lurk, it can be hard to know where they've been or where they might be hiding. Enter **Moonlight Dust**—a magical, glowing powder designed to reveal the Boogeyman's tracks. This special dust, when scattered around your room, glows softly in the dark and sticks to the Boogeyman's movements, allowing you to track his steps and anticipate his next move.

This chapter will teach you how to create your own **Moonlight Dust** at home, using safe and simple ingredients. It's a fun and effective way to monitor the Boogeyman's activity, giving you a clear advantage in your quest to keep him at bay. Kids and adults alike will enjoy making and using this powder, turning a potentially scary situation into an engaging activity filled with curiosity and discovery.

What is Moonlight Dust?

Moonlight Dust is a glowing powder that you can sprinkle around your room to reveal the presence of the Boogeyman. When the Boogeyman steps into an area where the dust has been spread, it clings to his feet, leaving behind glowing footprints. The luminescent glow of the dust allows you to follow his trail and see where he's been hiding, making it easier to set traps or defenses in those areas.

Moonlight Dust glows faintly in the dark, making it especially useful for tracking Boogeyman movements at night. Once applied, it can last for several hours, giving you enough time to observe and act accordingly. Whether you're setting a trap or just curious about where the Boogeyman might be hiding, Moonlight Dust gives you the ability to see his movements clearly.

Ingredients for Moonlight Dust

To make **Moonlight Dust**, you only need a few basic ingredients that can be easily found at home or in craft stores. These ingredients are safe to handle, making this a fun activity for children and parents to do together.

Here's what you'll need:

- **1 cup of cornstarch** – This forms the base of the powder, giving it a light and easily spreadable texture.
- **½ cup of baking soda** – Helps the powder stick to surfaces (and to the Boogeyman's feet).
- **1 tablespoon of glow-in-the-dark powder or paint** – The key ingredient that makes the dust glow when the lights are out. You can find glow-in-the-dark powder or paint at most craft stores.
- **1 teaspoon of fine glitter (optional)** – Adds a sparkling effect to the powder, making it more visually appealing.
- **Essential oil (optional)** – A few drops of lavender or eucalyptus oil can add a calming scent to the powder.

How to Make Moonlight Dust – Step-by-Step Instructions

Making **Moonlight Dust** is easy and fun! Here's a step-by-step guide to creating this magical powder at home.

Step 1: Gather Your Supplies

Before you start making Moonlight Dust, gather all your ingredients and set up your workspace. You'll need a mixing bowl, a spoon for stirring, and a jar or container to store the powder once it's made.

Step 2: Combine the Cornstarch and Baking Soda

In a large mixing bowl, combine **1 cup of cornstarch** and ½ **cup of baking soda**. Stir them together until the mixture is light and powdery. The cornstarch gives the Moonlight Dust its soft, easily spreadable texture, while the baking soda helps it stick to surfaces and Boogeyman tracks.

Step 3: Add the Glow-in-the-Dark Powder or Paint

Next, add **1 tablespoon of glow-in-the-dark powder** or **glow-in-the-dark paint** to the mixture. This is the key ingredient that will make your Moonlight Dust glow in the dark, allowing you to see Boogeyman tracks. Stir the powder or paint thoroughly into the cornstarch and baking soda mixture until it is evenly distributed.

If you're using glow-in-the-dark paint, make sure to mix it in slowly so that it blends smoothly with the dry ingredients.

Step 4: Add Glitter for Extra Sparkle (Optional)

If you want your Moonlight Dust to sparkle and shimmer, add **1 teaspoon of fine glitter** to the mixture. Stir it in well so that the glitter is spread evenly throughout the powder. The glitter adds a fun, magical touch that makes the dust even more exciting to use, especially for kids.

Step 5: Optional: Add a Calming Scent

If you'd like your Moonlight Dust to have a pleasant scent, you can add **a few drops of essential oil**. Lavender or eucalyptus oil are good choices, as they are known for their calming properties, which can help make the room feel safer and more comfortable. Stir the essential oil into the mixture, ensuring that the powder is lightly scented but not too strong.

Step 6: Store the Moonlight Dust

Once all the ingredients are thoroughly mixed, transfer your Moonlight Dust into an airtight container, such as a jar or resealable bag. This will keep the powder fresh and ready to use whenever you need it. Store it in a cool, dry place, and keep it out of direct sunlight to preserve the glow-in-the-dark effect.

How to Use Moonlight Dust to Track the Boogeyman

Now that you've made your **Moonlight Dust**, it's time to put it to use! Here are a few ways you can sprinkle and spread the powder to reveal the Boogeyman's tracks.

1. Sprinkle Moonlight Dust Around the Bed

One of the most common places the Boogeyman hides is under the bed. By sprinkling **Moonlight Dust** around the perimeter of the bed, you'll be able to see if the Boogeyman sneaks out during the night. The powder will cling to his feet, leaving behind glowing tracks as he moves.

- Spread a light layer of Moonlight Dust all around the bed, paying special attention to the edges where the Boogeyman is most likely to step.
- Check the powder in the morning (or during the night if you're feeling brave) to see if there are any glowing footprints.
- If you spot tracks, you'll know exactly where the Boogeyman has been and where to focus your defenses.

2. Use Moonlight Dust in the Closet

Closets are another favorite hiding spot for Boogeymen. You can use Moonlight Dust to track their movements in and out of the closet by sprinkling a line of the powder along the bottom edge of the closet door.

- Spread a thin line of Moonlight Dust across the doorway of the closet. If the Boogeyman tries to leave, his footprints will glow in the dark, revealing his path.
- If you notice glowing footprints leading out of the closet, you can be prepared to act and set up additional traps or defenses in that area.
- Alternatively, sprinkle some inside the closet to see if the Boogeyman moves while inside.

3. Track Movements Near Windows

If you suspect the Boogeyman might be using a window as an entry or exit point, sprinkle **Moonlight Dust** along the windowsill and below the window on the floor.

- The powder will cling to the Boogeyman's feet if he tries to enter or leave through the window, creating a glowing trail for you to follow.
- This method is particularly useful if you want to know whether the Boogeyman is coming from outside or moving between different areas in your room.

4. Create a "Boogeyman Detection Circle"

For a more comprehensive method, you can create a **detection circle** using Moonlight Dust. This circle will act as a barrier around your bed or favorite hiding places in the room, allowing you to see if the Boogeyman has crossed into those areas.

- Sprinkle a ring of Moonlight Dust around your bed or any key area where you suspect the Boogeyman may be hiding.
- Check the circle at night or in the morning. If the powder has glowing footprints, you'll know the Boogeyman has been moving within your space.
- This method not only helps you detect the Boogeyman's movements but also serves as a warning system, allowing you to prepare your defenses accordingly.

Enhancing the Moonlight Dust Experience

Using Moonlight Dust is already a fun and effective way to track the Boogeyman, but here are a few ways to enhance the experience and make it even more engaging for kids and adults alike:

1. Glow-in-the-Dark Patterns

Get creative with how you spread the Moonlight Dust by making **patterns or symbols**. Instead of just sprinkling it randomly, you can create stars, spirals, or even protective symbols around your bed or closet. These patterns not only look cool but can also make the tracking process more interactive and enjoyable.

2. Make a Boogeyman Map

Create a **Boogeyman Map** on paper where you draw the layout of your room. Each night, check the Moonlight Dust for footprints and mark the Boogeyman's tracks on your map. Over time, you'll build a detailed picture of where the Boogeyman likes to move and hide, helping you set up more effective defenses.

3. Combine Moonlight Dust with Other Defenses

Moonlight Dust works great in combination with other defenses. After tracking the Boogeyman's movements, you can set up **Boogey Goo**, light traps, or mirrors in areas where the dust reveals heavy Boogeyman activity. This multi-layered approach ensures that you're always one step ahead of the Boogeyman.

Safety Tips for Using Moonlight Dust

Moonlight Dust is safe to handle, but here are a few important safety reminders to keep in mind:

- **Not for Consumption**: While Moonlight Dust is made from safe household ingredients, it is not meant for eating. Be sure to explain to children that the powder is only for tracking the Boogeyman and should not be consumed.
- **Avoid Contact with Eyes**: If the powder gets into the eyes, rinse them immediately with clean water. Avoid touching your face while handling Moonlight Dust.
- **Supervision Recommended**: If younger children are involved, make sure an adult supervises the making and application of Moonlight Dust to ensure it is used safely.

Conclusion: Moonlight Dust – Illuminating the Boogeyman's Path

Moonlight Dust is a magical tool that gives you the upper hand in your fight against the Boogeyman. By revealing his tracks with glowing footprints, this dust allows you to see exactly where the Boogeyman has been and where he's likely to go next. Not only does it make Boogeyman detection easier, but it also turns a potentially frightening situation into a fun and creative activity for kids and parents to enjoy together.

With Moonlight Dust, you can stay one step ahead of the Boogeyman, tracking his movements, setting up defenses, and ensuring that no dark corner of your room goes unexplored. So get ready to sprinkle, track, and outsmart the Boogeyman with the glowing power of Moonlight Dust!

Part 8: Fighting the Final Battle

Chapter 33: Confronting the Boogeyman Head-On – Preparing for a Direct Encounter

After all the traps, defenses, and careful strategies you've learned to protect yourself from the Boogeyman, there may come a time when you have no choice but to face him directly. **Confronting the Boogeyman head-on** can be a frightening experience, but with the right preparation, knowledge, and mental fortitude, you can turn the tables and come out victorious. In this chapter, we'll explore how to prepare for a direct encounter, what tools and tactics to use, and how to maintain control over the situation.

Facing the Boogeyman requires not only physical defenses but also a strong mind and unshakable confidence. This chapter will help you master both, ensuring that when the time comes to confront the Boogeyman, you're ready.

1. Understanding the Nature of a Head-On Encounter

Before preparing for a direct encounter with the Boogeyman, it's important to understand what makes such a situation different from other types of interactions. When you confront the Boogeyman directly, you are stepping into a battle of both **physical and psychological strength**.

- **The Boogeyman Feeds on Fear**: The Boogeyman's primary weapon is fear. If you let fear control your actions, you give him power. The goal of a direct confrontation is to **face your fear** head-on and diminish the Boogeyman's ability to influence you.
- **Psychological Warfare**: Confronting the Boogeyman isn't just about physical strength or light-based defenses—it's about mental resilience. The Boogeyman will try to trick your mind, making you doubt yourself or feel overwhelmed. Learning how to stay calm and confident is key.
- **Timing Matters**: A head-on encounter often happens when other defenses have failed, or when the Boogeyman grows bold enough to face you. These encounters usually happen at night, when the shadows are thickest and fear is most palpable.

By understanding the nature of the confrontation, you can begin to prepare both mentally and physically for the encounter.

2. Mental Preparation – Mastering Your Fear

The most important part of preparing for a direct encounter with the Boogeyman is mastering your **fear**. Since the Boogeyman draws his power from your fear, learning to control it will weaken him before the confrontation even begins.

Visualization Techniques

Visualization is a powerful tool to mentally prepare for a direct encounter. Practice **visualizing yourself** standing strong in the face of the Boogeyman. Picture yourself surrounded by an aura of light or armor, blocking the Boogeyman's attempts to scare you. Imagine every breath you take pushing him back, weakening his power.

- **How to Visualize**: Find a quiet place to sit and close your eyes. Visualize yourself standing in a dark room, but picture your body glowing with an internal light. Imagine the Boogeyman trying to approach but unable to get close because of the strength of your light. Practice this regularly to build your mental defenses.

Positive Affirmations

Positive affirmations can help reinforce your mental strength. Repeating phrases like "I am not afraid," "I am stronger than the Boogeyman," and "Fear has no control over me" will help condition your mind to stay calm and in control when you confront him.

- **Examples of Affirmations**:
    - "I am in control of my mind and my space."
    - "The Boogeyman cannot scare me."
    - "I am stronger than fear."

Deep Breathing and Grounding

In moments of fear, your heart rate might increase, and panic can set in. Practice **deep breathing techniques** to calm yourself before and during a direct encounter. Grounding exercises, like pressing your feet into the floor or holding a familiar object, can help keep you centered and focused.

- **How to Practice Deep Breathing**: Inhale deeply for four counts, hold for four counts, and exhale for four counts. Focus on the rhythm of your breath, which will help reduce fear and anxiety in the moment.

3. Assembling Your Boogeyman Confrontation Kit

Just like any other encounter, facing the Boogeyman head-on requires the right **tools**. Here's how to prepare a **Boogeyman Confrontation Kit**, equipped with all the essentials you'll need to protect yourself and take control of the situation.

Light-Based Defenses

The Boogeyman thrives in darkness, so light is one of your strongest weapons. Make sure you have **multiple light sources** ready for your confrontation.

- **Flashlight**: A high-powered LED flashlight can be a game-changer in a direct encounter. Keep it by your bedside or in your confrontation kit, and shine it directly on the Boogeyman to weaken him.
- **Glowsticks**: Use glowsticks to create a safe zone around yourself. You can toss a few on the floor to light up dark areas where the Boogeyman might try to move.
- **Nightlight or Lantern**: Set up a lantern or plug in a nightlight near the area of confrontation. These lights will keep the room illuminated and diminish the Boogeyman's power.

Sound Tools

Certain **sounds** can disorient or repel the Boogeyman. Include sound-based tools in your kit to weaken him.

- **Whistles or Bells**: High-pitched noises, like a loud whistle or jingling bells, can confuse the Boogeyman and force him to retreat.
- **Tibetan Singing Bowls**: The vibrations from a singing bowl can disrupt the Boogeyman's form, making it harder for him to approach.
- **Clapping or Stomping**: Even something as simple as clapping your hands loudly or stomping your feet can startle the Boogeyman and give you the upper hand.

Physical Barriers

While mental strength is critical, having **physical barriers** can add extra layers of protection.

- **Salt or Chalk Circles**: Before the confrontation, draw a protective circle of salt or chalk around yourself or your bed. The Boogeyman won't be able to cross these boundaries.
- **Mirrors**: Use mirrors to reflect the Boogeyman's image back at him. Position them around the room so the Boogeyman sees his reflection from multiple angles, weakening his hold.
- **Boogey Goo**: If you've created Boogey Goo (from Chapter 30), keep some on hand to throw or place in key locations. If the Boogeyman steps in it, he'll get stuck.

4. Timing the Confrontation

Facing the Boogeyman requires strategy. While you may be ready to confront him, timing is critical. The Boogeyman is strongest in the shadows, so waiting for the right moment to confront him is key to gaining the upper hand.

Identifying the Right Time

- **Wait for Movement**: The Boogeyman often lurks in the shadows, but he'll reveal himself when he moves. Wait for him to step into the light or into a space where you've laid traps (such as with Moonlight Dust or Boogie Goo). Once he's exposed, you'll know it's the right time to act.
- **Strike During His Weakest Moment**: Boogeymen are vulnerable to sudden bursts of light, noise, or reflection. Use your tools at the moment when he hesitates or pauses, as this is when he's most susceptible.

Holding Your Ground

When the Boogeyman appears, don't panic. **Hold your ground** and use your prepared tools. Remember that fear gives him power, and by staying calm, you take that power away.

5. The Confrontation – What to Do When the Boogeyman Appears

When the Boogeyman finally reveals himself, it's time to take action. Follow these steps to ensure that the encounter ends with you in control.

Step 1: Shine Light on Him

As soon as you see the Boogeyman appear, **shine a bright light** directly at him. Whether it's from a flashlight, glowstick, or lantern, the light will weaken him and force him to stop moving. The brighter and more focused the light, the more disoriented he'll become.

- **Tip**: Move the light slowly but deliberately, following the Boogeyman's movements to keep him exposed. Don't let him slip back into the shadows.

Step 2: Speak with Authority

Use your voice to assert control over the Boogeyman. The Boogeyman thrives on fear, but when you speak with confidence and authority, you disrupt his power. **Command him to leave** your space.

- Say something like: "I see you, Boogeyman. You have no power here. Leave now and never return."
- Speak clearly and loudly. Even if you feel a bit scared, try to project strength through your words.

Step 3: Use Sound to Disorient Him

Once you've shone the light on the Boogeyman and spoken to him, use **sound** to further weaken him. Clap your hands, blow a whistle, or ring a bell. The sudden noise will disorient him, making it difficult for him to maintain his form.

Step 4: Establish a Physical Barrier

If the Boogeyman tries to approach, establish a **physical barrier** between yourself and him. Use a mirror to reflect his image, or throw a handful of salt or Boogey Goo in his direction to stop his advance. If you've drawn a protective circle of chalk or salt, stay inside that boundary, as the Boogeyman cannot cross it.

6. The Aftermath – Securing Your Space

Once you've confronted the Boogeyman and forced him to retreat, it's important to **secure your space** to prevent him from coming back. Here's what to do:

- **Reinforce Your Defenses**: Double-check all your protective barriers, including salt lines, light sources, and mirrors. Make sure everything is in place to keep the Boogeyman from returning.
- **Cleanse the Space**: Use sage or another cleansing herb to remove any lingering negative energy. Walk around the room, waving the smoke in areas where the Boogeyman appeared. Special Note: It is recommended to have Sage or Palo Santo on standby for Cleansing your space.
- **Maintain a Calm Environment**: Play calming music or set up a soothing nightlight to keep the atmosphere peaceful. This will discourage the Boogeyman from trying to return.

Conclusion: Confronting the Boogeyman Head-On – A Test of Courage

Confronting the Boogeyman head-on is a test of both mental and physical strength. By preparing yourself with light-based defenses, sound tools, and psychological resilience, you can face the Boogeyman without fear. Remember, the Boogeyman's greatest weapon is your fear, but when you refuse to let fear control you, you strip him of his power. With the right mindset, tools, and strategy, you can confront the Boogeyman, force him to retreat, and regain control of your space.

In the end, facing the Boogeyman isn't just about defeating a scary creature—it's about mastering your own fear and proving to yourself that you have the strength to overcome anything.

Chapter 34: Restoring Your Imaginary Friend – Can a Boogeyman Be Turned Back into a Friend?

Many children have had **imaginary friends**—comforting, playful companions who help them navigate the world of childhood fears, creativity, and imagination. But what if that once-friendly figure, who used to bring comfort, becomes something darker—a Boogeyman? Can you **turn a Boogeyman back into a friend**? Is it possible to restore the light to a being who now thrives on fear?

In this chapter, we'll explore the idea that a Boogeyman may not always be an enemy, but rather a former imaginary friend who has become twisted by fear, neglect, or loneliness. By confronting the Boogeyman with compassion, understanding, and creativity, you may be able to **restore** the positive relationship you once had. This chapter will guide you through the steps to try and transform the Boogeyman back into a friend—while also understanding when it's time to let go and move forward.

1. Understanding the Connection Between Imaginary Friends and Boogeymen

An **imaginary friend** is often born out of a child's imagination, creativity, and need for companionship. These friends provide comfort, helping children explore their emotions, confront fears, and learn how to navigate social situations. However, just like any relationship, the bond between a child and their imaginary friend can change over time.

As children grow, their needs and emotions evolve. In some cases, an imaginary friend may begin to fade or feel neglected as the child outgrows the need for them. In other situations, emotional changes such as new fears, anxieties, or life transitions (moving, school stress, etc.) may cause the imaginary friend to take on a more sinister form—eventually turning into a **Boogeyman**.

When an imaginary friend transforms into a Boogeyman, it's often because they've been **distorted by negative emotions**, such as fear or abandonment. Understanding this transformation is key to reversing it. Instead of treating the Boogeyman purely as an enemy, it may be helpful to approach them with compassion and an open mind.

2. Signs Your Boogeyman Was Once an Imaginary Friend

How do you know if your Boogeyman was once your imaginary friend? Here are some **clues** that can help you recognize a connection:

- **Familiar Traits**: If the Boogeyman resembles or mimics certain behaviors, names, or characteristics of your former imaginary friend, this could indicate that they share a connection.
- **Recognizable Patterns**: Does the Boogeyman appear at times when you feel lonely, stressed, or scared—times when your imaginary friend would have offered comfort? This suggests that the Boogeyman may have originated from those comforting moments.

- **Unusual Encounters**: The Boogeyman may interact with you in ways that feel oddly personal, almost as if they know you well. If the Boogeyman seems to understand your fears or weaknesses, it could be because they were once part of your inner world as a friend.

Recognizing these signs is the first step in understanding the Boogeyman's origins and opening the door to potentially **restoring** the relationship.

3. Emotional Healing – Confronting the Boogeyman with Compassion

Once you've recognized that the Boogeyman may have been your imaginary friend, it's time to begin the process of **healing**. This involves confronting the Boogeyman not with fear, but with **compassion**.

Step 1: Acknowledge the Change

Acknowledge that your relationship with your imaginary friend has changed. Speak directly to the Boogeyman, even if they remain hidden in the shadows. Saying something like, "I know you were once my friend, and things have changed, but I want to understand why," can open a dialogue between you and the Boogeyman.

Step 2: Address Your Fears

Be honest about the fears you've experienced since the transformation. Explain how the Boogeyman's actions have made you feel scared or uncomfortable, but also express a desire to **move past those fears**. The Boogeyman thrives on fear, so by addressing it openly, you begin to take away its power.

Step 3: Offer Compassion

Show compassion to the Boogeyman. If they were once your friend, they may feel lonely, abandoned, or confused by the change. Say something like, "I remember when we were friends. I know you might feel alone or lost, but I'm here to help." This acknowledgment can help start the healing process.

Step 4: Forgive and Let Go of Grudges

If the Boogeyman has frightened or hurt you, it's important to **forgive** those actions. Letting go of any anger or resentment can create space for healing and transformation. Forgiveness doesn't mean ignoring what happened; it's about recognizing the hurt and deciding to move forward without holding on to negative emotions.

4. Rebuilding Trust with the Boogeyman

Transforming a Boogeyman back into an imaginary friend requires **rebuilding trust**. This won't happen overnight, but with patience and consistency, you can re-establish a connection.

Step 1: Create a Safe Environment

The Boogeyman feeds on fear, but you can shift the environment by creating a **safe, inviting space** for healing. Light a soft, warm nightlight, play calming music, or use familiar scents (like lavender) to create a welcoming atmosphere. This can encourage the Boogeyman to come out of the shadows and begin interacting in a less frightening way.

Step 2: Encourage Positive Interaction

Encourage the Boogeyman to engage in positive ways. Instead of seeing the Boogeyman as a threat, try talking to them as if they're still your friend. Ask questions like, "What do you need to feel better?" or "Can we work together to help you feel less angry or scared?" By reframing the interaction, you shift the dynamic from fear to understanding.

Step 3: Reintroduce Shared Activities

If you once had fun or comforting activities with your imaginary friend, reintroduce those into your interactions with the Boogeyman. Maybe you used to draw together, play with toys, or tell stories. Inviting the Boogeyman back into these positive experiences can help remind them of the bond you once had, leading to gradual healing.

Step 4: Set Boundaries

While rebuilding trust is important, it's equally critical to set **boundaries** with the Boogeyman. Explain that fear and intimidation are not acceptable behaviors. You might say, "We can be friends again, but you can't scare me or hide in the dark anymore. If you want to be a part of my life, it has to be in a good way."

5. The Power of Imagination – Restoring the Friend

Imagination is a powerful tool in transforming the Boogeyman back into a friend. Since the Boogeyman was created in your mind, you also have the power to reshape them into something more positive.

Visualization Techniques

Use **visualization** to change the Boogeyman's form. Picture the Boogeyman in your mind, but instead of seeing them as a frightening figure, imagine them as the friend they once were. You can even give them a new appearance, making them look more like a friendly creature or character you admire.

For example, you might visualize the Boogeyman turning from a shadowy, scary figure into a gentle, glowing being who offers you protection instead of fear. Practice this visualization regularly to reshape your perception of the Boogeyman.

Imaginary Transformation Ritual

You can create a fun **ritual** to symbolize the transformation of the Boogeyman back into a friend. For example, draw a picture of what you want your Boogeyman-turned-friend to look like, and then fold it into an envelope or hide it under your pillow. Before bed, say, "I welcome you back as my friend. Let's leave fear behind and be kind to each other."

Another idea is to create a **magical object**—such as a toy, charm, or drawing—that represents the new version of your imaginary friend. Keep this object by your bed as a reminder of the transformation, and use it to reinforce the positive connection.

Storytelling for Healing

Tell stories where you and the Boogeyman work together as friends again. You might imagine going on adventures, helping each other solve problems, or defending each other from other fears. By weaving a narrative where the Boogeyman is an ally, not an enemy, you reshape the relationship into something empowering and positive.

6. Knowing When to Let Go – When Transformation Isn't Possible

In some cases, it may not be possible to fully transform the Boogeyman back into a friend. If the Boogeyman remains too tied to fear and negativity, it's important to know when to **let go**. Holding on to the idea of restoring a friend can sometimes keep you stuck in a loop of fear and confusion.

Accepting the Boogeyman's Role

It's okay to accept that the Boogeyman may no longer be a friend, but a symbol of something you've outgrown. By recognizing this, you give yourself permission to move forward and leave the Boogeyman behind.

Finding New Sources of Comfort

If the transformation isn't possible, focus on finding new **sources of comfort** and creativity. Surround yourself with supportive people, comforting objects, and positive activities that fill the space once held by the Boogeyman or your imaginary friend.

Closing the Chapter

Consider having a **farewell ritual** where you thank the Boogeyman (or your former imaginary friend) for the lessons and companionship they provided, but make it clear that it's time to move on. You can write a letter, draw a picture, or perform a small symbolic act—such as closing a door or blowing out a candle—to signify the end of that chapter.

Conclusion: Restoring Your Imaginary Friend – A Journey of Healing and Transformation

Restoring the **Boogeyman back into an imaginary friend** is a journey of compassion, creativity, and emotional healing. By confronting the Boogeyman with understanding rather than fear, you open the door to transforming the relationship back into something positive. Whether you choose to rebuild trust, reshape the Boogeyman through imagination, or let go and move forward, this chapter teaches you that you have the power to redefine your connection with the Boogeyman.

In the end, the transformation process is about reclaiming your imagination, healing from fear, and finding comfort in the world you create for yourself. Whether the Boogeyman becomes a friend again or remains a distant memory, you'll emerge stronger, wiser, and more empowered to face whatever comes next.

Conclusion

Chapter 35: The End of Fear – Banishing the Boogeyman Once and for All

After many encounters, defenses, and strategies, the time has come for you to face the ultimate challenge: banishing the Boogeyman **once and for all**. This chapter focuses on reclaiming your imagination, breaking free from the grip of fear, and ensuring that the Boogeyman no longer holds any power over you. By understanding the root of the fear that fuels the Boogeyman and applying key psychological and practical methods, you can rid yourself of his presence forever and live in peace, free from nighttime terror.

This process is not only about removing the Boogeyman from your life but also about reclaiming your imagination as a space for joy, creativity, and empowerment. The final victory over the Boogeyman represents a personal triumph over fear and an affirmation of your inner strength.

1. Understanding the Boogeyman's True Power – Fear

At his core, the Boogeyman thrives on one thing: **fear**. He is an embodiment of anxieties, insecurities, and the darker parts of the imagination. The more fear you give him, the stronger he becomes. Therefore, the key to banishing the Boogeyman is to **remove the source of his power**—your fear. Without fear to feed on, the Boogeyman cannot survive.

- **Fear as a Fuel**: The Boogeyman doesn't have physical strength; instead, he gains power from the emotions he draws out of you. The more you fear him, the more real and powerful he seems. But once you stop being afraid, his presence diminishes.
- **Imagination as a Source of Power**: While fear can distort your imagination into creating terrifying things, imagination itself is a neutral force. The Boogeyman is just one product of your mind, but you can just as easily use your imagination to **create something beautiful**—something that renders the Boogeyman powerless.

Understanding this dynamic is the first step toward banishing him. The more you control your emotions and imagination, the less power the Boogeyman has.

2. Confronting Your Fear – Owning the Darkness

The Boogeyman represents the parts of your imagination that have been twisted by fear, uncertainty, and the unknown. To banish him, you must **confront your fear** head-on and own the parts of yourself that scare you. Facing fear is never easy, but it's essential in reclaiming your power over the Boogeyman.

Step 1: Acknowledge Your Fears

Start by acknowledging the specific fears that the Boogeyman represents. Is it a fear of the dark? Of being alone? Of the unknown? By identifying what the Boogeyman symbolizes, you begin to demystify him.

- **Write It Down**: Take a moment to write down the fears that the Boogeyman represents for you. Seeing your fears on paper makes them tangible and less overwhelming.

- **Speak Your Fears Aloud**: Saying your fears out loud takes away their power. You might say, "I am afraid of the dark because it feels unknown," or "I'm scared of being alone at night." By speaking your fear, you begin to weaken its hold on you.

Step 2: Challenge Your Fear

Once you've acknowledged your fears, it's time to **challenge them**. Ask yourself, "What's the worst that can happen?" Often, fears are based on imagined scenarios that are unlikely or exaggerated. The Boogeyman thrives on these imagined fears, so by rationalizing them, you take away his strength.

- **Visualize the Worst Outcome**: Imagine the Boogeyman appearing. What would actually happen? Would he hurt you, or would he simply vanish when confronted? By playing out the scenario in your mind, you gain control over it.
- **Challenge the Fear with Facts**: Remind yourself that the Boogeyman is a product of your imagination. He doesn't have real-world power—he can't harm you physically. The more you remind yourself of this, the weaker the Boogeyman becomes.

3. Reclaiming Your Imagination – Turning Fear into Strength

Your imagination is a powerful tool that can either create terrifying things like the Boogeyman or beautiful things that empower and uplift you. Reclaiming your imagination means transforming the space where fear once lived into a place of **creativity and joy**.

Step 1: Visualization of Light and Strength

To take back control of your imagination, practice visualizing **light** and **strength** whenever you feel the Boogeyman's presence or fear creeping in.

- **Visualize a Bright Light**: Close your eyes and imagine a warm, bright light filling the room. Picture it as a golden or white light that radiates from you, pushing the darkness and the Boogeyman away. This light represents your confidence and strength.
- **Transform the Boogeyman**: Instead of seeing the Boogeyman as a dark, scary figure, visualize him changing into something harmless—like a shadow shrinking into the distance or a figure fading away. By reshaping the Boogeyman in your mind, you take control of your imagination.

Step 2: Imaginative Creations

Once you've cleared your mind of the Boogeyman, start filling your imagination with **positive creations**.

- **Create Imaginary Friends or Allies**: Imagine creating new friends or allies in your mind who can guard you against fear. These could be protective creatures, friendly animals, or even superhero-like figures who stand watch over you.

- **Build Safe Spaces in Your Mind**: Visualize places in your mind where you feel completely safe and at peace, like a cozy room filled with soft pillows or a bright, sunny field. These mental safe spaces will help keep fear at bay and remind you that you control your imagination.

By actively creating positive images, you replace the fear-based elements of your imagination with ones that empower and protect you.

4. Rituals to Banish the Boogeyman

Sometimes, rituals can provide a sense of closure and empowerment when banishing the Boogeyman. Performing a simple **banishing ritual** helps you symbolically and mentally close the chapter on fear.

The Boogeyman Banishment Ritual

Here's a ritual you can perform to banish the Boogeyman once and for all:

Materials Needed:

- A small piece of paper
- A pencil
- A candle (optional)
- Salt or chalk (optional)

Steps:

1. **Write the Boogeyman's Name**: On the piece of paper, write down the name of the Boogeyman or the specific fear he represents.
2. **State Your Intention**: Hold the paper and say, "I no longer fear you, Boogeyman. You have no power here. I banish you from my mind and my space."
3. **Visualize Light**: Picture the Boogeyman being surrounded by a powerful light that grows brighter and brighter until he fades away completely.
4. **Burn or Tear the Paper**: Safely burn the piece of paper in a candle flame (with adult supervision) or tear it into small pieces. As the paper disappears, imagine the Boogeyman being banished forever.
5. **Create a Protective Circle**: For added protection, you can create a circle of salt or chalk around your room or bed. This symbolizes a barrier that the Boogeyman cannot cross.

Performing this ritual gives you a sense of finality, reinforcing the idea that the Boogeyman no longer has any hold over you.

5. Building Long-Term Defenses – Creating a Fear-Free Environment

Once the Boogeyman is banished, it's important to maintain a **fear-free environment** to ensure he doesn't return. Here's how to build long-term defenses to keep your imagination safe.

Step 1: Light as a Constant Companion

Since the Boogeyman thrives in darkness, make **light** a constant presence in your space. Use soft nightlights, glow-in-the-dark stickers, or even LED candles to create a warm, inviting atmosphere in your room.

- **Nightlight Ritual**: Every night before bed, turn on your nightlight and say, "This light keeps me safe and free from fear. No Boogeyman can enter here."

Step 2: Positive Affirmations and Mantras

Continue to use **positive affirmations** to reinforce your confidence and strength. Each morning, repeat a mantra that reminds you of your power over fear.

- **Examples of Affirmations**:
  - "I am fearless and in control."
  - "My mind is my own, and fear has no place here."
  - "I create only joy and peace in my imagination."

Step 3: Gratitude for Your Imagination

Instead of seeing your imagination as a place where fear can take root, learn to appreciate it as a source of creativity and wonder. Every night before bed, take a moment to reflect on the positive things your imagination has brought you—whether it's dreams, creativity, or problem-solving abilities.

- **Gratitude Practice**: Before sleeping, say something like, "Thank you for my imagination. It is a gift that brings me light, joy, and endless possibilities."

6. Seeking Support – Strength in Numbers

While banishing the Boogeyman is something you can do on your own, it's always helpful to have **support** from others. Whether it's a parent, sibling, or friend, having someone by your side can provide extra encouragement and protection.

- **Sharing the Journey**: Talk to someone about your experience with the Boogeyman and how you're working to banish him. Sometimes, simply sharing your story can lessen the Boogeyman's hold over you.
- **Creating a Team**: Invite others to help you maintain a fear-free environment. You can perform banishing rituals together or simply talk through your feelings with someone who can offer reassurance.

7. Embracing a Fear-Free Future – Living Without the Boogeyman

With the Boogeyman banished, you are now free to live without fear. This freedom isn't just about eliminating a childhood monster—it's about embracing a life where you control your imagination, your emotions, and your inner world. Here's how to move forward:

Step 1: Celebrate Your Victory

Take a moment to **celebrate your success** in banishing the Boogeyman. Whether it's by drawing a picture, writing about your journey, or simply smiling at the thought of your newfound freedom, make sure to acknowledge your victory.

Step 2: Stay Mindful of Fear

While you've banished the Boogeyman, fear may still try to creep in from time to time. Stay mindful of your emotions and continue using the tools you've learned to manage and release fear before it grows into something larger.

Step 3: Create a Fear-Free Life

Moving forward, focus on building a life filled with **joy, creativity, and empowerment**. Surround yourself with positive influences, and continue practicing self-compassion and inner strength.

Conclusion: The End of Fear – Reclaiming Your Power Once and For All

The journey to banishing the Boogeyman is about more than defeating a childhood monster—it's about reclaiming your imagination, mastering your fears, and embracing your inner strength. By confronting fear head-on, transforming it through creativity, and performing rituals to finalize the Boogeyman's departure, you take back control of your mind and your life.

As you step into a future free from fear, remember that you hold the power to create the world you want to live in. The Boogeyman may have once seemed invincible, but now you know the truth: fear is powerless in the face of light, courage, and imagination.

Appendix

Appendix A: Glossary of Boogeyman Terms and Tools

This appendix serves as a comprehensive guide to the terminology, tools, and concepts used throughout the book. Whether you're new to the world of Boogeyman defense or simply need a refresher, this glossary will provide clear definitions and explanations of everything you need to understand when dealing with the Boogeyman and his many forms.

A

- **Affirmation Shield**: A mental defense technique that involves using positive affirmations, such as "I am strong" or "Fear has no power over me," to create an invisible barrier that protects you from the Boogeyman's influence. Affirmation Shields help build mental resilience against fear.
- **Astral Battle**: A mental or spiritual battle that takes place in the astral plane, or in the Boogeyman's dimension, often through dream-like experiences or deep imagination. Astral Battles require strong mental focus and the ability to project one's consciousness beyond the physical world.

B

- **Banishment Ritual**: A symbolic or literal ceremony performed to permanently expel the Boogeyman from your space. This can involve burning paper, chanting phrases of empowerment, or visualizing the Boogeyman disappearing in a bright light.
- **Bed Guard Routine**: A nightly habit of checking under the bed and ensuring the space is clean and free of any signs of Boogeyman activity. This routine helps maintain a safe and protected sleeping environment.
- **Boogey Goo**: A sticky, homemade substance designed to trap the Boogeyman when he steps into it. Boogey Goo can be placed around vulnerable areas like the bed or closet to immobilize the Boogeyman, giving you time to respond.
- **Boogey Light**: Any light source (such as a flashlight, nightlight, or lantern) that is used to weaken or repel the Boogeyman. Boogey Lights are particularly effective because the Boogeyman thrives in darkness, and light renders him powerless.
- **Boogeyman Binding Ritual**: A magical or symbolic act meant to "bind" the Boogeyman, limiting his ability to move or harm you. This might involve tying symbolic knots, placing objects under the bed, or drawing symbols to trap the Boogeyman's energy.
- **Boogeyman Confrontation Kit**: A set of tools assembled to help during a direct encounter with the Boogeyman. This kit typically includes light sources, sound devices, physical barriers, and mental defense strategies.

- **Boogeyman Duel**: A mental or psychological challenge in which you face the Boogeyman head-on, testing your willpower and ability to confront fear without backing down. The Boogeyman Duel is about mastering your fear, not necessarily defeating the Boogeyman physically.
- **Boogeyman Energy Detectors**: Devices designed to pick up on the Boogeyman's presence by detecting changes in energy, often using thermal or electromagnetic signals. These detectors help identify when the Boogeyman is near.
- **Boogeyman Traps**: A variety of setups designed to capture or immobilize the Boogeyman. These traps can be physical, such as strings, bells, or Boogey Goo, or they can be light-based, such as circles of glowsticks or mirrors.

C

- **Candy Bait**: Sweets, often in the form of **Sugar Trap Sweets**, that are used to lure the Boogeyman out of hiding. The candies appear harmless but are infused with sticky substances that trap the Boogeyman once he takes the bait.
- **Chalk Circles**: Circles drawn with chalk that serve as protective barriers against the Boogeyman. These circles are believed to prevent the Boogeyman from crossing into certain areas, particularly around beds or doorways.
- **Compartmentalizing Fear**: A mental technique that involves isolating your fear into a small, manageable part of your mind so that it doesn't overwhelm you. This makes it easier to focus on defending yourself against the Boogeyman.

D

- **Daylight Thinking**: A mental exercise in which you remind yourself that the Boogeyman is powerless during the day, helping you stay calm and confident. Daylight Thinking helps reduce the Boogeyman's hold over you by reinforcing the idea that he can't harm you in the light.
- **Dream Guardians**: Imaginary or spiritual protectors who guard your dreams from Boogeyman intrusion. These figures can be dragons, knights, or even superheroes, and they help ensure that the Boogeyman cannot infiltrate your dreams.
- **Dream Crafting**: The process of controlling or shaping your dreams to create safe environments or confront the Boogeyman directly within your dreams. Dream Crafting allows you to use your dreams as a space for battling or outsmarting the Boogeyman.

E

- **Element of Surprise**: A tactic used to catch the Boogeyman off guard by using unexpected defenses or strategies. The element of surprise can involve shifting your routine, using new defense tools, or deploying sudden attacks that the Boogeyman doesn't expect.

F

- **Fairy Dust Defense**: A magical powder, often represented by glitter or another sparkling substance, that is believed to ward off the Boogeyman. Fairy Dust is sprinkled around vulnerable areas like windows or doors to keep the Boogeyman away.
- **Fear Confrontation Practice**: A psychological exercise that involves exposing yourself to small amounts of fear in controlled environments to build resistance. Over time, this practice helps reduce your sensitivity to fear, weakening the Boogeyman's power.

G

- **Glowstick Barricades**: Barriers made of glowsticks, set up around your bed or door, that create a protective circle of light. The Boogeyman cannot cross these glowing barriers, as the light disrupts his ability to move freely.

H

- **Holy Water Spray**: Water that has been blessed or charged with positive energy and is used to repel the Boogeyman. Holy Water Sprays can be misted around the room, especially in dark corners or under the bed, to cleanse the space of negative energy.
- **Humor Defense**: Using laughter and humor to repel the Boogeyman. Since the Boogeyman feeds on fear, laughter weakens his influence. This defense involves making jokes about the Boogeyman or finding humor in the situation to reduce anxiety.

I

- **Imagination-Based Defenses**: Defense techniques that rely on the power of imagination, such as creating imaginary weapons, allies, or fortresses. These defenses turn your creativity into a shield, protecting you from the Boogeyman's influence.
- **Imaginary Friend Callbacks**: The act of summoning or reconnecting with your imaginary friend to protect you from the Boogeyman. By bringing back this positive figure, you regain a sense of safety and comfort.

J

- **Joint Imaginary Friend Power**: The combined power of multiple imaginary friends to defend against the Boogeyman. When you and others pool your imaginary allies together, their collective strength increases, making them more effective in combatting the Boogeyman.

L

- **Light Trap**: A defense mechanism that uses light to trap or weaken the Boogeyman. Light Traps can involve flashlights, lanterns, or glow-in-the-dark materials set in key locations to immobilize the Boogeyman when he steps into the light.

M

- **Mind Over Matter**: A mental technique in which you use your mind to reshape your reality, making yourself immune to the Boogeyman's influence. This technique requires strong mental focus and the ability to control your thoughts, even when fear is present.
- **Mirror Shields**: Mirrors placed strategically around the room to reflect the Boogeyman's image. Mirrors disrupt the Boogeyman's power by forcing him to see himself, which weakens his influence and prevents him from moving freely.
- **Moonlight Dust**: A glowing powder that can be sprinkled around the room to reveal the Boogeyman's tracks. When the Boogeyman steps in Moonlight Dust, it clings to his feet and leaves behind glowing footprints, helping you track his movements.

N

- **Nighttime Guardians**: Imaginary or spiritual protectors that watch over you while you sleep. These guardians help prevent the Boogeyman from approaching or disturbing your dreams.

P

- **Protective Circles**: Circles drawn with chalk, salt, or another protective material that create a barrier the Boogeyman cannot cross. These circles are commonly used around beds or windows to keep the Boogeyman at bay.

R

- **Reverse Psychology**: A tactic in which you confuse the Boogeyman by pretending you're not afraid or even inviting him closer. Reverse Psychology disrupts the Boogeyman's ability to feed on fear, often leaving him confused and unable to act.

S

- **Salt Line**: A line of salt laid around beds, doors, or windows to create a barrier that the Boogeyman cannot cross. Salt lines are a classic defense against supernatural creatures in folklore, including the Boogeyman.
- **Sound Barrier**: A defense technique that uses white noise, music, or other sounds to create a barrier that the Boogeyman cannot penetrate. Sound Barriers disrupt the Boogeyman's ability to move silently or sneak up on you.
- **Sugar Trap Sweets**: Special candies designed to attract the Boogeyman. These sweets contain sticky substances that trap him when he attempts to eat them, immobilizing him long enough for you to act.

T

- **Temporalfuge Device**: A unique invention that causes the Boogeyman to age rapidly, weakening him and rendering him powerless. The Temporalfuge Device is an advanced tool used for permanently disabling the Boogeyman's ability to scare.

U

- **Under-the-Bed Patrol**: The practice of regularly checking under the bed for signs of Boogeyman activity, often using a long-handled object like a broom. This patrol ensures that the Boogeyman isn't hiding in this common lurking place.

W

- **Whistle Alarm**: A high-pitched whistle that is blown to alert others of the Boogeyman's presence or to scare him away. The loud sound disrupts the Boogeyman's concentration and weakens his power.

Conclusion

This glossary provides a detailed overview of the terms and tools essential for understanding and combating the Boogeyman. From mental techniques like **Mind Over Matter** to physical tools like **Boogey Goo** and **Salt Lines**, these definitions serve as your guide to mastering fear and reclaiming your imagination. Keep this glossary handy whenever you need to refresh your knowledge or prepare for a new encounter with the Boogeyman.

Appendix B: Step-by-Step Instructions for Building the Temporalfuge Device

The **Temporalfuge Device** is a unique and powerful invention designed to weaken and neutralize the Boogeyman by rapidly aging him, rendering him too old and powerless to continue his mischief. This advanced tool combines elements of science, creativity, and imagination to create a temporal field that disrupts the Boogeyman's existence, accelerating his aging process in a matter of seconds. In this appendix, you will find **detailed, step-by-step instructions** on how to build your very own Temporalfuge Device at home.

While the concept of manipulating time might sound complex, the device itself is simple to construct, using easily obtainable materials. The Temporalfuge Device is not just a tool; it's a symbol of your ability to take control of the situation and face the Boogeyman with courage and ingenuity.

Materials Needed

Before beginning, make sure you have the following materials on hand. Most of these items can be found around the house or at a local craft store:

Core Components:

- **Plastic or metal tube** (about 12 inches long): This will serve as the main body of the device, housing the key components.
- **Small motor** (such as a motor from a small fan or toy): The motor will power the rotating mechanism, essential for creating the time-manipulating field.
- **Battery pack with AA batteries**: To power the motor.
- **LED lights**: These lights will help indicate when the device is active and can also serve as an additional visual deterrent to weaken the Boogeyman.
- **Wire connectors**: To connect the motor and the battery pack.
- **Toggle switch**: A simple on/off switch to control the power to the motor.
- **Small plastic or metal disc** (about 4-6 inches in diameter): This will act as the "time-rotation plate," responsible for generating the temporal field.

Supporting Elements:

- **Glow-in-the-dark paint or stickers**: To add an eerie, glowing effect to the device, reinforcing its supernatural purpose.
- **Reflective material (such as aluminum foil or small mirrors)**: Used to enhance the time-distortion field by reflecting light.
- **Tape or hot glue**: To secure components in place.
- **Small gears or pulleys**: To help connect the motor to the time-rotation plate for smooth spinning action.

Optional Enhancements:

- **Sound chip** (optional): To add sound effects (such as a whirring or ticking noise) when the device is activated, heightening its impact.
- **Colored glass beads** or **crystals**: To channel "energy" into the device, giving it a more mystical appearance.

Step-by-Step Assembly Instructions

Now that you have your materials, let's walk through the construction of your Temporalfuge Device. Follow these instructions carefully to ensure that the device functions correctly.

Step 1: Preparing the Tube (Main Body of the Device)

1. **Take your plastic or metal tube** and inspect it to make sure it is clean and free of any debris. This tube will house the key components, so it needs to be sturdy and long enough to fit everything inside comfortably.
2. **Optional Decoration**: If you want to paint or decorate the tube with glow-in-the-dark paint or stickers, now is the time to do so. This will give the device its glowing, time-altering appearance when it's active.

Step 2: Installing the Motor

1. **Place the small motor** inside one end of the tube. The motor should fit snugly, but if it is loose, use tape or hot glue to secure it in place. The motor will power the rotating plate that generates the time-altering field.
2. **Connect the motor's wires** to the battery pack using the wire connectors. Make sure the battery pack fits inside the tube or can be attached securely to the outside.

Step 3: Attaching the Time-Rotation Plate

1. **Take the small plastic or metal disc** and attach it to the motor's spindle or shaft using gears or pulleys, if necessary. This disc will rotate when the motor is activated, creating the effect of manipulating time.
2. **Test the rotation** by briefly connecting the battery pack to the motor to make sure the plate spins smoothly. Adjust the connection if it wobbles or doesn't spin properly.

Step 4: Adding LED Lights

1. **Attach the LED lights** around the outside of the tube or the time-rotation plate. The lights will indicate when the device is active and serve as an additional deterrent to the Boogeyman.

2. **Connect the LED lights** to the same battery pack that powers the motor. Make sure they light up when the motor is activated.

Step 5: Installing the Toggle Switch

1. **Install the toggle switch** in an easy-to-reach location on the outside of the tube. This switch will allow you to turn the device on and off without having to remove the battery pack.
2. **Wire the toggle switch** to the motor and the battery pack so that flipping the switch activates both the motor and the LED lights.

Step 6: Enhancing the Time-Distortion Effect

1. **Attach reflective material** (such as aluminum foil or small mirrors) around the time-rotation plate or on the inside of the tube. This reflective material will help "distort" light, creating the illusion of bending time.
2. **Add glow-in-the-dark elements**: Apply glow-in-the-dark paint or attach glow-in-the-dark stickers to the rotation plate and other key areas of the device. This gives the Temporalfuge Device an eerie, glowing effect when activated in the dark, enhancing its supernatural appearance.
3. **Optional**: If you are using **colored glass beads** or **crystals**, glue them around the outside of the tube or onto the time-rotation plate. These decorative elements symbolize the "energy" being channeled into the device, making it look even more powerful.

Step 7: Optional Sound Chip Installation

1. If you want to add **sound effects**, take a small sound chip (such as those used in greeting cards or toys) and attach it to the device. You can program the chip to emit a ticking, whirring, or even a mystical hum when the Temporalfuge Device is activated.
2. **Position the sound chip** near the motor or battery pack so that it activates when the device is turned on. This adds an extra layer of immersion to the device, making it more believable.

Step 8: Final Assembly and Testing

1. **Check all connections** to make sure the motor, lights, and switch are working properly. Tighten any loose wires and ensure that the battery pack is securely in place.
2. **Test the Temporalfuge Device** by turning on the switch. The motor should cause the time-rotation plate to spin, the LED lights should glow, and any sound effects should activate. The reflective materials will create a time-distortion effect, and the glow-in-the-dark elements will make the device appear otherworldly in low light.

3. **Fine-tune the design** as needed. If the rotation plate isn't spinning smoothly, adjust the motor alignment or add more gears. If the lights aren't bright enough, consider adding additional LEDs or upgrading to a more powerful battery pack.

How to Use the Temporalfuge Device

Once the Temporalfuge Device is complete, it's time to use it in your battle against the Boogeyman. Here's how to activate and wield it effectively:

1. **Activate the Device**: When you sense the Boogeyman's presence, flip the toggle switch to turn on the device. The lights will glow, the rotation plate will spin, and any sound effects will start, indicating that the Temporalfuge Device is active.
2. **Point the Device at the Boogeyman**: Aim the tube at the Boogeyman, especially in areas where he may be hiding (such as the closet, under the bed, or in dark corners). The spinning plate creates a time-manipulating field that disrupts the Boogeyman's existence, accelerating his aging process.
3. **Visualize the Boogeyman Aging**: As you point the device at the Boogeyman, imagine him rapidly aging. Picture his form becoming weaker and more fragile with each passing second. The glowing lights and spinning mechanism reinforce this image, helping to mentally project the effect.
4. **Continue Until He Disappears**: Keep the device active until the Boogeyman has aged to the point of being powerless. This could take several seconds or minutes, depending on the Boogeyman's strength. Once he disappears or retreats, turn off the device.

Troubleshooting and Maintenance

- **Motor Not Spinning**: Check the battery connections and ensure the motor is properly wired. If the motor still won't spin, try replacing the batteries or tightening any loose connections.
- **LED Lights Not Working**: If the LED lights aren't activating, make sure they are connected to the correct wires and that the switch is functioning properly.
- **Sound Effects Too Quiet**: If you added a sound chip but can barely hear the effects, try positioning the chip closer to the surface of the device or using a chip with louder sounds.
- **Loose Components**: Over time, parts of the Temporalfuge Device may come loose. Check all connections regularly and reapply glue or tape where needed to keep the device in working order.

Safety Note

While the Temporalfuge Device is designed to be fun and imaginative, always ensure safety when using tools like motors, batteries, and glue. If younger children are involved, an adult should supervise the assembly process. Remember, the Temporalfuge Device is not a real weapon, but rather a creative tool designed to help empower you in your battle against fear.

Conclusion: The Power of the Temporalfuge Device

By building the **Temporalfuge Device**, you've not only created a powerful tool to banish the Boogeyman but also demonstrated your ability to take control of fear through creativity and ingenuity. This device symbolizes your strength and resourcefulness, giving you the upper hand in any encounter with the Boogeyman. With the Temporalfuge Device in hand, the Boogeyman stands no chance—time itself is on your side!

Appendix C: Suggested Reading Material for Further Boogeyman Lore

For those intrigued by the world of Boogeymen and interested in expanding their knowledge, this appendix offers a curated list of books, stories, and resources that delve into the lore, mythology, and cultural significance of these shadowy figures. From ancient folklore to modern interpretations, these works explore the darker side of human imagination and the universal fears that Boogeymen represent. Whether you're looking to deepen your understanding of Boogeymen or simply enjoy tales of supernatural beings, this list will provide hours of fascinating reading.

Folklore and Mythology: The Origins of the Boogeyman

1. *The Dictionary of Demons: Names of the Damned* **by Michelle Belanger**

- This comprehensive resource offers insight into demonic entities and supernatural creatures from various cultures, including those that resemble the Boogeyman. It provides historical context and explores how the Boogeyman has been portrayed as a symbol of fear in many cultures.

2. *The Book of Hallowe'en* **by Ruth Edna Kelley**

- Written in 1919, this book delves into the origins of Halloween and the creatures associated with the holiday, including various Boogeyman-like figures. Kelley explores how fear of the unknown has shaped tales of dark beings that lurk in the shadows.

3. *Boogeymen: The Lore and Legends of Fearsome Creatures* **by Christopher Dewey**

- This book explores the Boogeyman from different cultural perspectives. It focuses on how each region of the world has its version of the Boogeyman, with unique traits and behaviors, showing that fear of this creature is universal.

4. *Encyclopedia of Spirits: The Ultimate Guide to the Magic of Fairies, Genies, Demons, Ghosts, Gods & Goddesses* **by Judika Illes**

- While not exclusively about Boogeymen, this encyclopedia offers a wealth of information on spirits and supernatural beings from folklore around the world, many of whom share characteristics with the Boogeyman. This book is a useful resource for understanding how the Boogeyman fits into the broader context of spiritual entities.

5. *Scary Stories to Tell in the Dark* **by Alvin Schwartz**

• A classic collection of folklore and urban legends that have haunted children for decades. Many of the tales in this series involve creatures or figures that resemble the Boogeyman, making it an essential read for those interested in understanding the intersection of folklore and childhood fears.

Classic Literature: Boogeyman in Fiction
6. *The King in Yellow* by Robert W. Chambers

• This collection of supernatural horror stories introduces the idea of an unseen, terrifying force that haunts the edges of the known world. While not a Boogeyman in the traditional sense, the entity known as the King in Yellow represents the existential fear of the unknown—a core trait of the Boogeyman myth.

7. *The Strange Case of Dr. Jekyll and Mr. Hyde* by Robert Louis Stevenson

• In this novella, Mr. Hyde embodies the concept of a dual nature, a hidden and monstrous side that emerges under cover of darkness. Hyde's transformation into a Boogeyman-like figure who embodies the fears of unchecked power and hidden evil makes this classic a great companion to understanding how fear of the self can fuel Boogeyman lore.

8. *The Turn of the Screw* by Henry James

• This novella explores the psychological terror of unseen forces and ambiguous figures, much like the Boogeyman. The story plays on the fear of invisible threats and the fine line between imagination and reality, key elements in many Boogeyman tales.

9. *Dracula* by Bram Stoker

• Count Dracula can be seen as a sophisticated version of the Boogeyman—an ancient figure who lurks in the shadows and preys upon the fears and vulnerabilities of his victims. Dracula represents the unknown and uncontrollable elements of the night, much like traditional Boogeymen.

10. *The Shadow Over Innsmouth* by H.P. Lovecraft

• Lovecraft's tale of horror and cosmic fear introduces the idea of creatures that lurk beneath the surface of normality, much like the Boogeyman. The fear of something alien hiding just out of sight taps into the same primal fears that the Boogeyman exploits.

Psychological Horror and Modern Interpretations
11. *It* by Stephen King

- King's novel introduces Pennywise, a shape-shifting entity that feeds on children's fears, very much like a Boogeyman. The book explores how fear and trauma affect children and how they must confront their inner demons, a recurring theme in Boogeyman stories.

12. *The Babadook* by Jennifer Kent (film and book adaptation)

- This story is a modern take on the Boogeyman myth, where the creature represents the protagonist's repressed grief and trauma. The Babadook's emergence as a menacing figure within the house mirrors the way Boogeymen often symbolize unresolved fears and anxieties.

13. *The Sandman* by Neil Gaiman

- This graphic novel series features a variety of supernatural beings, including creatures that resemble Boogeymen. Gaiman's interpretation of the Dream World and its inhabitants taps into the mythology of figures who control or exploit human fears and dreams.

14. *Coraline* by Neil Gaiman

- A dark, twisted fantasy where the Other Mother plays the role of a Boogeyman-like figure who preys on the protagonist's desires and fears. Coraline's battle to reclaim her family and her sense of self is a compelling take on the Boogeyman narrative, where the monster hides in plain sight.

15. *House of Leaves* by Mark Z. Danielewski

- This novel explores the fear of the unknown in physical spaces, particularly the labyrinthine house at the center of the story. The Boogeyman here is the house itself, which seems to shift and grow, much like how a child's fear of the Boogeyman can feel overwhelming and infinite.

Anthologies and Collections on Fear
16. *Dark Tales: Folklore Retold* edited by Alice Hudson

- A collection of modern retellings of folklore, many of which involve creatures that can be interpreted as Boogeymen. These stories highlight how ancient fears continue to resonate in modern culture and how Boogeyman-like figures still haunt the fringes of our imagination.

17. *The Haunted: A Social History of Ghosts* **by Owen Davies**

- This book explores the history of ghosts and haunting, including figures like the Boogeyman who represent the darker side of the supernatural. It offers a social perspective on how these figures have been used to explain fear and control behavior throughout history.

18. *The Weird: A Compendium of Strange and Dark Stories* **edited by Ann and Jeff Van-derMeer**

- This anthology features over 100 years of strange and eerie fiction, including stories that re-volve around fearsome creatures like the Boogeyman. The collection offers a deep dive into weird fiction, where the boundaries between fear, imagination, and reality blur.

Children's Books on the Boogeyman
19. *There's a Nightmare in My Closet* **by Mercer Mayer**

- This classic children's book introduces the concept of the Boogeyman in a gentle, humorous way. It's an excellent starting point for children dealing with fears of monsters in the dark, of-fering a lighthearted resolution that can help children feel empowered.

20. *The Dark* **by Lemony Snicket and illustrated by Jon Klassen**

- A beautifully illustrated children's book that addresses the fear of darkness, personifying the dark as a character. It provides a subtle way of helping children confront their fear of what might be lurking in the shadows—potentially the Boogeyman.

21. *I Need My Monster* **by Amanda Noll**

- A playful twist on the Boogeyman concept, this story follows a boy who discovers that his monster is missing, and he needs him back! It's a fun exploration of how children relate to imaginary creatures and how they can be both frightening and comforting at the same time.

Scholarly Works on Fear and Monsters
22. *The Monstrous-Feminine: Film, Feminism, Psychoanalysis* **by Barbara Creed**

- This scholarly text delves into the representation of monsters in film, including figures that can be interpreted as Boogeymen. While more academic in tone, it provides an insightful analysis of how gender and psychology play a role in our perceptions of fear and monsters.

23. *The Philosophy of Horror* by Noël Carroll

- Carroll's book explores the nature of horror, monsters, and the psychology of fear. The Boogeyman, as a classic horror figure, is analyzed through the lens of philosophical inquiry into why we are drawn to stories and characters that scare us.

24. *Monsters in the Closet: Homosexuality and the Horror Film* by Harry Benshoff

- This book explores the symbolism of monsters, including Boogeymen, in the horror genre. Benshoff examines how monsters represent societal fears, anxieties, and taboos, offering a unique perspective on how the Boogeyman fits into broader themes of fear.

25. *Fears of Childhood: Psychoanalysis of the Monstrous* by Marjorie S. Kahane

- A psychological exploration of the fears that children experience and how figures like the Boogeyman represent these deep-seated anxieties. This book delves into the ways in which childhood fears manifest and how they can be confronted and overcome.

Conclusion: The Continuing Legacy of the Boogeyman

The Boogeyman is more than just a childhood monster; he is a **symbol of fear** that has permeated cultures, stories, and imaginations for centuries. Whether you're reading about ancient folklore or modern horror stories, the Boogeyman represents the darker side of human experience—the part that grapples with the unknown, the unexplainable, and the uncontrollable. These suggested readings will give you a deeper appreciation for the complexity and universality of Boogeyman lore, helping you to understand his origins and why he continues to haunt the fringes of our world.

By immersing yourself in these works, you'll gain not only an understanding of the Boogeyman but also insights into the broader themes of fear, imagination, and the human psyche. Happy reading!

<u>Message from the Author:</u>

I hope you enjoyed this book, I love astrology and knew there was not a book such as this out on the shelf. I love metaphysical items as well. Please check out my other books:

-Life of Government Benefits

-My life of Hell

-My life with Hydrocephalus

-Red Sky

-World Domination:Woman's rule

-World Domination:Woman's Rule 2: The War

-Life and Banishment of Apophis: book 1

-The Kidney Friendly Diet

-The Ultimate Hemp Cookbook

-Creating a Dispensary(legally)

-Cleanliness throughout life: the importance of showering from childhood to adulthood.

-Strong Roots: The Risks of Overcoddling children

-Hemp Horoscopes: Cosmic Insights and Earthly Healing

- Celestial Hemp Navigating the Zodiac: Through the Green Cosmos

-Astrological Hemp: Aligning The Stars with Earth's Ancient Herb

-The Astrological Guide to Hemp: Stars, Signs, and Sacred Leaves

-Green Growth: Innovative Marketing Strategies for your Hemp Products and Dispensary

-Cosmic Cannabis

-Astrological Munchies

-Henry The Hemp

-Zodiacal Roots: The Astrological Soul Of Hemp

- Green Constellations: Intersection of Hemp and Zodiac

-Hemp in The Houses: An astrological Adventure Through The Cannabis Galaxy

-Galactic Ganja Guide

Heavenly Hemp

Zodiac Leaves

Doctor Who Astrology

Cannastrology

Stellar Satvias and Cosmic Indicas

<u>Celestial Cannabis: A Zodiac Journey</u>

AstroHerbology: The Sky and The Soil: Volume 1

AstroHerbology:Celestial Cannabis:Volume 2

Cosmic Cannabis Cultivation

The Starry Guide to Herbal Harmony: Volume 1

The Starry Guide to Herbal Harmony: Cannabis Universe: Volume 2

Yugioh Astrology: Astrological Guide to Deck, Duels and more

Nightmare Mansion: Echoes of The Abyss

Nightmare Mansion 2: Legacy of Shadows

Nightmare Mansion 3: Shadows of the Forgotten

Nightmare Mansion 4: Echoes of the Damned

The Life and Banishment of Apophis: Book 2

Nightmare Mansion: Halls of Despair

<u>Healing with Herb: Cannabis and Hydrocephalus</u>

<u>Planetary Pot: Aligning with Astrological Herbs: Volume 1</u>

Fast Track to Freedom: 30 Days to Financial Independence Using AI, Assets, and Agile Hustles

<u>Cosmic Hemp Pathways</u>

How to Become Financially Free in 30 Days: 10,000 Paths to Prosperity

Zodiacal Herbage: Astrological Insights: Volume 1

Nightmare Mansion: Whispers in the Walls

The Daleks Invade Atlantis

Henry the hemp and Hydrocephalus

10X The Kidney Friendly Diet

Cannabis Universe: Adult coloring book

Hemp Astrology: The Healing Power of the Stars

Zodiacal Herbage: Astrological Insights: Cannabis Universe: Volume 2

<u>Planetary Pot: Aligning with Astrological Herbs: Cannabis Universes: Volume 2</u>

Doctor Who Meets the Replicators and SG-1: The Ultimate Battle for Survival

Nightmare Mansion: Curse of the Blood Moon

<u>The Celestial Stoner: A Guide to the Zodiac</u>

Cosmic Pleasures: Sex Toy Astrology for Every Sign

Hydrocephalus Astrology: Navigating the Stars and Healing Waters

Lapis and the Mischievous Chocolate Bar

Celestial Positions: Sexual Astrology for Every Sign

Apophis's Shadow Work Journal: **:** A Journey of Self-Discovery and Healing

Kinky Cosmos: Sexual Kink Astrology for Every Sign

Digital Cosmos: The Astrological Digimon Compendium

Stellar Seeds: The Cosmic Guide to Growing with Astrology

Apophis's Daily Gratitude Journal

Cat Astrology: Feline Mysteries of the Cosmos

The Cosmic Kama Sutra: An Astrological Guide to Sexual Positions

Unleash Your Potential: A Guided Journal Powered by AI Insights

Whispers of the Enchanted Grove

Cosmic Pleasures: An Astrological Guide to Sexual Kinks
369, 12 Manifestation Journal
Whisper of the nocturne journal(blank journal for writing or drawing)

AstroPaws: The Celestial Guide to Your Dog's Zodiac Destiny

If you want solar for your home go here: https://www.harborsolar.live/apophisenterprises/

get some solar here
Matthew Petchinsky

Get Some Tarot cards: https://www.makeplayingcards.com/sell/apophis-occult-shop

get some tarot mats and cards here

Matthew Petchinsky

<u>Get some shirts: https://www.bonfire.com/store/apophis-shirt-emporium/</u>

get some shirts here
Matthew Petchinsky

<u>Instagrams:</u>
@apophis_enterprises,
@apophisbookemporium,
@apophisscardshop

Twitter: @apophisenterpr1

 Tiktok:@apophisenterprise

Youtube: @sg1fan23477, @FiresideRetreatKingdom

Podcast: Apophis Chat Zone: https://open.spotify.com/show/5zXbr-CLEV2xzCp8ybrfHsk?si=fb4d4fdbdce44dec

listen to my podcast here
Matthew Petchinsky

Newsletter: https://apophiss-newsletter-27c897.beehiiv.com/

join my newsletter here
Matthew Petchinsky

www.ingramcontent.com/pod-product-compliance
Lightning Source LLC
Chambersburg PA
CBHW081358130726
47998CB00011B/3000